THE
REFERENCE
SHELF

REPRESENTATIVE AMERICAN

SPEECHES, 1990–1991

edited by Owen Peterson
Professor, Department of Speech Communication
Louisiana State University

THE REFERENCE SHELF

Volume 63 Number 6

THE H. W. WILSON COMPANY

New York   1991

THE REFERENCE SHELF

The books in this series contain reprints of articles, excerpts from books, and addresses on current issues and social trends in the United States and other countries. There are six separately bound numbers in each volume, all of which are generally published in the same calendar year. One number is a collection of recent speeches; each of the others is devoted to a single subject and gives background information and discussion from various points of view, concluding with a comprehensive bibliography that contains books and pamphlets and abstracts of additional articles on the subject. Books in the series may be purchased individually or on subscription.

The Library of Congress has cataloged this serial title as follows:

Representative American speeches.   1937/38–
New York, H. W. Wilson Co.
v.   21 cm.   (The Reference shelf)
Annual.
Indexes:
Author index: 1937/38–1959/60, with 1959/60;
1960/61–1969/70, with 1969/70; 1970/71–1979/80,
with 1979/80; 1980/81–1989/90, with 1990.
Editors: 1937/38–1958/59, A. C. Baird.—1959/60–69/70, L.
Thonssen.—1970/71–1979/80, W. W. Braden.—1980/81–   O.
Peterson.
ISSN 0197-6923Representative American speeches.
1. Speeches, addresses, etc., American.   2. Speeches, addresses, etc.
I. Baird, Albert Craig, 1883–   ed.   II. Thonssen,
Lester, 1904–   ed.   III. Braden, Waldo Warder, 1911–   ed.
IV. Peterson, Owen, 1924–   ed.   V. Series.
PS668.B3   815.5082   38-27962
                                                       MARC-S

Library of Congress   [8503r85]rev4

Printed in the United States of America

CONTENTS

PREFACE

The great events of 1989 and 1990 included the decline of communism and the emergence of democracy and free enterprise in the Soviet Union and eastern Europe. After more than 45 years, the Cold War suddenly was over. One logically might have expected that interest and public discourse in the United States would focus on these momentous events and changes. And with a recently elected administration led by President George Bush, one might also have expected public attention to be concentrated on such domestic matters as the huge federal deficit, the failure of many of the nation's savings and loans institutions, poverty, and the spiralling cost of health care.

These expectations might well have been fulfilled had Iraq not invaded Kuwait in August, 1990. From that moment, all other issues were overshadowed, as the debate over the United States response, the declaration of war, the progress of the conflict, and the eventual victory and patriotic celebrations all dominated public interest. During the period of crisis, war, and resolution—from the time of the invasion of Kuwait to the victory parades of June, 1991—almost all domestic issues and other international problems received scant attention.

Public address during the midterm November 1990 elections was also influenced by events in the Middle East. Only six months earlier, politicians had been debating issues like whether to support a constitutional amendment banning flag burning, how to spend the savings from cuts in military expenditures, and whether the government should fund art projects that some people deemed "obscene." Suddenly, these issues evaporated as politicians of both parties struggled with or rallied behind President Bush's Middle East policies. Continuing a long-standing downward trend, with voter turnout estimated at 36.4 per cent of those eligible to vote, the lowest percentage in 50 years.

Although the Persian Gulf events eclipsed interest in other problems, some speakers during 1990 and 1991 continued to address the issues of abortion, AIDS, crime, poverty, education, and the environment. The selection of speeches in this volume of *Representative American Speeches* attempts to reflect this broader range of subjects.

In preparing this collection, many people provided valuable assistance. Foremost this year are Bill McPherson, whose research provided important information about the speakers, speeches, audiences, and occasions, and Julie Bradford, who for two years has helped obtain information about the speeches and has prepared the manuscripts and introductions. I thank Ginger Conrad and Lisa Landry for their continued cooperation and help.

I also thank my Louisiana State University colleagues and students: Timothy Caboni, Sam Cangiamilla, Ann Carriger, Stephen L. Cooper, Mary Frances Hopkins, and Harold Mixon.

Others who have provided useful information are Michael Adee, Waldo W. Braden, Lynne V. Cheney, Barbara Conly, Keith Donahue, Alan Shawn Feinstein, Dwight W. Gee, Vera Glaser, Susan L. Gonzales, Dan Herrernan, Cassie Hughes, Robert C. Jeffrey, Cal Logue, George F. Moriarty, Jr., Bonita Mulanax, Robert Nichols, Anna Perez, Judi Risk, Mick Rood, Albert Scardino, Ellen Schorr, Barbara Snow, Rose O. Stone, Robert M. Wachter, William T. Walker, Jr.

OWEN PETERSON

Baton Rouge, Louisiana
June 15, 1991

CRISIS IN THE MIDDLE EAST

WESTERN CIVILIZATION: A VIEW FROM THE EAST[1]
THE JEFFERSON LECTURE IN THE HUMANITIES
Bernard Lewis[2]

In 1972 the National Endowment for the Humanities established the Jefferson Lecture in the Humanities as the higheest official award the federal government bestows for distinguished intellectual achievement in the humanities. The lecture provides the opportunity for an outstanding thinker to explore, in a public forum, matters of broad concern in the humanities and the intellectual, moral, and political traditions of our civilization. The award includes a stipend of $10,000. Each year the lecturer is chosen by the National Council on the Humanities.

Dr. Bernard Lewis, Cleveland E. Dodge Professor Emeritus of Near Eastern Studies at Princeton University, was invited to deliver the l9th Jefferson Lecture in May, 1990. Over the years, previous speakers have come from the disciplines of literature, law, history, sociology, physics, archeology, religion, philosophy, and psychoanalysis, and included such scholars as Lionel Trilling, Robert Penn Warren, Saul Bellow, C. Vann Woodward, Barbara Tuchman, Sidney Hook, Cleanth Brooks, and Walker Percy.

Born in London, England, Lewis earned his B. A. and Ph. D. degrees at the University of London and a *diplôme des études semiteques* at the University of Paris. From 1949 to 1974, he taught history in the University of London's School of Oriental and African Studies. In 1974 he immigrated to the United States, where he was appointed professor of Near Eastern Studies at Princeton. In 1982 he became a naturalized citizen of the United States.

Recognized as the ranking scholar of Islamic and Middle Eastern history, Lewis has written more than twenty books in that field. His books have been translated into nineteen foreign languages. Lewis has also written articles for leading journals and periodicals. He holds five honorary degrees and has been the recipient of many honors and awards.

For the Jefferson lecture, Lewis chose as his topic, "Western Civilization: A View from the East." He delivered it at 6:30 P.M. on Wednesday, May 2, 1990, in the Departmental Auditorium of the National Endowment for the Humanities in Washington, D. C. The program began with a welcome and remarks by Lynne V. Cheney, chairman of the N.E.H.,

---

[1]Delivered at 6:30 P.M., Wednesday, May 2, 1990, in the Departmental Auditorium of the National Endowment for the Humanities in Washington, D. C.

[2]For biographical note, see Appendix.

and an introduction by Hillel Fradkin of the Bradley Foundation. Following the lecture, a reception was held at the National Museum of American History. As is customary with the Jefferson Lecturer, Lewis presented his address a second time, on May 10, 1990, at the Hoover Institution at Stanford University in Palo Alto, California. The format for the second was almost identical to that for his Washington presentation.

Although those who selected Lewis to deliver the 1990 lecture had no way for foreseeing the events that were to develop in the Persian Gulf later that year, their choice of an expert on the Middle East to discuss differences between western and eastern civilization seems almost prescient.

While the popular press devoted little attention to the lecture, it was given extensive coverage in the *Chronicle of Higher Education* (May 9, 1990, p. A4) and in *Humanities*, the bimonthly review published by the National Endowment for the Humanities (May/June, 1990, pp. 4-26). The lecture, with minor changes, was also published as an article in *The Atlantic Monthly* of September 1990. Later, after the war with Iraq had begun, the *Wall Street Journal* carried a lengthy article by Lewis in which he elaborated on some of the ideas discussed in the lecture ("Who'll Win, Who'll Lose in the Gulf," February 20,1991, p. A14)

Bernard Lewis's speech:In one of Thomas Jefferson's letters he remarks, on the question of the relations between church and state, that in matters of religion "the maxim of civil government" should be reversed, and we should rather say: "divided we stand, united we fall."

In this remark Jefferson was setting forth, with classic terseness, an idea that has come to be regarded as essentially American, on the separation of church and state. This idea was not entirely new and had some precedents in the writings of Spinoza, Locke, and the philosophers of the European Enlightenment. It was, however, in the United States that the principle was first given the force of law and gradually, in the course of two centuries, became a reality.

If the idea that religion and politics should be separated is relatively new, dating back a mere 300 years, the idea that they are distinct dates back almost to the beginnings of Christianity. Christians are enjoined in their Scriptures to "render unto Caesar the things which are Caesar's and unto God the things which are God's." While opinions have differed as to the real intention of this phrase, it has generally been interpreted as legitimizing a situation in which two institutions exist side by side, each with its own laws and chain of authority, one concerned with religion, called the church, the other concerned with politics, called the state. And since there are two, they may be joined or separated, subordinate or independent, and conflicts may arise between them over questions of demarcation and jurisdiction.

This formulation of the problems posed by the relations between religion and politics and the possible solutions within that formulation arises from Christian, not universal, principles and experience. There are other religious traditions in which religion and politics are differently perceived, and in which therefore the problems, and in consequence the solutions, are radically different from those we know in the West. Most of these traditions, despite their often very high level of sophistication and achievement, remained or became local, limited to one region, or one culture, or one people. There is one, however, which in its worldwide distribution, its continuing vitality, and its universalist aspirations, can be compared with Christianity, and that is Islam.

Islam is one of the world's great religions. Let me be explicit on what I mean by that. It has brought comfort and peace of mind to countless millions of men. It has given dignity and meaning to drab and impoverished lives. It has taught men of different races to live in brotherhood and people of different creeds to live side by side in reasonable tolerance. It inspired a great civilization in which others besides Muslims lived creative and useful lives and which, by its achievement, enriched the whole world. But Islam, like other religions, has also known periods when it inspired in some of its followers a mood of hatred and violence. It is our misfortune that we have to confront part, though by no means all or even most, of the Muslim world while it is going through such a period and when much, though again not all, of that hatred is directed against us.

Why? We should not exaggerate the dimensions of the problem. The Muslim world is far from unanimous in its rejection of the West, nor have the Muslim regions of the Third World been the most passionate and the most extreme in their hostility. There are still significant numbers, in some quarters perhaps a majority, of Muslims with whom we share certain basic cultural and moral, social and political beliefs and aspirations; there is still an imposing Western presence, cultural, economic, diplomatic, in Muslim lands, some of which are Western allies. Certainly, nowhere in the Muslim world, neither in the Middle East nor elsewhere, has American policy suffered disasters or encountered problems comparable with those of Southeast Asia or Central America. There is no Cuba, no Vietnam in the Muslim world, and no place where American forces are involved as combatants or even as "advisers." But there is a Libya, an Iran, and a Lebanon, and a surge of hatred that distresses, alarms, and above all baffles Americans.

At times, this hatred goes beyond the level of hostility to specific interests or actions or policies or even countries, and becomes a rejection of Western civilization as such, not only what it does but what it is, and of the principles and values that it practices and professes. These indeed are seen as innately evil, and those who promote or accept them [are seen] as the "enemies of God."

This phrase, which recurs so frequently in the statements of the Iranian leadership, both in their judicial proceedings and in their political pronouncements, must seem very strange to the modern outsider, whether secular or religious. The idea that God has enemies, and needs human help in order to identify and dispose of them, is a little difficult to assimilate. It is not, however, all that alien. The concept of the enemies of God is familiar in pre-classical and classical antiquity and in both the Old and New Testaments, as well as in the Qur'an. A particularly relevant version of the idea occurs in the dualist religions of ancient Iran, which believed not in one but in two supreme powers. The Zoroastrian devil, unlike the Christian or Muslim or Jewish devil, is not one of God's creatures performing some of God's more mysterious tasks, but is an independent power, a supreme force of evil engaged in a cosmic struggle against God. This belief influenced a number of Christian, Muslim, and Jewish sects through Manichaeism and other routes. The forgotten but not extinct religion of the Manichees has given its name to the perception of problems as a stark and simple conflict between matching forces of pure good and pure evil.

The Qur'an is, of course, strictly monotheistic and recognizes one God, one universal power only. There is a struggle in men's hearts between good and evil, between God's commandments and the tempter, but this is seen as a struggle ordained by God with its outcome preordained by God, serving as a test of mankind, and not, as in some of the old dualist religions, a struggle in which mankind has a crucial part to play in bringing about the victory of good over evil. Despite this monotheism, Islam, like Judaism and Christianity, was at various stages in its development influenced, especially in Iran, by the dualist idea of a cosmic clash of good and evil, light and darkness, order and chaos, truth and falsehood, God and the Adversary, variously known as devil, Iblis, Satan, and other names.

In Islam, the struggle of good and evil acquired, from the start, political and even military dimensions. Muhammad, it will be recalled, was not only a prophet and a teacher, like the founders of other religions; he was also the head of a polity and of a community, a ruler and a soldier. Hence his struggle involved a state and its armed forces. If the fighters in the war for Islam, the holy war "in the path of God," are fighting for God, it follows that their opponents are fighting against God. And since God is in principle the sovereign, the supreme head of the Islamic state, with the Prophet, and after the Prophet the caliphs, as His vicegerents, then God as sovereign commands the army. The army is God's army and the enemy is God's enemy. The duty of God's soldiers is to dispatch God's enemies as quickly as possible to the place where God will chastise them, that is to say, in the afterlife.

Clearly related to this is the basic division of mankind as perceived in Islam. Most, probably all, human societies have a way of distinguishing between themselves and others: insider and outsider, in-group and out-group, kinsman or neighbor and foreigner. We all have a definition which not only defines the outsider but also, and perhaps more particularly, helps to define and illustrate our perception of ourselves.

In the classical Islamic view, to which many are again beginning to return, the world and all mankind are divided into two: the House of Islam, where the Muslim law and faith prevail, and the rest, variously known as the House of Unbelief and the House of War, which it is the duty of Muslims ultimately to bring to Islam. But the greater part of the world is still outside Islam, and even inside the Islamic lands, according to the view of the Muslim radicals, the faith of Islam has been undermined, and the law of Islam has been abrogated. The obligation of holy war, therefore, begins at home and continues abroad against the self-same infidel enemy.

Like every other civilization known to human history, the Muslim world in its heyday saw itself as the center of truth and enlightenment, surrounded on all sides by infidel barbarians whom it would in due course civilize and enlighten. But between these different groups of barbarians there was a crucial difference. The barbarians to the east and the south were polytheists and idolaters, offering no serious threat and no competition at all to Islam. In the north and west, in contrast, Muslims from an early date recognized a genuine rival: a world religion with universalist aspirations, a distinctive civilization inspired by that religion, and an empire which, though much smaller than theirs, was no less ambitious in its claims and aspirations. This was the entity which was known to itself and others as Christendom, and which for long was almost identical with Europe.

The struggle between these two rival systems has now lasted for some fourteen centuries.It began with the advent of Islam in the seventh century and has continued virtually to the present day. It has consisted of a long series of attacks and counterattacks, jihads and crusades, conquests and reconquests. For the first thousand years, lslam was advancing, Christendom in retreat and under threat. The new faith conquered the old Christian lands of the Levant and North Africa and invaded Europe, ruling for a while in Sicily, Spain, Portugal, and even parts of France. The attempt by the Crusaders to recover the lost lands of Christendom in the east was held and thrown back, and even the loss of southwest Europe to the Reconquista was amply compensated by the advance into southeast Europe, twice reaching as far as Vienna. For the last 300 years, since the failure of the second Turkish siege of Vienna in 1683 and the rise of the European colonial empires in Asia and Africa, Islam has been on the defensive, and the Christian and post-Christian civilization of Europe and her daughters has brought the whole world, including Islam, within its orbit.

For a long time now there has been a rising tide of rebellion against Western paramountcy, and a desire to reassert Muslim values and restore Muslim greatness. The Muslim has suffered successive stages of defeat. The first was his loss of domination in the world to the advancing power of Russia and the West. The second was the undermining of his authority in his own country, through the invasion of foreign ideas and laws and ways of life and sometimes even foreign rulers or settlers, and the enfranchisement of native non-Muslim elements. The third, the last straw, was the loss of his mastery in his own house as a result of the abolition of slavery and the emancipation of women. It was too much to endure, and the outbreak of rage was inevitable against these alien, infidel, and incomprehensible forces that had subverted his dominance, disrupted his society, devalued his values, impoverished and subjugated him, and finally violated the sanctuary of his home. It was also natural that this rage should be directed primarily against the millennial enemy and should draw its strength from ancient beliefs and loyalties.

Europe and her daughters? The phrase may seem odd to Americans, whose national myths, since the beginning of their nationhood and even earlier, have usually defined their very identity in opposition to Europe as something new and radically different from the old European ways. This is not, however, the way that others have seen it, not often in Europe, and hardly ever elsewhere.

Though people of other races and cultures participated, for the most part involuntarily, in the discovery and creation of the Americas, this was, and in the eyes of the rest of the world for long remained, a European enterprise, in which Europeans predominated and dominated, and to which Europeans gave their languages, their religions, and much of their way of life.

For a very long time voluntary immigration to America was almost exclusively European. There were indeed some who came from the Muslim lands in the Middle East and North Africa, but they were, with few exceptions, members of the Christian and, to a lesser extent, the Jewish minorities in those countries. Their departure for America and their subsequent presence in America would not have lessened, but would rather have strengthened the European image of America in Muslim eyes.

In the lands of Islam remarkably little was known about America. At first, the voyages of discovery aroused some interest: the only surviving copy of Columbus's own map of America is a Turkish translation and adaptation, still preserved in the Topkapi Palace Museum in Istanbul. A sixteenth-century Turkish geographer's account of the discovery of the New World, entitled *The History of Western India*, was one of the first books printed in Turkey. But thereafter interest seems to have waned, and not much is said about America in Turkish, Arabic, or other Muslim languages until a relatively late date. A Moroccan ambassador who was in Spain at the time wrote what must surely be the first Arabic account of the American Revolution. The sultan of Morocco signed a treaty of friendship with the United States in 1787, and thereafter the new republic had a number of dealings, some friendly, some hostile, mostly commercial, with other Muslim states. These seem to have had little impact on either side. The

American Revolution and the American republic to which it gave birth for long remained unnoticed and unknown. Even the small but growing American presence in the nineteenth century— merchants, consuls, missionaries, and teachers—aroused little or no curiosity and is almost unmentioned in the Muslim literature and the newspapers of the time.

The Second World War, the oil industry, and postwar developments brought many Americans to the Islamic lands; increasing numbers of Muslims also came to America, at first as students, then as teachers, as businessmen or other visitors, eventually as immigrants. Cinema and later television brought the American way of life, or at any rate a certain version of it, before countless millions to whom the very name of America had previously been meaningless or unknown. A wide range of American products, particularly in the immediate postwar years when European competition was virtually eliminated and Japanese competition had not yet arisen, reached into the remotest markets of the Muslim world, winning new customers and, perhaps more important, creating new tastes and ambitions. For some, America represented freedom and justice and opportunity. For many more, it represented wealth and power and success, at a time when these qualities were not regarded as sins or crimes.

And then came the great change, when the leaders of a widespread and widening religious revival sought out and identified their enemies as the enemies of God, and gave them "a local habitation and a name" in the Western hemisphere. Suddenly, or so it seemed, America had become the archenemy, the incarnation of evil, the diabolic opponent of all that is good, and specifically, for Muslims, of Islam. Why?

Among the components in the mood of anti-Westernism, and more especially of anti-Americanism, were certain intellectual influences coming from Europe. One of these was from Germany, where a negative view of America formed part of a school of thought by no means limited to the Nazis, but including writers as diverse as Rainer Maria Rilke, Oswald Spengler, Ernst Jünger, and Martin Heidegger. In this perception, America was the ultimate example of civilization without culture; rich and comfortable, materially advanced but soulless and artificial; assembled or at best constructed, not grown; mechanical not organic; technologically complex, but without the spirituality and vitality of the rooted, human, national cultures of the Germans and other "authentic" peoples. German philosophy and particularly the philosophy of education enjoyed a considerable vogue among Arab and some other Muslim intellectuals in the thirties and early forties, and this philosophic anti-Americanism was part of the message.

After the collapse of the Third Reich and the temporary ending of German influence, another philosophy, even more anti-American, took its place: the Soviet version of Marxism, with its denunciation of Western capitalism and of America as its most advanced and dangerous form. And when Soviet influence began to fade, there was yet another to take its place or at least to supplement its working: the influence of the new mystique of Third Worldism, emanating from Western Europe, particularly from France, and later also from the United States, and drawing at times on both these earlier philosophies. This mystique was helped by the universal human tendency to invent a golden age in the past, and the specifically European propensity to locate it elsewhere. A new variant of the old, golden age myth placed it in the Third World, where the innocence of the non-Western Adam and Eve was ruined by the Western serpent. This view took as axiomatic the goodness and purity of the East and the wickedness of the West, expanding in an exponential curve of evil from Western Europe to the United States. These ideas too fell on fertile ground and won widespread support.

But though these imported philosophies helped to provide intellectual expression for anti-Westernism and anti-Americanism, they did not cause it, and certainly they do not explain the widespread anti-Westernism which made so many in the Middle East and elsewhere in the Islamic world receptive to such ideas.

It must be surely clear that what won support for such totally diverse doctrines was not Nazi race theory, which can have had little appeal for Arabs, nor Soviet atheist communism, which can have little appeal for Muslims, but rather their basic anti-Westernism. Nazism and communism were the main forces opposed to the West, both as a way of life and as a power in the world, and as such they could count on at least the sympathy if not on the support of those who saw in the West their principal enemy.

But why? If we turn from the general to the specific, there is no lack of individual policies and actions pursued and taken by individual Western governments, which have aroused the passion-

ate anger of Middle Eastern and other Islamic peoples. Yet all too
often, when these policies are abandoned and the problems resolved, there is only a local and temporary alleviation. The
French have left Algeria, the British have left Egypt, the Western
oil companies have left their oil wells, the westernizing Shah has
left Iran, yet the generalized resentment against the West remains and grows and is not appeased.

Clearly, something deeper is involved than these specific
grievances, numerous and important as they may be, something
deeper which turns every disagreement into a problem and
makes every problem insoluble.

This revulsion against America, more generally against the
West, is by no means limited to the Muslim world, nor have Muslims, with the exception of the Iranian mullahs and their disciples
elsewhere, experienced and exhibited its more virulent forms.
This mood of disillusionment and hostility has affected many other parts of the world and even reached some elements in the United States. It is from these last, speaking for themselves and
claiming to speak for the oppressed peoples of the Third World,
that the most publicized explanations, and justifications, of this
rejection of Western civilization and its values have of late been
heard.

The accusations are familiar. We of the West are accused of
sexism, racism, and imperialism, institutionalized in patriarchy
and slavery, tyranny, and exploitation. To these charges, and to
others as heinous, we have no option but to plead guilty, not as
Americans, nor yet as Westerners, but simply as human beings,
as members of the human race. In all these sins, we are not the
only sinners, and in some of them we are very far from being the
worst. The treatment of women in the Western world, and more
generally in Christendom, has always been unequal and often oppressive, but even at its worst it was rather better than the rule
of polygamy and concubinage that has otherwise been the almost
universal lot of womankind on this planet.

Is racism then the main grievance? Certainly the word figures
prominently in publicity addressed to Western, East European,
and some Third World audiences. It figures less prominently in
what is written and published at home and has become a generalized and meaningless term of abuse, rather like "fascism," which
is now imputed to opponents even by spokesmen for one-party,
nationalist dictatorships of various complexions.

Slavery is today universally denounced as an offense against humanity, but within living memory it has been practiced and even defended as a necessary institution, established and regulated by divine law. The peculiarity of the peculiar institution, as Americans call it, lay not in its existence but in its abolition. It was Westerners who were the first to break the consensus of acceptance and to outlaw slavery, first at home, then in the other territories that they controlled, and finally wherever in the world they were able to exercise power or influence, in a word, by means of imperialism.

Is imperialism then the grievance? Some Western powers, and in a sense Western civilization as a whole, have certainly been guilty of imperialism, but are we really to believe that in the expansion of Western Europe there was a quality of moral delinquency lacking in such earlier, relatively innocent expansions as those of the Arabs or Mongols or Ottomans, or in more recent expansions such as that which brought the rulers of Muscovy to the Black Sea, the Caspian, the Hindu Kush, and the Pacific Ocean? In having practiced sexism, racism, and imperialism, the West was merely following the common practice of mankind through the millennia of recorded history. Where it is unique and distinct from all others is in having recognized, named, and tried, not entirely without success, to remedy these historic diseases. And that is surely a matter for congratulation, not condemnation. We do not hold Western medical science in general, or Dr. Parkinson and Dr. Alzheimer in particular, responsible for the diseases which they diagnosed and to which they gave their names.

Of all these offenses, the one that is most widely, frequently, and vehemently denounced is undoubtedly imperialism, sometimes just Western, sometimes Eastern (i.e., Soviet) and Western alike. But in the literature of Islamic fundamentalists, the use of this term often suggests that it may not carry quite the same meaning for them as for its Western critics. In many of these writings, the term "imperialist" is given a distinctively religious significance, being used in association, and sometimes interchangeably, with "missionary," and denoting a form of attack which includes the Crusades and the reconquest of Spain as well as the modern colonial empires. One also sometimes gets the impression that the offense of imperialism is not, as for Western critics, the domination by one people over another, but rather the allocation of roles in this process. What is truly evil and unacceptable is the domination of infidels over true believers. For true believers to rule mis-believers is proper and natural, since this provides for the maintenance of the holy law and gives the misbelievers both the opportunity and the incentive to embrace the true faith. But for misbelievers to rule over true believers is blasphemous and unnat-ural, since it leads to the corruption of religion and morality in society and to the flouting or even the abrogation of God's law. In the same spirit, spokesmen for the new Muslim minorities in Western Europe demand for Islam a degree of legal protection which those countries no longer give to Christianity and have never given to Judaism. Nor, of course, did the governments of their countries of origin ever accord such protection to religions other than their own. In their perception, there is no contradic-tion in these attitudes. The true faith, based on God's final revela-tion, must be protected from insult and abuse; other faiths, which may be false or incomplete, have no right to any such protection.

There are other difficulties in the way of accepting imperial-ism as an explanation of this hostility, even if we define imperial-ism, narrowly and specifically, as the invasion and domination of Muslim countries by non-Muslims. If the hostility is directed against imperialism in that sense, why has it been so much strong-er against Western Europe, which has relinquished all its Muslim possessions and dependencies, and so much weaker against Rus-sia, which still rules, with no light hand, over many millions of re-luctant Muslim subjects and over ancient Muslim cities and countries? And why should it include the United States, which has never ruled any Muslim country?

The last surviving European empire with Muslim subjects, that of Russia, far from being the target of criticism and attack, has been almost exempt. Even the most recent repressions of Muslim revolts in the southern and central Asian republics of the USSR incurred no more than relatively mild words of expostula-tion, coupled with a disclaimer of any desire to interfere in what are called the "internal affairs" of the USSR and a request for the preservation of order and tranquillity on the frontier.

One reason for this somewhat surprising restraint is to be found in the nature of events in Azerbaijan. Islam is obviously an important and potentially a growing element in the Azerbaijani sense of identity, but it is not at present a dominant element, and the Azerbaijani movement has more in common with the liberal patriotism of Europe than with Islamic fundamentalism. Such a movement would not arouse the sympathy of the rulers of the Islamic Republic. It might even alarm them, since a genuinely democratic national state run by the people of Soviet Azerbaijan would exercise a powerful attraction on their kinsmen immediately to the south in the Iranian province of Azerbaijan.

Another reason for this relative lack of concern for the sixty or so million Muslims under Soviet rule may be a calculation of risk and advantage. Russia is near, along the northern frontiers of Turkey, Iran, and Afghanistan; America and even Western Europe are far away. More to the point, it has not hitherto been the practice of the Soviets to quell disturbances with water cannon and rubber bullets, with TV cameras in attendance, nor to release arrested persons on bail and allow them access to domestic and foreign media. They do not interview their harshest critics on prime time, nor tempt them with teaching, lecturing, and writing engagements. On the contrary, their ways of indicating displeasure with such criticism can often be quite unpleasant.

But fear of Russian reprisals, though no doubt important, is not the only or perhaps even the major reason for the relatively minor place assigned to Russia, as compared to the West, in the demonology of fundamentalism. It was after all from the West, not from Russia, that the great social and intellectual and economic changes emerged, which have transformed most of the Islamic world and given rise to such commonly denounced Western evils as consumerism and secularism. No one could accuse the Soviets of consumerism; their materialism is philosophic, to be precise dialectical, and has little or nothing to do with providing the good things of life. Such provision represents another kind of materialism, often designated by its opponents as crass. It is associated with the capitalist West, and not with the communist East, which, on the contrary, has practiced, or at least imposed on its subjects, a degree of austerity that would impress a Sufi saint.

Nor had the Soviets, until very recently, been vulnerable to charges of secularism, the other great fundamentalist accusation against the West. Though atheist, they are not godless, and had in fact created an elaborate state apparatus to impose the worship of their gods, an apparatus with its own orthodoxy, a hierarchy to define and enforce it, and an armed inquisition to detect and extirpate heresy. The separation of religion from the state does not mean the establishment of irreligion by the state, still less the forcible imposition of an anti-religious philosophy. Soviet secularism, like Soviet consumerism, holds no temptation for the Muslim masses and is losing what appeal it had for Muslim intellectuals. More than ever before, it is Western capitalism and democracy that still provide an authentic and attractive alternative to traditional ways of thought and life. Fundamentalist leaders are not mistaken in seeing in Western civilization the greatest challenge to the way of life that they wish to retain or restore for their people.

The origins of secularism in the West may be found in two circumstances: in early Christian teachings, and still more, experience, which created two institutions, church and state, and in later Christian conflicts, which drove them apart.

Muslims too had their religious disagreements, but there was nothing remotely approaching the ferocity of the Christian struggles between Protestants and Catholics, which devastated Christian Europe in the 16th and 17th centuries and finally drove Christians in desperation to evolve a doctrine of the separation of religion from the state. Only by depriving religious institutions of coercive power, so it seemed at the time, could Christendom restrain the murderous intolerance and persecution which Christians had visited on followers of other religions and, most of all, on those who professed other forms of their own. Muslims experienced no such need and evolved no such doctrine. There was no need for secularism in Islam, and even its pluralism was very different from that of the pagan Roman Empire so vividly described by Edward Gibbon, who remarked that "the various modes of worship which prevailed in the Roman world were all considered by the common people equally true, by the philosophers equally false, and by magistrates equally useful." Islam was never prepared, either in theory or in practice, to accord full equality to those who held other beliefs and practiced other forms of worship, least of all to religions subsequent to itself. It did, however, accord to the holders of partial truth a degree of practical as well as theoretical tolerance rarely paralleled in the Christian world until the adoption of a measure of secularism in the late seventeenth and eighteenth centuries.

At first the Muslim response to Western civilization was one of admiration and emulation, an immense respect for the achievements of the West and a desire to imitate and adopt them. This desire arose from a keen and growing awareness of the relative weakness, poverty, and backwardness of the Islamic world as compared with the advancing West. This disparity first became apparent on the battlefield, but soon spread to other areas of human activity. Muslim writers observed and wrote about the wealth and power of the West, its science and technology, its manufactures and its forms of government. For a time, the secret of Western success was seen to lie in two achievements: economic advancement and especially industry; political institutions and especially freedom. Several generations of reformers and modernizers tried to adapt these and introduce them to their own countries, in the hope that thereby they would be able to achieve equality with the West and perhaps restore their lost superiority.

In our own time, this mood of admiration and emulation has given way to one of hostility and rejection. In part this mood is surely due to a feeling of humiliation, a growing awareness, among the heirs of an old, proud, and for long dominant civilization, of having been overtaken, overborne, and overwhelmed by those whom they had long regarded as their inferiors. In part, this change is due to events in the Western world itself. One factor of major importance was certainly the impact of two great suicidal wars in which Western civilization tore itself apart, bringing untold destruction to its own and other peoples, and in which the belligerents conducted an immense propaganda effort in the Islamic world and elsewhere to discredit and undermine each other. The message they brought found many listeners, the more ready to respond, in that their own experience of Western ways was not happy. The introduction of Western commercial, financial, and industrial methods did indeed bring great wealth, but it accrued, in the first instance, to transplanted Westerners and members of Westernized minorities and to only a few among the main Muslim population. In time these few became more numerous, but they remained isolated from the masses, differing from them even in their dress and style of life. Inevitably they were seen as agents and collaborators of what was once again regarded as a hostile world. Even the political institutions that had come from the West were discredited, being judged not by their Western originals but by their local imitators. These, operating in a situation beyond their control, using imported and inappropriate methods which they did not fully understand, were unable to cope with the rapidly developing crises and were one by one overthrown. For vast numbers of Middle Easterners, Western-style economic methods brought poverty, Western-style political institutions brought tyranny, even Western-style warfare brought defeat. It is hardly surprising that so many were willing to listen to voices telling them that the old Islamic ways were best and that their only solution was to throw aside the pagan and infidel innovations of the reformers and to return to the True Path which God had prescribed for his people.

Ultimately, the struggle of the fundamentalists is against two enemies, secularism and modernism. The war against secularism is conscious and explicit, and there is by now a whole literature denouncing secularism as an evil, neo-pagan force in the modern world and attributing it variously to the Jews, the West, and the United States. The war against modernity is for the most part neither conscious nor explicit, and is directed against the whole process of change that has taken place in the Islamic world in the last century or more and has transformed the political, economic, social, and even cultural structures of Muslim countries. Islamic fundamentalism has given an aim and a form to the otherwise aimless and formless resentment and anger of the Muslim masses at the forces that have disrupted their societies, subverted their institutions, denied or destroyed traditional values and loyalties, aggravated and emphasized their disparities and in the final analysis, robbed them of their beliefs, their aspirations, their dignity, and to an increasing extent, even their livelihood.

The instinct of the masses is not false in locating the ultimate source of these cataclysmic changes in the West and in attributing the disruption of their old way of life to the impact of Western domination, Western influence, or Western precept and example. And since America is the legitimate heir of European civilization and the recognized and unchallenged leader of the West, it is America that has inherited the resulting grievances and become the focus on which their pent-up hate and anger converge. It should by now be clear that we are facing a mood and a movement far transcending the level of issues and policies and the governments that pursue them. This is no less than a clash of civilizations, the perhaps irrational but surely historic reaction of an ancient rival against our Judeo-Christian heritage, our secular present, and the worldwide expansion of both. It is crucially important that we on our side should study their heritage and understand their present, and that we should not be provoked into an equally historic but also equally irrational reaction against them.

Not all the ideas imported from the West by Western intruders or native Westernizers were rejected. Some were accepted even by the most radical Islamic fundamentalists, usually without acknowledgment of source, and suffering a sea change into something rarely rich but often strange. One such was political freedom, with the associated notions and practices of representation, election, and constitutional government. Even the Islamic Republic of Iran has a written constitution and an elected assembly, as well as a kind of episcopate, for none of which is there any prescription in Islamic teaching or any precedent in the Islamic past. Both are clearly adapted from Western models. They have also retained many of the cultural and social customs of the West and the symbols which express them, as for example the form and style of male (and to a much lesser extent female) clothing, notably in the military. The use of Western-invented guns and tanks and planes is a military necessity, but the continued use of fitted tunics and peaked caps is a cultural choice. From constitutions to Coca-Cola, from tanks and television to T-shirts, the symbols and artifacts, and through them the ideas, of the West have retained, even strengthened, their appeal.

The movement which is nowadays called fundamentalism is not the only Islamic tradition. There are others, more tolerant, more open, which helped to inspire the great achievements of Islamic civilization in the past, and we may hope that these other traditions will in time prevail. But before this issue is decided there will be a hard struggle, in which we of the West can do little or nothing. Even the attempt might do harm, for these are issues which Muslims, and only Muslims, must decide among themselves. And in the meantime, we must take great care, on all sides, to avoid the danger of a new era of religious wars, arising from the exacerbation of differences and the revival of ancient, long-forgotten prejudices.

We must then strive to achieve a better appreciation of other religious and political cultures through the study of their history, their literature, and their achievements. At the same time we may hope that they too will try to achieve a better understanding of ours, and especially that they will understand and respect, even if they do not choose to adopt for themselves, our Western perception of the proper relationship between religion and politics.

To describe this perception, I shall end as I began, with a quotation from an American president, this time not from the justly

celebrated Thomas Jefferson, but from the somewhat unjustly
neglected John Tyler, who, in a letter dated July 10, 1843, gave
eloquent and indeed prophetic expression to the principle of religious freedom:

> The United States have adventured upon a great and noble experiment, which is believed to have been hazarded in the absence of all
> previous precedent: that of total separation of Church and State. No
> religious establishment *by law* exists among us. The conscience is left
> free from all restraint and each is permitted to worship his Maker
> after his own judgement. The offices of the Government are open
> alike to all. No tithes are levied to support an established Hierarchy,
> nor is the fallible judgement of man set up as the sure and infallible
> creed of faith. The Mahommedan, if he will to come among us would
> have the privilege guaranteed to him by the constitution to worship
> according to the Koran; and the East Indian might erect a shrine to
> Brahma if it so pleased him. Such is the spirit of toleration inculcated
> by our political Institutions. . . . The Hebrew persecuted and down
> trodden in other regions takes up his abode among us with none to
> make him afraid. . . . He may even more turn his eye to Judea resting with confidence on the promise that is made him of his restoration to that holy land and he may worship the God of his fathers after
> the manner that that worship was conducted by Aaron and his successors in the priesthood, and the Aegis of the Government is over
> him to defend and protect him. Such is the great experiment which
> we have tried, and such are the happy fruits which have resulted
> from it; our system of free government would be imperfect without
> it.
>
> The body may be oppressed and manacled and yet survive; but
> if the mind of man be fettered, its energies and faculties perish, and
> what remains is of the earth, earthly. Mind should be free as the light
> or as the air.

FIRST COMMIT THE NATION,
THEN COMMIT THE TROOPS[1]
H. Ross Perot[2]

At 2:00 A.M. (Baghdad time) on August 2, 1990, eighty thousand troops from Iraq's Republican Guard pushed across the border with Kuwait and headed south toward Kuwait City, the emirate's capital. Kuwait's crown prince telephoned the American Embassy asking for immediate military help to stop the invasion. Reportedly, the Bush administration in Washington replied that the United States simply did not have the military resources in place to send help. The question in Washington at that time was whether the Iraqis would move farther south into Saudi Arabia.

Public outrage in the United States, coupled with reports of atrocities in Kuwait and alleged mistreatment of Western hostages—including their use as "human shields" at military and industrial installations—prompted many policy-makers to support a policy of sending troops to the Persian Gulf at once. Others favored a strategy of sanctions and waiting out the Iraqis.

Fearing a repetition of the events that had led to American involvement and eventual withdrawal in an undeclared war in Vietnam, many responsible leaders urged caution. While willing to support sanctions against Iraq, they opposed any commitment of troops to military action in the Persian Gulf without prior Congressional approval. One of the spokesmen for this point of view was H. Ross Perot, a self-made Texas multimillionaire.

Perot was described by *Current Biography* as "a paragon of the Protestant ethic [who] has dazzled Wall Street with his business acumen and captured headlines with his patriotic zeal in behalf of United States prisoners of war in North Vietnam" (July 1971). Perit also made the front page when he was able through his own initiative to arrange the escape of all employees of the Perot Systems Industries from Iran during the hostage crisis in the late 1970s.

Although an extremely successful corporation executive, Perot believes that his initiative and individuality should not be confined to the business world. Greatly influenced by Henry David Thoreau's observation, "The mass of men lead lives of quiet desperation," he decided early that he should do what he could to help the less privileged. In 1969 he formed the Perot Foundation, a non-profit corporation to handle his contributions to projects he considers deserving. Perot also feels a responsibility to speak out on issues affecting the country on behalf of those people who may not have access to power.

On December 6, 1990, Perot addressed the National Press Club in Washington, D.C. In his speech, Perot expressed his love for the country, its principles, and its people. He then said, "Today, I would like to speak on behalf of millions of American citizens who never get to speak at the National Press Club, or present their views to a national television audience." Senator Ernest Hollings inserted Perot's speech in the *Congressional Record* with the following observations:

> I know that many of my colleagues in this body share my opinion that Ross Perot is a national treasure—both as a superb, innovative businessman and innovator, and as a font of old-fashioned, hard-nosed common sense about the needs and priorities of the nation. Ross Perot is one man who looks beyond party affiliation and parochial regional loyalties to address the true national interest of the United States of America.
>
> The latest example of Ross Perot's uncanny knack for straight talk—straight talk that rings true and clear as a bell—was his speech before the National Press Club on December 6. The speech covers a broad range of issues, but is especially acute on the matter of the Persian Gulf. I urge every member of the Senate to study this speech, to get a feel for what this man is saying. We ignore his counsel at our own risk. (January 14, 1991, p. S428).

Perot delivered the address to a capacity audience of approximately 400 people at 1:00 P.M. in the ballroom of the National Press Club. In addition to the audience of club members and their guests, the speech was covered live by National Public Radio and cable stations affiliated with C-SPAN.

Mick Rood, chairman of the Speakers Committee at the National Press Club, commented on the speech saying "Perot has been the best-received speaker at the NPC in recent years, based on requests for tapes of the speech."

Ross Perot's speech: I love this great country. I love the principles on which it was founded. I love its people.

Today, I would like to speak on behalf of millions of American citizens who never get to speak at the National Press Club or present their views to a national television audience. I am deeply concerned that the most important people in our country are becoming disillusioned and cynical.

[1]Delivered at a luncheon meeting at the National Press Club ballroom in Washington, D.C., to an audience of approximately 400 at 1:00 P.M., December 6, 1990.

[2]For biographical note, see Appendix.

The people I am concerned about represent the majority of our nation's voters. They elect our political leaders. After elections, the people I am concerned about go back to their jobs and families. They are not organized into special interest groups. Their daily presence is not felt in Washington, the state capitols, or even at the city halls. More and more, they feel they have no effective voice.

Who are these people? These are people who work hard, play by the rules, operate in the center of the field of ethical behavior—not on the sidelines—obey the law, [and] rear good children. They are patriots, active in their schools and churches. They attend PTA meetings, teach Sunday school, lead the scout troops, and coach the little league teams. They come from all races, all religions. They are the steel and concrete that hold our nation together. They are givers in a world of takers. They are the people de Tocqueville wrote about when he toured America to learn why we were such a great country. He concluded, "America is great because her people are good."

The people I am concerned about represent the heart of this country's tax base. They pay the bills for our mistakes. Today, they are spending hundreds of billions of their hard-earned dollars to make government work and to clean up problems created by others. They are the majority of the electorate.

And, finally and most importantly, these are the people whose husbands, wives, sons, and daughters make up the military forces in the deserts of Saudi Arabia.

Why are these people so frustrated? They pay substantial taxes at the local, state, and national level, and yet they are receiving very poor services in return from their government. Their money is being poorly spent, and they know it.

Let's look at the facts. Just ten years ago, our great country was the largest creditor nation in the world. Today, we are the largest debtor nation in the history of man.

Our country is the most violent, crime-ridden society in the industrialized world. We have 450,000 men and women in the battlefield in the Middle East because of the rape, pillage, and plunder in Kuwait, and yet we are unwilling to put the same emphasis on the same problems—yes, we have rape, pillage, and plunder in our cities and this city, Washington, D.C., the murder capital of the United States.

Fifty-seven percent of our people are afraid to walk in their own neighborhoods at night. Entire sections of our cities have been abandoned to crime. Millions of the people I am talking about have been wrongfully put in jail. They have had to put bars on their windows and doors.

Our leaders are willing to commit billions to solve problems in the Middle East, but are content to hold press conferences about these same problems in our own country.

This country now ranks at the bottom of the industrialized world in academic achievement. We have the largest number of functional illiterates in the industrialized world.

Our system of justice has failed the people. We are the most litigious society in the industrialized world. We have five percent of the world's population, two-thirds of the world's lawyers. Yet, it takes years for a citizen to get through our court system. And, an average citizen can't even afford to hire a lawyer. Judges are the lowest paid members of the legal profession, while lawyers just out of law school make $80,000 a year.

Our prison system is a mess. It costs more to keep a person in prison for a year than to send him to Harvard for one year.

Our people live in a nation with five percent of the world's population and fifty percent of the world's cocaine use.

And yet we are willing to go to war in the Middle East because of Iraq's potential to produce chemical weapons, while we do little to solve the problems of chemical warfare that is being conducted every day against our children on the streets of this country.

The people are frustrated that organized special interest groups have taken control of our political process. The book, *Agents of Influence*, tells the story. For example: The Japanese spend $400 million a year lobbying—an amount equal to the cost of all elections for the House and Senate in 1988—to protect the $50 billion a year Japanese trade surplus. Not a bad return.

The Japanese wanted their trucks declared as cars when they arrived in this country to reduce the imports fee from twenty-five percent to two and one-half percent. Once they arrived at the dealer, the Japanese wanted them declared as trucks again to avoid paying the penalties for high emissions and low mileage. The Japanese spend three million dollars lobbying for this, over the opposition of U.S. automobile manufacturers. The Japanese won. Their three million dollar one-time investment saves them five hundred million dollars per year in tariffs, not a bad return. In a nation operating at a deficit, guess who picks up the five hundred million dollar tab: the ordinary citizen.

Congressional staffers routinely leak information to curry favor to position themselves for six-figure income lobbying jobs later. Between 1973 and 1990, one-third of the principal trade officials in the Office of the U.S. Trade Commission left to become foreign agents. In 1990, during the trade talks on advanced technology, one senior State Department official, who had helped draft the position papers, attended interagency meetings, had access to confidential U.S. information, knew the U.S. strategy, left to become a foreign lobbyist.

A former president received a two million dollar fee from the Japanese. The presidency is not for sale, now or later.

This practice is corrupting the U.S. political and economic system. It corrupts our institutions. We have put U.S. integrity and national honor up for sale. The people are disgusted, and they should be. No wonder we are in a recession.

The first three words of the Constitution are "We the people." If we were drafting this great document today and if we were honest with ourselves, the first words would have to be: "We the special interests," or "We the big PAC contributors," or "We the international lobbyists," or "We the image makers, spin doctors, and sound-bite specialists," or "We the arrogant White House staffers," or perhaps it should be, "We the summiteers."

We seem to have two-day summits on everything from education to spending—lots of talk, lots of press, lots of TV, no results. Remember Lech Walesa's words to Congress: "Words are plentiful, but deeds are precious." This is the core problem on domestic issues.

The people are frustrated that the business leaders of our country have allowed the job base to deteriorate. Only a handful of people can create jobs. As one hard-working citizen said after his company closed its doors, "I didn't quit my job; my job quit me."

In 1960, seventy-five percent of the vehicles made in the world were made in Detroit. Today that number is twenty-five percent. Go home tonight and look at the brand names on your television, VCR, compact disc, and other electronics. We created this industry. The electronics industry and its jobs have gone overseas. The two principal exports from New York harbor are scrap steel and scrap paper.

We are becoming a third-world country, shipping lumber, iron ore, and other basic products across the world to be manufactured into finished products and returned to our country to be sold. The good jobs paying top salaries are in producing the finished products. They have gone overseas and our tax base is damaged.

Our people are disillusioned that the White House and Congress cynically covered up the savings and loan crisis until after the 1988 elections. It was obvious in 1986. The delay, driven by personal political ambitions, increased the size of this problem from fifty million dollars to five hundred billion dollars, and the burden for paying for this mess rests squarely on the shoulders of the ordinary citizen. Who was in charge of deregulation at this time? Vice President Bush.

These people are frustrated by a government that stood by idly allowing hundreds of thousands of jobs to be destroyed and countless companies to be wrecked by the junk bond fiasco.

It is difficult for the people to understand a system of justice that allows Michael Milken to illegally make over a billion dollars, pay a six hundred million dollar fine, but keep four hundred million. They wonder if someone steals four hubcaps, will the judge let them keep two?

The people are disgusted by transactions like RJR Nabisco, where the beautiful people of Wall Street made nine hundred million dollars in up-front fees in a few weeks. They keep this money even if RJR Nabisco fails. This is not capitalism. This is piracy. Sooner or later, the people will realize that the price of Cheese Ritz crackers has gone up thirty percent since the junk bond deal, and that they are paying the bill for this fiasco each time they buy a box of crackers. Ask yourself, again, who was in charge of deregulation during the 1980s?

The ordinary citizen's frustration reached a new high during the budget and tax negotiations. Whatever happened to "Read my lips—no new taxes"? This was a cynical campaign tactic first stated by Lenin when he said, "Tell the people what they want to hear." It also worked in the United States, a free society.

The tax bubble, lowering the income tax rate for the wealthiest Americans, made no sense. Congress made the White House drop this one. The fifteen percent capital gains tax made no sense. Again, Congress refused to let this one slip through. The deficit gets bigger each year, while our leaders campaign that they will control spending and get rid of waste in government. The people are tired of being used.

The people are frustrated by the budget shell game that forecasted unrealistic economic growth rates, and four percent interest rates at the recent budget summit. We won't grow that fast. Interest rates won't go that low. No wonder the people are cynical.

Only the most cynical at the budget summit would have suggested that by reducing future proposed expenditures, we were actually cutting expenses and saving *real* money. The average citizen is just now beginning to understand that we did not cut our current level of real expenditure at all. We increased taxes and played a fool's game with the numbers, tricking the American people, serving special interests, and further weakening our economy. The confrontational attitude of the White House staff during the tax and budget negotiations was unacceptable.

Our President blames the recession on the war in the Middle East. Don't be fooled. The recession is the result of ten years of gross excess spending and mismanagement in our country. Using the Middle East as an excuse is being untruthful with the people.

Who weakened the buying power of your dollars in 1987–88 after the October 1987 stock market crash—to delay a recession—until after the 1988 election? Look it up. What is this person doing today? Jim Baker, then Secretary of Treasury, today Secretary of State.

These domestic issues are our real problems. They should carry the highest priority. Our single biggest problem is that we are going broke. Bluntly stated, we can't afford to be in the Middle East. The cost is five hundred million dollars a day, fifteen billion dollars a month.

We have been so rich for so long that we just assume we can fund any program or war we can come up with. But we have let it slip away. This great engine created millions of jobs, millions of taxpayers. We had this economic strength for so long that we continue to pretend we have it.

If we have any time or money left over after we once again make our country work for the benefit of our people and pay our bills, I suggest that the highest priority should be to help Eastern Europe succeed in its revolution. Getting involved with Iraq and the Middle East in such a dominant role wouldn't even make a rational priority list.

Our leaders don't give domestic problems the proper priority because they are controversial and difficult to resolve; working on them is comparable to cleaning out the barn or taking out the trash; it is far more exciting to leave the problems behind and flit around the world, appearing briefly at summits, meeting with heads of state, and even putting hundreds of thousands of Americans in the desert as an expression of power.

The press loves it. Such sound-bite activity is made for television. It is exciting to watch, until you think about the lives at risk and the cost. While it may be entertaining, it does not serve the people's needs. While these domestic issues are our real problems, all of these concerns have been temporarily swept aside by the people because of their concerns for members of their families in the Middle East.

This morning I visited the Vietnam Memorial. I urge you to go there and think about current events. On many occasions over the past twenty years, I have promised the men and women of our armed forces, the widows, children, and parents of the men killed in action, and the wounded who will never again lead normal lives that, before this country goes to war again, I would use the resources at my disposal to see that we first commit the nation and then commit the troops. That is the lesson of Vietnam.

I will keep that promise. I hope that my years of service to this country have earned me the right to constructively criticize events occurring at this time.

Who is in the Middle East? The sons and daughters of the people I am speaking about today are in the Middle East. Since we deployed troops in August I have spoken to over eight thousand people. Only eight had immediate family members in the Middle East. Only two members of Congress have family members in the Middle East. The people who work *for* the business executives I spoke to have sons and daughters in the Middle East. These people have worked hard and sacrificed for their children. Many of these parents will only realize their personal dreams through their children's successes. Their sons and daughters may be all they have; their children are their treasures.

A rich woman dressed in her jewelry and furs was walking down the street to the opera. She approached a poor woman with her two children, one in each hand. As they met, the rich lady looked haughtily at the poor woman and asked, "And where are your pearls?" The poor woman drew herself up proudly, pointed to her children and said, "These are my pearls." Never forget, we have 450,000 lives—450,000 pearls—in the Middle East. We must not waste them. We must first commit the nation.

Why are we in the Middle East? In "The Charge of the Light Brigade," Tennyson wrote, "Theirs was not to reason why. Theirs was but to do or die." That may apply to kings, but in our country we have to know why. We cannot commit the nation until we get that one straight.

Our Commander in Chief cannot make up his mind why we are there. At one time it was the price of oil. We caused the price of oil to go up by imposing an embargo. Iraq would dearly love to sell its oil. Never forget, if the devil himself controls the Middle East, oil is worthless until he sells it.

At another time we were there for jobs. Jobs are not worth dying for. I would give up my job in an instant to keep one person from dying—millions of others would too. Each human life is precious. Sooner or later, somebody had better convince us that this is a cause worth dying for.

Still later, the reason was we are fighting for a new world order. What is the new world order? No one can explain it. It is just another sound bite.

Then, our mission was to eliminate Hussein's nuclear and chemical capability and try him in a Nuremberg setting as a war criminal. The earlier Israeli air strike on Iraq is a good example how to take care of this problem without putting 450,000 people in the desert.

Have we forgotten that we have already dealt with a dictator who created chemical warfare weapons? Kaddafi. It didn't take 450,000 people. We didn't clear it with the U.N. We launched an air strike. Kaddafi became a choir boy overnight.

Initially, we were told we were fighting for the American way of life. Nobody bought that one. The Arabs must have laughed.

Lately, it seems that it is a combination of all of the above.

I believe that, in fact, we have developed a pattern of fighting to cover up our past mistakes. We are erasing human errors with human lives. For example, Noriega was a sorry devil, but he was our sorry devil. We gave him money and arms for years. Our government let him deal drugs into our country and brutally abuse his own people. We thought we could control him. We lost control. We captured him using a Panamanian major, failed to pick him up, allowed him to execute the major, and, then, we were embarrassed.

We attacked Panama, took the country, arrested Noriega, destroyed certain areas, and abandoned Panama's people as soon as it was off the front pages. Now, we won't let Noriega have access to his money to pay his lawyers. Some element of our government had to be involved in passing the tapes to CNN. Our government controlled the tapes. These two actions help increase the probability that Noriega cannot be tried. If Noriega does go to trial, some of our most senior officials will really be embarrassed because of their past dealings with him. Noriega could go free. Because we walked away from Panama and left it in ruins, and the people disillusioned, Noriega could, possibly, get reelected in an honest election. This would be a sad ending for the men and women who died and were wounded in Panama.

Who fired the missiles that struck the U.S.S. *Stark*? Saddam Hussein. We supported him since 1982. We gave him billions. We ignored his atrocities. We knew he was trying to build nuclear weapons: allies helped him. The State Department resisted any nuclear sanctions against Iraq until after the invasion of Kuwait. We gave him five billion dollars in agricultural support; he used two billion dollars to buy arms. We winked. Honeywell sold propane bomb materials to Iraq. Our government allowed it. We didn't complain when our allies, France and Germany, assisted him in developing chemical and nuclear weapons. According to *Der Speigel*, the German newspaper, the Germans are still operating the Iraq chemical warfare plants at this moment. Last year we were helping Germany to reunite. They have short memories.

The people certainly don't understand why our ambassador to Iraq, with written approval from our Secretary of State, told Hussein that the U.S. had "no opinion on Arab-Arab conflicts, like your border dispute with Kuwait".

When you negotiate with Arabs, always remember they are smarter than we are; they will skin you. I would like to read and excerpt from one of Kipling's poems regarding dealing with Arabs: "The end of the fight is a tombstone white, And the name of the late deceased, And the epitaph drear—'a fool lies here, Who tried to hustle the east'."

Our State Department gave Hussein a green light to take part of Kuwait. The U.S. oil industry and the C.I.A. warned the President that Iraq was about to attack Kuwait. Our leaders knew Hussein was going to take some of Kuwait and they did nothing. When Hussein took the entire country, we were embarrassed.

Now, like Noriega, Hussein is out of control and we must both defeat him and bring him to trial.

Do you see a pattern? The people wonder why we gave Noriega and Hussein billions, knowing full well that they were sorry, worthless devils. The people can't understand why we are now embracing Syria and its leader, Assad. They remember that Assad was involved in killing two hundred and fifty Marines in Lebanon and in destroying Pan Am flight 103. How can this man possibly become our ally? It is unthinkable that our President would meet with this terrorist who killed our people. Assad of Syria, our new bad-boy friend in the Middle East, has committed the same atrocities in Lebanon since August that Hussein has committed in Kuwait, and yet we ignore Assad's atrocities. If we fight and win, Assad will be the new strong man of the Middle East.

The American people can't understand why their sons and daughters are preparing to fight for kings and emirs. Americans don't fight and die for despots who think they can buy anything including million-dollar-a-year blondes. Americans fight only for great causes. If you have seen Arab royalty on the streets of New York and London, you can understand that they are living a definition of the phrase "absolute decadence". Read the book *The Mayflower Madam*, with careful attention to the Arab stories. Talk to the managers of luxury hotels throughout the world, and you will be appalled.

The Arabs should not be allowed to censor our fighting forces' mail. If we are going to fight and die in the Middle East for them, our forces ought to be able to practice their own religious beliefs. They ought to be allowed to display the American flag. They ought to be allowed to have Bibles. They ought to be able to say a prayer of Thanksgiving with the President. We ought to be able to send USO shows with girls to entertain them. Having seen the beautiful people of the Arab world in New York and London, I can assure you, we don't need any lessons from them on morality.

The approach we are taking will not create a new world order or stabilize the Middle East. In fact, if we had a total military victory over Iraq, we would destabilize the Middle East. If you have questions on this, we can discuss them during the question-and-answer period.

The people ask: How do we commit the nation? Read the Constitution, Article 1, Section 8: Only Congress can declare war—and commit the nation to death on the battlefield. It is illegal and it is wrong for any one person in our country to put 450,000 lives at risk. Our system of government is based on checks and balances. If the President can't even appoint his cabinet or spend money without Congressional approval, do you think there is any possibility that the framers of the Constitution intended for the President to have the unilateral right to put lives at risk? Of course not. The words of the Constitution are simple and plain. Here they are: "The Congress shall have the right to declare war."

The lesson of Vietnam is: first commit the nation, then commit the troops. It is Congress's job to commit the nation and the troops. The President's job is to lead the nation and the troops after Congress gives him the authority.

The people are disgusted that our leaders are running around the world using our money to literally buy the approval of the Security Council members so that we can go to war in the Middle East. Why aren't our leaders seeking the permission of the American people through Congress to put 450,000 lives at risk. I don't believe the American people are interested in having countries like China, Yemen, Columbia, Kuwait, Saudi Arabia, and even France, who sold uranium to Hussein and made it possible for him to create nuclear weapons, decide whether our fighting men live or die. This is our responsibility. Congress must decide the matter. First commit the nation, then commit the troops.

This conflict is a U.N. problem, not solely a U.S. problem. We have five per cent of the world's population, yet we are bearing most of the burden in the Middle East. I can hear the Washington establishment whining now: "But how would it look if the American people don't want to fight in the Middle East?" Let's stop worrying about how things look. Nothing looks worse than American casualties lost in a war that the American people neither understand nor support.

The Declaration of Independence promises life, liberty, and the pursuit of happiness. Life is first. We are risking 450,000 lives, and even the President can't tell us why. Walk past the Vietnam Memorial and through Arlington Cemetery. Ask yourself, would you be willing for one of your loved ones to die for this cause.

Congress has the constitutional responsibility to declare war. It must first commit the nation, then we can commit the troops. Congress does not have to wait for a Presidential request.

Two days ago I spoke to 3,500 mayors at their national convention. I urged them to mobilize the people in their cities and towns, to fully inform the people, to debate this issue, to include their Congressmen, and decide what we should do. Here is what you can do: keep our commitment to our fighting men and women; go to city hall; help organize town hall meetings; involve your congressman; get tapes of this speech from the National Press Club; call or write me if you need help: Ross Perot, Box D, Dallas, Texas 75208.

You, the people, own this country. The elected officials are your servants. Decide what course of action we should take in the Middle East. You hold 450,000 lives in the palms of your hands.

If you decide we must go to war, direct Congress to do it. At that point, we will all face East—no whining, no dissension, total commitment—and get the job done. You ask, can ordinary Americans really do this? Remember Lech Walesa, a Polish shipyard worker. He changed Eastern Europe. Of course you can do it. First commit the nation, then commit the troops. I know the American people will make the right decision.

May God watch over our fighting forces. God bless you all. God bless America.

OPERATION DESERT STORM[1]
GEORGE H.W. BUSH[2]

Almost immediately after the invasion of Kuwait by Iraq on August 2, 1990, the Bush administration began planning an offensive campaign to dislodge the Iraqi forces. Although administration officials insisted that the only mission of United States forces was to defend Saudi Arabia and enforce United Nations sanctions against Iraq, the possibility of war had been clear "ever since Bush said, on August 5th, that the aggression against Kuwait 'will not stand'." (Thomas Freidman and Patrick Tyler,

[1]This nationally televised address was delivered in the Oval Office of the White House in Washington, D.C. at 9 P.M. on January 16, 1991.
[2]For biographical note, see Appendix.

New York Times, March 3, 1991, p. 1.)
  Elizabeth Drew explained:

> It was evident from conversations with Administration officials from
> very early on that some of them believed it would come to war—and
> some thought that just as well. Once the President committed the na-
> tion to the liberation of Kuwait, the policy of starting with sanctions
> and of at least appearing to pursue the diplomatic course while the
> troops and equipment were dispatched to the Gulf region had its
> own logic, whether the outcome was to be a peaceful solution or war.
> It was clear from very early on that some officials saw sanctions and
> diplomacy as the necessary precursors of war. (*New Yorker*, February
> 4, 1991, p. 82).

  After securing authorization for the use of military force from twenty
United Nations members, shortly after 7:00 P.M. on January 16, 1991, a
presidential spokesman read a three sentence statement by President
Bush announcing the start of a military attack on Baghdad and Kuwait.
At 9:00 P.M. in an address from the Oval Office of the White House carried on national television, President Bush confirmed the military action.
  How does one find the right words for declaring war? "How does a
speech use rhetoric to comfort and rally a nation?" Elizabeth Bickley
asked. "How do you frame the issue so the people are behind you?" (*Insight
on the News*, January 14, 1991, p. 56). Clearly this is no problem if you are
an American president responding to a Japanese attack on Pearl Harbor
or a British prime minister exhorting his people to withstand an impending invasion by Nazi Germany. But how does one tell the American public
that it should go to war to liberate a small, undemocratic kingdom in the
Persian Gulf that most of them had never heard of six months earlier.
This was a problem which the President and his aides faced in preparing
his speech. According to R.W. Apple, Jr.:

> Since the beginning of the crisis in the Persian Gulf . . . Mr. Bush
> has sought to liken his struggle against Saddam Hussein and Iraq to
> that against Hitler and Germany, a struggle that united the Ameri-
> can people and much of the world and ended gloriously for the coali-
> tion against fascism. Indeed, the President . . . repeatedly called
> Saddam Hussein a Hitler, said that he would not repeat Chamber-
> lain's appeasement of Germany at Munich, and compared Iraqi use
> of poison gas in earlier wars to Nazi atrocities. (*New York Times*, Janu-
> ary 17, 1991, p. A8)

  The importance of the speech in the President's mind is underlined
by reports of his deep involvement in its preparation. According to Maureen Dowd," . . . aides said he had written at least four drafts over the last
two or three weeks." (*New York Times*, January 17, 1991, p A8).

Bush's address to the nation on the air strikes which began Operation Desert Storm brought the country to a virtual standstill. A reported seventy-nine per cent of the country's households watched the speech on television, a percentage exceeded only by the viewers of the funeral of President John F. Kennedy in 1963. James Barron described the event:

In one long moment yesterday, word that the United States had attacked Baghdad swept the country. In split-level suburban homes on the East Coast where dinner was in the oven, in big-city restaurants in the Midwest where bars were jammed with the happy-hour crowd and in skyscraper offices on the West Coast where people were still at work, there was an odd mixture of apprehension, sadness and relief.

In malls, shoppers emptied out of stores and cried. In supermarkets, cashiers rushed to call relatives and share the news that after five months of waiting and wondering America was at war. In department stores, people crowded in front of television sets, with some saying they were stunned that Presidnt Bush had decided to act so soon after the United Nations deadline for Iraq to withdraw from Kuwait.

Suddenly, in places where people gather, there was an unusual silence, erie rather than giddy. . . . The word that waves of air attacks were striking targets in Iraq silenced black-tie galas in Manhattan and crowds in a Houston hotel, where the chatter around the bar stoppped when the President began his speech from the Oval Office. (*New York Times*, January 17, 1991, p. 1)

*President Bush's speech:*Five months ago, Saddam Hussein started this cruel war against Kuwait; tonight the battle has been joined. This military action, taken in accord with United Nations resolutions and with the consent of the United States Congress, follows months of constant and virtually endless diplomatic activity on the part of the United Nations, the United States and many, many other countries.

Arab leaders sought what became known as an Arab solution, only to conclude that Saddam Hussein was unwilling to leave Kuwait. Others travelled to Baghdad in a variety of efforts to restore peace and justice. Our Secretary of State James Baker held an historic meeting in Geneva only to be totally rebuffed.

This past weekend, in a last ditch effort, the Secretary General of the United Nations went to the Middle East with peace in his heart, his second such mission, and he came back from Baghdad with no progress at all in getting Saddam Hussein to withdraw from Kuwait.

Now, the 28 countries with forces in the Gulf area have exhausted all reasonable efforts to reach a peaceful resolution, have no choice but to drive Saddam from Kuwait by force. We will not fail.

As I report to you, air attacks are under way against military targets in Iraq. We are determined to knock out Saddam Hussein's nuclear bomb potential. We will also destroy his chemical weapons facilities. Much of Saddam's artillery and tanks will be destroyed.

Our operations are designed to best protect the lives of all the coalition forces by targeting Saddam's vast military arsenal.

Initial reports from General Schwarzkopf are that our operations are proceeding according to plan.

Our objectives are clear. Saddam Hussein's forces will leave Kuwait. The legitimate government of Kuwait will be restored to its rightful place and Kuwait will once again be free.

Iraq will eventually comply with all relevant United Nations resolutions and then when peace is restored, it is our hope that Iraq will live as a peaceful and cooperative member of the family of nations, thus enhancing the security and stability of the Gulf.

Some may ask, "Why act now? Why not wait?" The answer is clear. The world could wait no longer.

Sanctions, though having some effect, showed no signs of accomplishing their objective. Sanctions were tried for well over five months and we and our allies concluded that sanctions alone would not force Saddam from Kuwait.

While the world waited, Saddam Hussein systematically raped, pillaged and plundered a tiny nation—no threat to his own. He subjected the people of Kuwait to unspeakable atrocities, and among those maimed and murdered—innocent children. While the world waited Saddam sought to add to the chemical weapons arsenal he now possesses an infinitely more dangerous weapon of mass destruction, a nuclear weapon.

And while the world waited, while the world talked peace and withdrawal, Saddam Hussein dug in and moved massive forces into Kuwait. While the world waited, while Saddam stalled, more damage was being done to the fragile economies of the Third World, the emerging democracies of Eastern Europe, to the entire world, including to our own economy.

The United States, together with the United Nations, exhausted every means at our disposal to bring this crisis to a peaceful end.

However, Saddam clearly felt that by stalling and threatening and defying the United Nations he could weaken the forces arrayed against him.

While the world waited Saddam Hussein met every overture of peace with open contempt. While the world prayed for peace Saddam prepared for war.

I had hoped that when the United States Congress, in historic debate, took its resolute action Saddam would realize he could not prevail and would move out of Kuwait in accord with the United Nations resolutions. He did not do that.

Instead, he remained intransigent, certain that time was on his side. Saddam was warned over and over again to comply with the will of the United Nations—leave Kuwait or be driven out. Saddam has arrogantly rejected all warnings. Instead, he tried to make this a dispute between Iraq and the United States of America.

Well, he failed. Tonight, 28 nations, countries from five continents—Europe and Asia, Africa and the Arab League—have forces in the Gulf area standing shoulder-to-shoulder against Saddam Hussein. These countries had hoped the use of force could be avoided. Regrettably, we now believe that only force will make him leave.

Prior to ordering our forces into battle, I instructed our military commanders to take every necessary step to prevail as quickly as possible and with the greatest degree of protection possible for American people before that this will not be another Vietnam.

And I repeat this here tonight. Our troops will have the best possible support in the entire world. And they will not be asked to fight with one hand tied behind their back.

I'm hopeful that this fighting will not go on for long and that casualties will be held to an absolute minimum. This is an historic moment. We have in this past year made great progress in ending the long era of conflict and Cold War. We have before us the opportunity to forge for ourselves and for future generations a new world order, a world where the rule of law, not the law of the jungle, governs the conduct of nations. When we are successful, and we will be, we have a real chance at this new world order, an order in which a credible United Nations can use its peacekeeping role to fulfil the promise and vision of the U.N.'s founders.

We have no argument with the people of Iraq. Indeed, for the innocents caught in this conflict, I pray for their safety. Our goal is not the conquest of Iraq. It is the liberation of Kuwait.

It is my hope that somehow the Iraqi people can even now convince their dictator that he must lay down his arms, leave Kuwait and let Iraq itself rejoin the family of peace-loving nations.

Thomas Paine wrote many years ago: "These are the times that try men's souls." Those well-known words are so very true today.

But even as planes of the multinational forces attack Iraq, I prefer to think of peace, not war. I am convinced not only that we will prevail, but that out of the horror of combat will come the recognition that no nation can stand against a world united, no nation will be permitted to brutally assault its neighbor.

No president can easily commit our sons and daughters to war.

They are the nation's finest. Ours is an all-volunteer force, magnificently trained, highly motivated. The troops know why they're there. And listen to what they say, for they've said it better than any president or prime minister ever could. Listen to Hollywood Huddleston, Marine lance corporal.

He says, "Let's free these people so we can go home and be free again." And he's right. The terrible crimes and tortures committed by Saddam's henchmen against the innocent people of Kuwait are an affront to mankind and a challenge to the freedom of all.

Listen to one of our great officers out there, Marine Lieutenant General Walter Boomer. He said, "There are things worth fighting for. A world in which brutality and lawlessness are allowed to go unchecked isn't the kind of world we're going to want to live in."

Listen to Master Sergeant J.K. Kendall of the 82nd Airborne. "We're here for more than just the price of a gallon of gas. What we're doing is going to chart the future of the world for the next 100 years. It's better to deal with this guy now than five years from now."

And finally, we should all sit up and listen to Jackie Jones, an Army lieutenant, when she says, "If we let him get away with this, who knows what's going to be next?" I've called upon Hollywood and Walter and J.P. and Jackie and all their courageous comrades in arms to do what must be done.

Tonight America and the world are deeply grateful to them and to their families.

And let me say to everyone listening or watching tonight: When the troops we've sent in finish their work, I'm determined to bring them home as soon as possible. Tonight, as our forces fight, they and their families are in our prayers.

May God bless each and every one of them and the coalition forces at our side in the Gulf, and may He continue to bless our nation, the United States of America.

THE WAR IS OVER:
A FRAMEWORK FOR PEACE[1]
George H. W. Bush[2]

On March 6, 1991, less than two months after announcing the military attack on Iraq, President George Bush addressed a joint session of Congress in a nationally televised speech proclaiming victory in the war in the Middle East and proposing measures to promote peace. He promised that he would not back away from America's difficult new responsibilities in the Middle East.

Maureen Dowd, reporting the address, wrote:

> The speech, capping a half-year of extraordinary diplomatic and military maneuvers that put the nation on an emotional roller-coaster, was a time for the President to savor the nearly unanimous accolades for his skill in cementing a disparate coalition and conducting a swift and victorious war. (*New York Times*, March 7, 1991, p. A4.)

In a *New York Times*/CBS News poll the same week, Bush received an eighty-seven per cent approval rating that matched the highest level ever recorded for a president—that given Harry S. Truman after the end of World War II.

Bush delivered the speech at 8:00 P.M. His wife, Barbara Bush, sat in the balcony as he spoke, surrounded by a daughter, daughter-in-law, the wife of the vice president, and spouses of cabinet members.

---

[1]Delivered to a joint session of Congress held in the House of Representatives, Washington, D.C., at 8:00P.M. on March 6, 1991.
[2]For biographical note, see Appendix.

President Bush's speech: Mr. President. Mr. Speaker. Members of Congress: Five short weeks ago, I came to this House to speak to you about the State of the Union. We met then in time of war. Tonight, we meet in a world blessed by the promise of peace.

From the moment Operation Desert Storm commenced on Jan. 16, until the time the guns fell silent at midnight one week ago, this nation has watched its sons and daughters with pride, watched over them with prayer. As Commander in Chief, I can report to you: Our armed forces fought with honor and valor. As President, I can report to the nation: aggression is defeated. The war is over.

This is a victory for every country in the coalition, and for the United Nations. A victory for unprecedented international cooperation and diplomacy, so well led by our Secretary of State James Baker. It is a victory for the rule of law and for what is right.

Desert Storm's success belongs to the team that so ably leads our armed forces, our Secretary of Defense and our Chairman of the Joint Chiefs: Dick Cheney and Colin Powell.

And, of course, this military victory also belongs to the one the British call the "Man of the Match"—the tower of calm at the eye of Desert Storm—General Norman Schwarzkopf.

And let us not forget Saudi General Khalid, or Britain's General de la Billiere, or General Roquejoffra of France, and all the others whose leadership played such a vital role. And most importantly, all those who served in the field.

I thank the members of this Congress. Support here for our troops in battle was overwhelming. And above all, I thank those whose unfailing love and support sustained our courageous men and women: I thank the American people.

Tonight, I come to this House to speak about the world, the world after war.

The recent challenge could not have been clearer. Saddam Hussein was the villain; Kuwait the victim. To the aid of this small country came nations from North America and Europe, from Asia and South America, from Africa and the Arab world, all united against aggression.

Our uncommon coalition must now work in common purpose to forge a future that should never again be held hostage to the darker side of human nature.

Tonight in Iraq, Saddam walks amidst ruin. His war machine is crushed. His ability to threaten mass destruction is itself destroyed. His people have been lied to, denied the truth. And when his defeated legions come home, all Iraqis will see and feel the havoc he has wrought. And this I promise you: For all that Saddam has done to his own people, to the Kuwaitis, and to the entire world, Saddam and those around him are accountable.

All of us grieve for the victims of war, for the people of Kuwait and the suffering that scars the soul of the proud nation. We grieve for all our fallen soldiers and their families, for all the innocents caught up in this conflict. And yes, we grieve for the people of Iraq, a people who have never been our enemy. My hope is that one day we will once again welcome them as friends into the community of nations.

Our commitment to peace in the Middle East does not end with the liberation of Kuwait. So tonight, let me outline four key challenges to be met:

First, we must work together to create shared security arrangements in the region. Our friends and allies in the Middle East recognize that they will bear the bulk of the responsibility for regional security. But we want them to know that just as we stood with them to repel aggression so now America stands ready to work with them to secure the peace.

This does not mean stationing U.S. ground forces on the Arabian Peninsula, but it does mean American participation in joint exercises involving both air and ground forces. And it means maintaining a capable U.S. naval presence in the region, just as we have for over 40 years. Let it be clear: our vital national interests depend on a stable and secure gulf.

Second, we must act to control the proliferation of weapons of mass destruction and the missiles used to deliver them. It would be tragic if the nations of the Middle East and Persian Gulf were now, in the wake of war, to embark on a new arms race. Iraq requires special vigilance. Until Iraq convinces the world of its peaceful intentions, that its leaders will not use new revenues to rearm and rebuild its menacing war machine, Iraq must not have access to the instruments of war.

Third, we must work to create new opportunities for peace and stability in the Middle East. On the night I announced Operation Desert Storm, I expressed my hope that out of the horrors of war might come new momentum for peace. We have learned in the modern age, geography cannot guarantee security and does not come from military power alone.

All of us know the depth of bitterness that has made the dispute between Israel and its neighbors so painful and intractable. Yet, in the conflict just concluded, Israel and many of the Arab states have for the first time found themselves confronting the same aggressor. By now, it should be plain to all parties that peacemaking in the Middle East requires compromise. At the same time, peace brings real benefits to everyone. We must do all that we can to close the gap between Israel and the Arab states and between Israelis and Palestinians. The tactics of terror lead nowhere: there can be no substitute for diplomacy.

A comprehensive peace must be grounded in United Nations Security Council Resolutions 242 and 338 and the principle of territory for peace. This principle must be elaborated to provide for Israel's security and recognition, and at the same time for legitimate Palestinian political rights. Anything else would fail the twin tests of fairness and security. The time has come to put an end to Arab-Israel conflict.

The war with Iraq is over. The quest for solutions to the problems in Lebanon, in the Arab-Israel dispute, and in the gulf must go forward with new vigor and determination. I guarantee you: no one will work harder for a stable peace in the region than we will.

Fourth, we must foster economic development for the sake of peace and progress. The Persian Gulf and Middle East form a region rich in natural resources with a wealth of untapped human potential. Resources once squandered on military might must be redirected to more peaceful ends. We are already addressing the immediate economic consequences of Iraq's aggression. Now, the challenge is to reach higher, to foster economic freedom and prosperity for all people of the region.

By meeting these four challenges we can build a framework for peace. I have asked Secretary of State Baker to go to the Middle East to begin this process. He will go to listen, to probe, to offer suggestions, and to advance the search for peace and stability. I have also asked him to raise the plight of the hostages held in Lebanon. We have not forgotten them. We will not forget them.

To all the challenges that confront this region of the world, there is no single solution, no solely American answer. But we can make a difference. America will work tirelessly as a catalyst for positive change.

But we can not lead a new world abroad if, at home, it's politics as usual on American defense and diplomacy. It's time to turn away from the temptation to protect unneeded weapons systems and obsolete bases. It's time to put an end to micro-management of foreign and security assistanc e programs, micro-management that humiliates our friends and allies and hamstrings our diplomacy. It's time to rise above the parochial and the pork barrel, to do what is necessary, what's right, and what will enable this nation to play the leadership role required of us.

The consequences of the conflict in the gulf reach far beyond the confines of the Middle East. Twice before in this century, an entire world was convulsed by war. Twice this century, out of the horrors of war hope emerged for enduring peace. Twice before, those hopes proved to be a distant dream, beyond the grasp of man.

Until now, the world we've known has been a world divided, a world of barbed wire and concrete block, conflict and cold war.

Now, we can see a new world coming into view, a world in which there is the very real prospect of a new world order. In the words of Winston Churchill, a "world order" in which "the principles of justice and fair play . . . protect the weak against the strong. . . . " A world where the United Nations, freed from cold war stalemate, is poised to fulfill the historic vision of its founders. A world in which freedom and respect for human rights find a home among all nations.

The Gulf War put this new world to its first test. And my fellow Americans: We passed that test.

For the sake of our principles, for the sake of the Kuwaiti people, we stood our ground. Because the world would not look the other way, Ambassador Al-Sabah, tonight, Kuwait is free.

Tonight, as our troops begin to come home, let us recognize that the hard work of freedom still calls us forward. We've learned the hard lessons of history. The victory over Iraq was not waged as "a war to end all wars." Even the new world order cannot guarantee an era of perpetual peace. But enduring peace must be our mission.

Our success in the gulf will shape not only the new world order we seek but our mission here at home.

In the war just ended, there were clearcut objectives, timetables, and, above all, an overriding imperative to achieve results. We must bring that same sense of self-discipline, that same sense of urgency, to the way we meet challenges here at home.

In my State of the Union Address and in my budget, I defined a comprehensive agenda to prepare for the next American century.

Our first priority is to get this economy rolling again. The fear and uncertainty caused by the crisis in the gulf were understandable. But now that the war is over, oil prices are down, interest rates are down, and confidence is rightly coming back. Americans can move forward to lend, spend and invest in this, the strongest economy on earth.

We must also enact the legislation that is key to building a better America. For example in 1990, we enacted an historic Clean Air Act. Now we've proposed a national energy strategy. We passed a child care bill that put power in the hands of parents. Today, we're ready to do the same thing with our schools, and expand choice in education. We passed a crime bill that made a useful start in fighting crime and drugs. This year we're sending to Congress our comprehensive crime package to finish the job. We passed the landmark Americans With Disabilities Act. Now we've sent forward our civil rights bill. We also passed the aviation bill. This year we've sent up our new highway bill.

And these are just a few of our pending proposals for reform and renewal.

Tonight, I call on Congress to move forward aggressively on our domestic front. Let's begin with two initiatives we should be able to agree on quickly: transportation and crime. And then, let's build on success with those and enact the rest of our agenda. If our forces could win the ground war in 100 hours, then surely the Congress can pass this legislation in 100 days. Let that be a promise we make tonight to the American people.

When I spoke in this House about the state of our union, I asked all of you: If we can selflessly confront evil for the sake of good in a land so far away, then surely we can make this land all that it should be. In the time since then, the brave men and women of Desert Storm accomplished more than even they may realize. They set out to confront an enemy abroad, and in the process, they transformed a nation at home.

Think of the way they went about their mission: with confidence and quiet pride. Think about their sense of duty, about all they taught us, about our values, about ourselves.

We hear so often about our young people in turmoil; how our children fall short; how our schools fails us; how American products and American workers are second class. Well, don't you believe it. The America we saw in Desert Storm was first-class talent.

And they did it using America's state-of-the art technology. We saw the excellence embodied in the Patriot missile and the patriots who made it work.

And we saw soldiers who know about honor and bravery and duty and country and the world-shaking power of these simple words.

There is something noble and majestic about the pride, about the patriotism, that we feel tonight.

So, to everyone here, and everyone watching at home, think about the men and women of Desert Storm. Let us honor them with our gratitude. Let us comfort the families of the fallen and remember each precious life lost.

Let us learn from them as well. Let us honor those who have served us by serving others.

Let us honor them as individuals, men and women of every race, all creeds and colors, by setting the face of this nation against discrimination, bigotry and hate.

I'm sure many of you saw on television the unforgettable scene of four terrified Iraqi soldiers, surrendering. They emerged from their bunker, broken, tears streaming from their eyes, fearing the worst. And then there was the American soldier. Remember what he said? He said: "It's O.K. You're all right now. You're all right now."

That scene says a lot about America, a lot about who we are. Americans are a caring people. We are a good people, a generous people. Let us always be caring and good and generous in all we do.

Soon, our troops will begin the march we've all been waiting for, their march home. I have directed Secretary Cheney to begin the immediate return of American combat units from the gulf.

Less than two hours from now, the first planeload of American soldiers will lift off from Saudi Arabia headed for the U.S.A. It will carry men and women of the 24th Mechanized Infantry Division bound for Fort Stewart, Ga. This is just the beginning of a steady flow of American troops coming home.

Let their return remind us that all those who have gone before are linked with us in the long line of freedom's march. Americans have always tried to serve, to sacrifice nobly for what we believe to be right.

Tonight, I ask every community in this country to make this coming Fourth of July a day of special celebration for our returning troops. They may have missed Thanksgiving and Christmas, but I can tell you this: for them and for their families, we can make this a holiday they'll never forget.

In a very real sense, this victory belongs to them: to the privates and the pilots, to the sergeants and the supply officers, to the men and women in the machines, and the men and women who made them work. It belongs to the regulars, to the Reserves, to the Guard. This victory belongs to the finest fighting force this nation has ever known.

We went halfway around the world to do what is moral and just and right. We fought hard, and with others we won the war. We lifted the yoke of aggression and tyranny from a small country that many Americans had never even heard of, and we ask nothing in return.

We're coming home now proud, confident, heads high. There is much that we must do at home and abroad. And we will do it. We are Americans.

May God bless this great nation, the United States of America.

GLOBAL CHALLENGES OF THE 1990s

SAVING THE ENVIRONMENT[1]
ROBERT REDFORD[2]

Robert Redford is best known as an actor. He has appeared in many successful motion pictures and, earlier, in several popular Broadway plays. In 1988 he won an Academy Award for his direction of the film "Ordinary People". Less well known is Redford's commitment to environmental protection and improvement. In 1982, he founded the Institute for Resource Management to bring together environmentalists, business leaders, energy producers, utilities, and others in an effort to find solutions to the conflicts over the way we use our national resources.

Redford addressed the National Press Club at one of its "newsmaker" luncheons at 1:00 P.M. on October 1, 1990. The club sponsors 70 such luncheons a year to which presidents, prime ministers, and prominent persons in every field are invited to deliver addresses. Redford was invited because of his distinguished record as an actor, director, and environmentalist. The speech, presented in the club's ballroom, drew a capacity audience of more than four hundred members, guests, and other journalists. Both the NPR and reporters noted that the audience was predominantly female. Judith Weintraub described the occasion as follows:

> At the press club, polite pandemonium reigned as the audience, mostly women and mostly over forty—make that over fifty-five—crowded into the ballroom (discreet little snapshot cameras in hand) for standard chicken, rice and string bean fare. No one was heard complaining about the food. The attraction was the speaker. (*Washington Post*, October 2, 1990, p. E4)

Vera Glaser, chairman of the club's speakers committee, introduced Redford.

Later, Redford also spoke to a capacity audience at the Smithsonian Institute. While many may have attended the speeches because of the "star" status of the speaker, the response to Redford's message on both occasions was favorable.

---

[1]Delivered in the ballroom of the National Press Club, Washington, D.C. at 1:00 P.M. on October 1, 1990.

[2] For biographical note, see Appendix.

At both events, Redford delivered a thoughtful speech, adroitly mixing information . . . rhetoric . . . and politics. . . . At the end of the day, Redford was weary, and clearly a little uncomfortable with all the fuss. Why did he come? "Because I care about the environment," he said. "It may sound square, and I guess I'm old fashioned. But I want to put something back into my own society— and right now it needs all the help it can get. (*Washington Post*, October 2, 1990, p. E4)

The speech was carried by both C-Span and National Public Radio.

In accompanying remarks, Congressman George Miller of California observed:

. . . for many years I have admired Robert Redford's commitment to environmental protection and improvement. His dedication is a deep and personal one to which he has devoted enormous amounts of effort and resources. (*Congressional Record*, October 2, 1990, p. E3079).

After commending the Institute for Resource Management for its efforts to resolve longstanding environmental conflicts, Miller praised Redford for looking:

. . . beyond our domestic disputes, recognizing that many of our toughest ecological problems cannot be addressed on a nation by nation basis. Nuclear waste, ozone depletion, acid rain, global warming—all require innovative international cooperation. With that goal in mind, IRM has begun a valuable exchange with the Soviet Union, bringing scientists, political leaders, and environmentalists together. (*Congressional Record*, October 2, 1990, E3079)

Robert Redford's speech:It's always a challenge to step outside the role of an actor. You never know what's going to come your way.

During the 1988 campaign, I spoke at one of the 25,000 toxic dump sites in this country and tried to say that the "environmental candidate," should give us an inkling as to how we can clean these places up.

When I finished my talk, one of the best-known national news reporters came running after me with his network crew, and I braced myself for a tough question on the waste problem. He got the camera in my face and shouted, who did I think was better-looking, me or Dan Quayle?

I guess Sam, let's call him Sam, Sam thought I was trying to pull a cover-up on this burning issue. Sometimes I have to face the facts that on some days, that's my environmental impact.

I'm here to share a concern on our environment. I'm not alone in realizing the environment has reached a point of no return. For years the struggle was to raise awareness, but now, thanks partly to the attention from the media, it is not any longer the issue. The issue is, what are we going to do about it?

I guess my involvement began before I even knew it, when I was growing up in Los Angeles at the end of the Depression and during and after World War II. I remember the excitement when the country began to open up after the war and rebuild itself. We were the most powerful nation on earth, no doubt about it. We had won the war, we had kept the world free. Our idea of progress was to build with no limit. It was exciting. We were taught this was our manifest destiny. But then something happened. I watched as the green, open spaces turned into concrete malls and freeways, and the clean, pure air turned into smog alerts. I watched as unbridled development became the order of the day. Oil drills appeared off the beaches, along with oilspills in the water and hunks of tar on the sand. The smell of orange blossoms turned into exhaust fumes.

It felt like my home was being taken away from me. I felt my roots being pulled out from under me. And I began to take it personally.

I had to go farther and farther away to find places where the natural environment still existed.

We are finding that we can't keep using up one place and moving on to the next. We have created a world that is tipping dangerously out of balance.

Like most people in my generation, I was brought up to believe in progress. I still do. But we're at a point where we have to ask ourselves if we are the beneficiaries of our progress, or the victims? Manifest destiny doesn't work anymore. Progress from now on has to mean something different. We are running out of places, we're running out of the resources, and we're running out of time.

Scientists tell us the struggle to sustain life in this earth's environment could be won in the next decade, or lost. As we approach the year 2000, we've now heard the hard facts.

Over 100 million people, half of our population, already breathe air that is unhealthy.

Health experts tell us not to eat the fish from our own rivers, lakes, and oceans.

We've got chemical and nuclear wastes piling up at dump sites and leeching into our land and water.

Our oceans are warming, our ozone layer's got a hole that's getting bigger and, according to Carl Sagan, a whole football field of rain forests are vanishing—not every hour, not every minute, but every second! With each tick, a field of trees are gone.

It's a pretty lousy legacy we've left for our children. We should be apologizing.

Native Americans try to live with seven generations in mind. Recently we have been plunging ahead blindly, without plans for even one generation.

The environmental movement has been growing for over 20 years, and in the seventies, it seemed for a while the Government was responding, passing regulations, supporting research for things like alternative fuels. Some corporations came up with energy plans, and some discovered conservation is good business. But today, when people in every community put more and more concern into the environment, the government in Washington seems to treat it as just one more special interest to be appeased.

What happened? There was so much good work done in the seventies. Where did we go off track? In the eighties, we had an executive branch whose major policy seemed to be to set loose selfishness. The idea was to open up all our institutions— banking, housing, real estate, energy—to fast-buck kings with a minimum of regulations. What a step backwards!

The results have been catastrophic. I think for the environment, there's never been such a time of naked greed and exploitation as we have seen in the last decade. The damage done, we'll feel for a long time.

The Reagan administration filled key appointments with agents of private profit who were put in place to sell off or pay out public assets. There seemed to be a mean-spirited attitude behind them. Their idea of land use policy was just more real estate development. James Watt, Ann Burford, Rita LaValle, Samuel Pierce, all foxes guarding the chicken coop.

When the occasional critic got up to ask if something was going wrong, the strategy was to give a superior little chuckle and dismiss the "prophets of gloom and doom, running down America."

Well, I'm not a prophet of gloom and doom. I've always assumed love of land and love of country go together. I think I'm like a lot of other people who are tired of being humored and handled.

A high-water mark for trying to sucker the voters came during the 1988 campaign. No wonder so many Americans stayed home and didn't vote. The big issue we were always hearing about was who was most effective at manipulating the public.

So instead of policy-makers you hire image-makers. You create some backdrop like a Salem cigarette ad and you announce, "I'm an environmentalist!"

We all remember that famous Bush-for-President ad with sewage pipes emptying into Boston Harbor. But after the election, who was watching when the administration cut $400 million from funds to do the job?

When the President was campaigning and was pressed on global warming and the greenhouse effect, he said, "Wait till you see the White House effect!" We've seen it: it's a call for more study. Well, that's an old stall.

Of course scientists disagree on some things, but what they agree on in this matter is more than enough to take action. America has played a big role in causing this problem, and the world looks to us to take the lead in solving it.

You don't solve these problems just by labelling yourself an environmentalist. You solve them by planning and commitment.

I think the press taking political ads and holding them up against the facts is a good thing. I hope we see more of it. And it's important that you're beginning to analyze the contributions to Congress from vested interests. It makes sense to me to trace contributions to congressmen and senators from industries connected to the savings and loan scandal. But maybe we should start doing the same thing for the environment.

We need more perspective on messages like "Read my lips." There's no point reading lips, if the lips aren't saying anything. That's called lip service. And it's no answer.

It used to be that environmentalism in the minds of some meant camping out, eating granola, and hugging a tree.

I remember Senator Jake Garn of Utah once called environmentalists "back-packing kooks." It later became clear the Senator was out in space.

Today, three out of every four Americans call themselves environmentalists.

Times have changed. More people see, for instance, that saving the environment is not a trade-off for losing jobs. Saying it is just an old political dodge. Environmentalism is good business. Advances in environmentally safe products can open new economic horizons. Whole industries will be created through energy conservation. And retooling existing industries will create more jobs than it takes away. Jobs with a sense of accomplishment and connection to others. A more human side to economics.

There is some good news. Almost every major city in the United States now has recycling programs: citizens are beginning to question the need when developers come into their neighborhoods. There are wonderful examples all over the country of people and communities taking things into their own hands. But individual action alone cannot solve our environmental problems. Pollution has no boundaries. Solutions require leadership.

We have seen in the last year people rising all over the world asking more from their leaders and beginning to get it. Poll after poll indicates that the people are way ahead of the politicians.

We can't wait around anymore for solutions to come from the top. It isn't going to happen. And as for Congress, the action there is too late, too slow, and too full of compromise.

American democracy has a long history of change won by popular movements: women's suffrage, labor laws, the civil rights movement, the end of the Vietnam War. It seems to me the grassroots activism we see around the country is evidence that there is a movement underway that wants action on behalf of the environment.

What we're living with is the result of human choices. And it can be changed by making better, wiser choices. As we've learned in the past, the media can play an important role in these events. I hope the work continues.

MAN AND NATURE:
THE FUTURE OF GLOBAL ENVIRONMENT[1]
JESSICA TUCHMAN MATHEWS[2]

In May, 1990, the North American Conference on Religion and Ecology, in collaboration with thirty environmental organizations, key scientists, educators, and leaders from the public and private sectors of society, launched the 1990s as the Decade of the Environment with a four-day intercontinental conference on "Caring for Creation."

The North American Conference on Religion and Ecology is an interfaith organization designed to help people enter the environmental movement in the 1990s with a more informed understanding, a deeper commitment, and a dynamic sense of environmental ministry. The invitation to the conference stated:

> Only when we develop a profound environmental ethic for the Creation will we be sufficiently motivated to clean up our soil, water, and air. Only when we ourselves become involved in environmental mission will we learn to heal, sustain, and regenerate our earth.

The conference was held on the sixty-acre grounds of the recently completed Washington National Cathedral and in the nearby Omni Shoreham Hotel. Activities during the conference included speeches, some 30 topical workshop, interfaith religious services, audiovisual presentations, receptions, a picnic, luncheons, a banquet, organ recital, and an ecology fair. Speakers addressing the conference included prominent environmentals, theologians, economists, ecumenists, United Nations officials, authors, and elected office holders.

While most activities during the first three days of the festival took place at the Omni Shoreham Hotel, the events of the last day took place at the Washington National Cathedral. "A Festival of Creation," held from 10:00 A.M. to 5:00 P.M. on Saturday, May 19, was open to the public and free of charge. Reverend Canon Michael P. Hamilton, director of the festival, explained its purpose:

> The festival was planned to examine these issues and to call for a partnership between the religious and conservation communities. Religious people need to learn the new facts about ecology from scientists; our society needs a moral and religious framework in which

[1]Delivered to an audience of 2,500 at the Festival of Creation in the Washington National Cathedral, Washington, D. C., at 10:00 A.M. on May 19, 1990.
[2]For biographical note, see Appendix.

to make the most beneficial use of those facts. To further these purposes, the cathedral invited three prominent speakers from different walks of life to challenge us to new thinking and action. (Forward to the program, "A Festival of Creation," Cathedral Papers, Washington National Cathedral, Washington, D. C.)

The three speakers were William K. Reilly, Administrator of the Environmental Protection Agency, Dr. Jurgen Moltman, theologian at Tubingen University in Germany, and Dr. Jessica T. Mathews, an environmentalist.

Jessica Mathews, whose speech is reprinted here, is Vice President of the World Resources Institute, an organization that carries out policy research on issues of international and global significance concerning the management of natural resources and the environment. Previously, she served as the Director of Global Issues of the National Security Council and a member of the editorial board of the *Washington Post*.

Preceded by His Royal Highness Prince Philip, Duke of Edinburgh, who spoke briefly, Dr. Mathews presented her speech in the nave of the Washington National Cathedral to an audience of 2,500 people that included both conference participants and non-members attracted to the public event.

Dr. Mathews' speech: The great French biologist and Nobel laureate Jacques Monod concluded not long ago, that "Mankind was mother nature's only serious mistake." A newspaper reader attentive to the health of the global environment in the 1980s, might almost have been tempted to agree.

Consider for a moment a few of the events of this past decade: the oil price rise and widespread shortages at its beginning; the chemical accident at Bhopal; the decimation of European and high-altitude U.S. forests from acid rain and other air pollutants; the explosion at Chernobyl; ozone depletion and the discovery of a "hole" in the ozone layer over Antarctica; drought and famine in Africa; the Rhine river chemical spill; the homeless freighter that sailed the world for two years without finding a place to unload its toxic cargo; steadily rising rates of tropical deforestation and of species extinction; closed beaches from Western Europe to the Baltic to New Jersey; the Exxon Valdez oil spill; and, as the decade closed, an outbreak of freakish weather—drought and record-breaking heat in the U.S., devastating floods in Bangladesh, the most powerful hurricane ever measured, and the warmest winter in Moscow in more than a century—all bringing intense new concern to the possibilities of global warming.

There were more hungry people on the planet as the 1980s drew to a close than ever before. Seven hundred to eight hundred million people, outside of China, eat fewer calories than are necessary for an active life. Malnutrition is a major factor in the deaths of twenty-five thousand infants and children under five each *day*. Even where adequate calories are available, clean water, which is equally essential, often is not. Waterborne disease, whose solutions are environmental, rather than medical, remains a scourge. Two hundred million people are sick with schistosomiasis, 175 million with malaria, 450 million with hookworm, river blindness and sleeping sickness affect 20 million each.

The 1980s also brought rich new scientific insights. As scientists studied the chemical elements essential to life—carbon, nitrogen, phosphorous and sulfur—they quickly found that their natural cycles through earth, air, water and living things were being affected on a global scale by human activities. Non-chemical changes are equally massive. On land, soil erosion and deforestation are accelerating the flow of sediments and nutrients to the ocean in some places, while dams built for irrigation and electricity interrupt the natural flow in others. The permanent loss of species—now estimated to stand at four per hour—utterly disrupts the natural balance between speciation and extinction.

The more closely scientists looked at the planet's structure and metabolism, from the top of the stratosphere to the ocean canyons, the more the evidence of rapid change accumulated. A sense of urgency gradually filtered through to governments that man is now the principal agent of environmental change on the planet, and that if humanity is to live successfully with its ability to alter natural systems it must first understand those systems and the ways in which human society depends on their normal functioning. Unless policies change, some scientists warn, man's impacts on the planet are so profound and are accumulating so rapidly that irreversible damage could occur—to put it bluntly—before we have any idea of what we are doing. Since man's ability to tinker inadvertently with the basic physiology of the planet is new in history, it is worth spending a few minutes to look at these changes in more detail.

At the core of all environmental trends lies population growth. It took 130 years for world population to grow from 1 billion to 2 billion; it will take just this decade to climb from 5 billion to 6 billion. Though the *rate* of growth is slowing, the human family grows by 93 million each year, a larger increment than ever before. Africa, already mired in poverty and struggling against a falling per capita GNP, will add more than the present population of the U.S. between 1980 and 2000. If fertility continues to decline at its present slow rate, demographers predict that the human population will level off at a staggering 14 billion, almost triple today's population, not at the 9 or 10 billion that seemed most likely just a few years ago.

No simple relationship links population levels and the resource base. Policies, technologies and institutions intervene between population growth and its impacts and can spell the difference between a highly stressed, degraded environment and one that could sustainably provide for many more people. Sometimes absolute numbers are crucial. Most often, though, the *rate* of growth is most important. Whereas a government might be fully capable of providing food, housing, jobs and health care for a population growing at one percent per year (and therefore doubling in 72 years), it might be completely overwhelmed by an annual growth rate of three percent, which would double the population in 24 years.

While the U.S. and the Soviet Union are each growing at just under one percent per year, and Europe only half that fast, Africa is expanding by about three percent annually and Asia and Latin America by about two percent. By 2025 the working age population in the developing countries alone will be larger than the world's current total population. Clearly these countries face an urgent choice. For many of them, current rates of growth mean that available capital will be swallowed up in meeting the needs of today's populations rather than invested in the job creation and resource conservation that will be needed to sustain their children. And of course, there are global impacts as well.

The most serious form of renewable resource decline is tropical deforestation. Globally, ten trees are being cut down for every one that is replanted, and an area twice the size of Austria is deforested each year. These luxuriant forests are deceptively fragile. Once disturbed, the entire ecosystem can unravel. The loss of the trees interrupts nutrient cycling; the soil loses fertility; plant and animal species lose their habitat and disappear; acute fuelwood shortages arise (especially in the dry tropical forests); without groundcover the soil erodes, and downstream rivers suffer siltation, causing both flooding and droughts, and damage to expensive irrigation and hydroelectric systems on which hopes for economic growth are pinned. Planned to last for 50–100 years, the dams can silt up almost overnight, leaving only foreign debt as a legacy. The record is probably held by a large dam in China which silted up completely in 4 years.

Traced through its effects on agriculture, energy supply and water resources, deforestation impoverishes about a billion people, and often leaves political as well as economic chaos in its wake. In Haiti, many of the boat people who fled to the U.S. left because of the brutality of the Duvaliers. But many were forced into the boats by the impossible task of farming the bare rock left behind by near total deforestation and soil erosion. Haitians are by no means the only environmental refugees. No one knows the true numbers, but in Indonesia, Central America, and sub-Saharan Africa, millions have been forced to leave their homes in part because the loss of plant cover and the consequent disappearance of soil have made it impossible to grow food. Where the refugees settle, they add to the local demand for food and put new burdens on the land, spreading the environmental stress that forced them from their homes like a disease. Resource mismanagement is not the only cause of these mass movements, of course. Religious and ethnic conflicts, political repression and other forces are at work. The environmental causes are simply the most often ignored.

The tropical forests also harbor most of the planet's genetic wealth, the heritage of 3.5 billion years of evolution. This diversity is therefore vanishing on a scale not seen since the disappearance of the dinosaurs. Extinction is a normal part of nature, but today's rate is 1,000 to 10,000 times greater than the natural rate. With the loss already at 100 species per day, one-fifth of all the species living in 1980 may be gone by the end of this decade.

The loss will be felt aesthetically, scientifically, and economically. Its costs are impossible even to estimate. A few years ago, a Mexican graduate student stumbled upon a primitive form of perennial corn which appears to exist nowhere else in the world but on that single hilltop, and which would have been quickly wiped out but for his alertness. If the perennial character can be bred into commercial corn its environmental and economic value will be enormous.

Genetic diversity is a virtually untapped resource. Man currently makes use of less than one percent of what is available.

Among the vast numbers of unused types of edible plants, for example, are a great many with equal or greater potential than the few that now form the basis of the human diet. The bitter irony is that genetic diversity is being lost on a grand scale at the very moment when biotechnology makes it possible to fully exploit the resource for the first time.

The most truly global and potentially threatening of environmental trends is greenhouse warming. The greenhouse effect results from the fact that the planet's atmosphere is largely transparent to incoming radiation from the sun but absorbs much of the lower energy radiation re-emitted by the earth. The effect is a natural phenomenon that makes the earth warm enough to support life. But as emissions of greenhouse gases increase, the planet warms *un*naturally. Carbon dioxide, the product of all combustion and therefore of all fossil fuel use, is the principal greenhouse gas.

There are many uncertainties about greenhouse climate change, but a scientific consensus exists on its central features: the soundness of the theory; the identity of the greenhouse gases; the rate at which their concentrations are growing, and in most cases, the reasons for that increase. There is also agreement that global average temperature has risen by slightly more than half a degree centigrade since the industrial revolution began, at the low end of the range the theory predicts. The uncertainties arise over how much warming will result from added greenhouse gases, and how fast it will occur. The questions, in short, are not whether, but when and how much.

Hotter temperatures are only one of the expected results. Precipitation patterns would shift, perhaps causing Dust Bowl-like conditions in key grain producing areas. Ocean currents may also shift, dramatically altering climate. A diversion of the Gulf Stream, for example, would make Western Europe far colder than it is today. Sea level would rise due to thermal expansion of the oceans and the melting of land-based ice. The predicted rise would inundate large coastal regions, erode shorelines, destroy coastal marshes and swamps (both areas of very high biological productivity), affect water supplies through the intrusion of salt water, and put at high risk the vastly disproportionate share of the world's economic infrastructure that is packed along coastlines. The great low-lying river deltas, from the Mississippi to the Nile and the Ganges, would likely be flooded. Some island nations would disappear altogether.

There would be positive consequences as well. Some plants would grow more quickly (though many, alas, will be weeds), fertilized by the additional carbon dioxide. Rainfall may rise in what are now arid but potentially fertile regions. Conditions for agriculture may also improve in some northern regions. The net effect, however, is almost certain to prove costly to all countries because all depend so heavily on the normal, predictable functioning of the climate system. Adapting to a changing climate, where that is possible, and when the impacts can be predicted in time, will be very expensive. Developing countries, with small reserves of capital, few scientists and engineers, and weak central governments, will be especially hard hit. Many needed adaptations will be prohibitively costly, and some of the most severe impacts, such as those on wildlife and ecosystems, will be beyond the reach of human correction.

Greenhouse warming is closely linked to stratospheric ozone depletion, which is caused by a group of manmade compounds known as chlorofluorocarbons, or CFCs. These, it turns out, are also potent greenhouse gases. The increased ultraviolet radiation caused by ozone loss will produce an increase in skin cancers, eye damage, crop loss and other as yet unknown impacts on plants and animals, including perhaps the suppression of immune systems.

Ozone depletion is a valuable object lesson in environmental humility. Chlorofluorocarbons were thoroughly tested when first introduced and found to be completely benign. Their possible effect on the remote stratosphere was simply never considered. More than a decade after the effect was discovered, a related phenomenon came to light, that led to a continent-sized "hole" in the layer over Antarctica. This history reminds us that our present knowledge of planetary mechanisms is scanty. The possibility of surprise, possibly a quite nasty surprise, must be placed rather high on the list of likely outcomes. The greatest risk may well come from a completely unanticipated direction, for we lack both crucial knowledge and early warning signals.

Do all these trends mean that the human prospect is bleak? Certainly, we—the human species—cannot go on as we are without fundamental change. Without it there is no way the planet can accommodate a doubling or more of population, at least a fivefold rise in economic output and a tripling of energy use all by the middle of the next century. We will need to redesign our technologies from the inside out, rather than continue to fiddle with what comes out the end of the pipe. The new designs must follow nature's example in which there are few if any wastes, materials are used with high efficiency, and every byproduct is used as the starting point in other processes. Look in a biochemistry text and you will see that all of nature's systems are circular designs. Nothing is linear, as most manmade processes are.

Such change is well within our technological capacity. With only a modest effort many of our present practices could be made to look primitive. The U.S. could cut its energy use in half with presently available technologies, and there is no telling what could be achieved through a determined research effort. We use a billion pounds of pesticide each year, less than one percent of which reaches a target pest. It should not be beyond us to increase that number three, five or ten fold. Our transportation system uses marginal improvements on fifty- and one hundred-year-old technologies. The hottest thing in mass transit right now is so-called "light rail," which is just another name for the trolley car, a technology that was introduced in the 1880s. We have not begun to use the revolutionary power of information and communications technologies to transform transportation just as they have transformed banking, publishing, retailing and just about everything else. In short, we have not yet really tried to make technology serve nature instead of letting nature serve technology as a source of resources and repository for wastes.

Yet even with that ambitious goal, technological change will be the easiest part of the challenge that lies ahead. The difficult part will be understanding what we are doing to the planet before it is too late, summoning the will to choose a different future, and developing the new rules and institutions that will enable us to travel that different path. That is a tall order, I know, but notice what is not included. I do not believe that we need to change human nature or human values. We will have to change how we think—especially about the future—and how we behave, especially as a global community. But change in thought and behavior, even in deeply ingrained habit, is well within what history tells us is possible. Indeed, thought and behavior can change quickly and profoundly as conditions and institutions change. Human slavery once seemed essential to economic success, morally acceptable, even ordinary. Now it is unthinkable.

How we act is a function of what we see in the world around us, and what we see is a function of what we understand. Thus science is a powerful shaper of human behavior. From Newton to Einstein our concept of the physical universe changed our way of thinking. Darwin certainly did too. Perhaps now it is Lovelock's turn. Lovelock proposes a theory he calls Gaia after the Greek earth goddess. Gaia sees the earth as a living organism in which the non-living realm is continuously shaped by the presence of life. Not just species evolve in the Gaian view, but species and their living and non-living environment together. Thus, the apparent planning and sense of purpose that natural selection produces—and which has always been so hard to grasp—is broadened to include the entire planet. It is far too early to say that Lovelock is correct, but the theory has generated exciting research, which is always suggestive. If Gaia is correct, it will force us to shift our focus from an overriding concern for the welfare of our own species to that of the planet as a whole.

Science regularly makes a fool of anyone who tries to predict its future. Darwin himself wrote in his *Autobiography*, "I rejoice that I have avoided controversies." But I will take the risk and hazard a guess that the revolutionary sciences of our time (just as astronomy and physics have been in the past) will be ecology and the study of earth as a living whole.

From that science will come the realization that despite technology, and what our major religions have taught, beginning with Genesis, man does *not* exercise dominion over nature. The reverse may well be closer to the truth: nature rules man, both because it shapes our minds, bodies and spirit and because we are, and will always remain, so economically dependent upon it. Our world view now is that man is not only above, but separate from nature, which exists solely to serve his purposes. We do not need to go to the other extreme as some suggest, and see ourselves as no different from nor better than a chimpanzee or a guppy. We can continue to view ourselves as the peak of creation, but we must discard our misguided sense of separateness. In that endeavor lies a great task for organized religion.

Those whose work keeps them closest to nature understand this best. They learn that, except in a narrow sense, or over a short term, it is hard to do better than nature. Let me give you a very simple example. When foresters first began to plant trees where old forests had been cut, they had a terrible time. The new forests looked nice, full of young, healthy trees with clean trunks and without crumbling dead trees in the way, but they didn't grow well. Slowly the foresters learned that everything in the natural forest served a purpose: without the dead hollow trees for owls and woodpeckers to nest in, insect populations got out of control; without the lichen that coats the trunks of old trees, forests could not fix enough nitrogen from the air to fertilize themselves.

Usually, the connections are harder to trace. The human system appears to outperform nature, but only till we count the cost in some other place or at some later time. This is a lesson that will have to be learned again and again. As human demands on the planet accelerate, we will learn the lesson on a larger and larger scale, until eventually we learn to incorporate it into how we think and behave.

The influence of nature on man's spirit should also be a positive force for change. It is the source of man's creativity. Probably the original inspiration for stained glass, like the magnificence that surrounds us, came from someone who had seen how sunlight filters through the leaves of a high tree canopy. Each of us has experienced the force with which a beautiful day lifts the spirit even in the middle of a city. We know the strength of our connection to certain species: witness all the fuss over the three trapped whales a few years ago. And we need wilderness, not just for recreation, but as Wallace Stegner wrote, "for spiritual renewal, the recognition of identity, and the birth of awe." I may be too optimistic here, because of course these connections have always been with us and in recent centuries haven't been notably influential. But perhaps as nature grows ever more threatened, its value will seem more obvious and urgent. Or perhaps as we see less of nature, it will be all the easier to lose.

If science, religion, and man's emotional connections to nature can reshape how we perceive our role on the planet, then institutional changes can pave the way to new policies and economic behavior. Prosaic and rather simple changes will have a sweeping impact. For example, economic indicators currently ignore environmental costs. When countries calculate their national income accounts—their GNP—they value and depreciate everything manmade, even intangibles like knowledge. But the accounts completely ignore environmental resources. The result is policies that can not distinguish between using income—say, the sustainable yield of lumber or fish—and using up a capital asset, namely the forest or fishery itself. In the private sector, we have indicators that measure how efficiently labor and capital are used, but nothing that measures environmental productivity—how much resources are used and emissions produced per unit of economic output. Changing these and other signals, to which policymakers are exquisitely tuned, will automatically and effortlessly go a long way toward turning bad policies into good ones.

Global environmental trends all pose potentially serious losses to national economies, are immune to solution by one or a few countries, and render geographic borders irrelevant. The internationalization of finance and industry and the boundary-erasing effects of remote sensing technology and linked computers, have the same effect. Even the amount we travel makes health policy, once solely a domestic prerogative, into an international issue. These invasions of national sovereignty make governments less central than they once were. I don't mean to suggest that nation states will disappear, but some of the powers they have held will be inherited by other actors: by individuals, the business sector and international organizations.

Individuals have a particularly important role to play. First, because changes in thought and understanding come from people, not institutions. Individuals will also provide much of the impetus toward a functioning global community in place of today's collection of nations. Working through their own international communities—science, business, labor, citizen activism, and so on—people offset the centrifugal forces that govern relations among states. Jean Monnet, the father of the European Community, knew this when he described his intention as "not to form coalitions between states, but union among people." That Monnet's wild dream is now a reality, and that Europe is in the longest period of peace in its history, is to me another hopeful portent.

Whether each of our individual preferences is for scholarship or business, civic action or research, the nudge of a petition or the slap of a lawsuit, all of us must believe and behave as if, to paraphrase another famous Frenchman, the fate of the planet is too important to be left to governments. Individual efforts in the face of problems which have a global dimension may seem inadequate, even futile. But, in aggregate, they are not. "Your actions may seem insignificant", Gandhi said, "but it's crucial that you do them".

For all that can be achieved outside of government, changes in national policy are also absolutely vital. Looking at the United States today and over the past decade, one cannot be very hopeful about the prospects for leadership in the Executive or the Congressional branch. Despite the manifest flaws in our political system as it functions today, I cannot put all of the blame on politicians, because leadership is a two-way street.

Leaders need followers who are willing to be led. We Americans have given no sign that we would reward leadership no matter how enlightened or beneficial. We need to care a lot more about our federal government and demand a lot more of it. We should insist that it provide what we want, while being more honest in matching those expectations with our willingness to pay. We must stop being diverted by phony debates over manufactured symbols and images. We need to care more about the budget and less about flag burning. Let's get rid of those who are content to do nothing more than nurse along a manifestly inadequate status quo, and seek out those who are determined to do better. And when we find leaders like that let's do what's necessary to elect them and then hold them accountable.

You will have gathered by this time that I am optimistic about our ability as a species to develop a permanent *modus vivendi* with the earth. Being an intensely practical person I have no other option. But I do not underestimate the challenge. Indeed it is in part because present policies are so bad that I see so much room for improvement. I also believe that a positive outlook is an essential ingredient of success. If our aim is merely to make a bad thing marginally better, we will never unleash the necessary energy and motivation. We need to believe in something bigger than fear of the consequences of inaction.

The historian Barbara Tuchman wrote that "We cannot reckon on the better impulses predominating in the world, only that they will always appear." They are appearing now, in thousands of gatherings like this one that would not have taken place even a few years ago. Our job is to seize this fleeting opportunity and to blow the scattered sparks into a bonfire for change.

THE SHAME OF HUNGER[1]
Elie Wiesel[2]

Alan Shawn Feinstein is the author of a highly successful investment newsletter and a syndicated column for investors, as well as several best-selling financial guides, a novel, and several children's books. More important, Feinstein believes that no one in this world should go hungry, and he has sought to make that belief a reality by putting his wealth back into the community. He has founded food banks and contributed to a wide range of charitable causes benefitting children and the elderly.

On April 5, 1990, the fourth annual Alan Shawn Feinstein Awards for the Prevention and Reduction of World Hunger were presented at Brown University. The keynote speaker at the evening ceremony was Elie Wiesel, the writer, educator, and philosopher once described as "the spiritual archivist of the Holocaust." Wiesel's humanitarian efforts have earned him the Congressional Gold Medal of Achievement, the Medal of Liberty, and the 1986 Nobel Prize for Peace. (See *Representative American Speeches, 1986–87*, pp. 71–74, for his Nobel prize acceptance speech.)

Wiesel, who lost his parents and a sister in the Holocaust and was himself imprisoned in concentration camps at Auschwitz and Buchenwald, had known hunger first hand, as he vividly described in his speech at the awards ceremony:

> I have been obsessed with the idea of hunger for years and years because I have seen what hunger can do to human beings. It is the easiest way for a tormenter to dehumanize another human being. When I think of hunger, I see images: emaciated bodies, swollen bodies, long bony arms pleading for mercy, motionless skeletons. How can one look at these images without losing sleep. And eyes, my God, eyes. Eyes that pierce your consciousness and tear your heart. How can one run away from those eyes?

Wiesel delivered his address at 8:00 P.M. in Salomon Hall of the Salomon Center Teaching to a standing-room-only crowd of approximately 800 in an auditorium with a seating capacity of 595. The speech was simulcast to a separate room with a capacity of 200, which also was full. The audience included students and faculty of Brown University, members of the Providence Community, and participants in the third annual Confer-

---

[1]Delivered at the fourth annual Alan Shawn Feinstein Awards for the Prevention and Reduction of World Hunger ceremony in Salomon Hall at Brown University, Providence, Rhode Island, to an audience of approximately 800 at 8:00 P.M. on April 5, 1990.

[2]For biographical note, see Appendix.

ence on Hunger Research Briefing and Exchange.

A welcome by the director of the Alan Shawn Feinstein World Hunger Program, remarks by Brown University President Vartan Gregorian, and two video presentations on hunger in the 1990s preceded Wiesel's address. Following the speech, Gregorian and television correspondent Morley Safer presented the awards. Feinstein spoke at the closing of the ceremonies.

The speech was reprinted in *Why* (World Hunger Year) magazine, and was inserted in the *Congressional Record* of January 30, 1991, by Senator Paul Simon.

Elie Wiesel's speech: I have been obsessed with the idea of hunger for years and years because I have seen what hunger can do to human beings. It is the easiest way for a tormenter to dehumanize another human being. When I think of hunger, I see images: emaciated bodies, swollen bellies, long bony arms pleading for mercy, motionless skeletons. How can one look at these images without losing sleep?

And eyes, my God, eyes. Eyes that pierce your consciousness and tear your heart. How can one run away from those eyes? The eyes of a mother who carries her dead child in her arms, not knowing where to go, or where to stop. At one moment you think that she would keep on going, going, going—to the end of the world. Except she wouldn't go very far, for the end of the world, for her, is there. Or the eyes of the old grandfather, who probably wonders where creation had gone wrong, and whether it was all worthwhile to create a family, to have faith in the future, to transmit misery from generation to generation, whether it was worth it to wager on humankind.

And then, the eyes of all eyes, the eyes of children, so dark, so immense, so deep, so focused and yet at the same time, so wide and so vague. What do they see? What do hungry children's eyes see? Death? Nothingness? God? And what if they saw us, all of us, in our complacency if not complicity? And what if their eyes are the eyes of our judges?

Hunger and death, death and starvation, starvation and shame. Poor men and women who yesterday were proud members of their tribes, bearers of ancient culture and lore, and who are now wandering among corpses. What is so horrifying in hunger is that it makes the individual death an anonymous death. In times of hunger, the individual death has lost its uniqueness. Scores of hungry people die daily, and those who mourn for them will die the next day, and the others will have no strength left to mourn.

Hunger in ancient times represented the ultimate malediction to society. Rich and poor, young and old, kings and servants, lived in fear of drought. They joined the priests in prayer for rain. Rain meant harvest, harvest meant food, food meant life, just as lack of food meant death. It still does.

Hunger and humiliation. A hungry person experiences an overwhelming feeling of shame. All desires, all aspirations, all dreams lose their lofty qualities and relate to food alone. I may testify to something that I have witnessed, in certain places at certain times, those people who were reduced by hunger, diminished by hunger, they did not think about theology, nor did they think about God or philosophy or literature. They thought of a piece of bread. A piece of bread was, to them, God, because a piece of bread then filled one's universe. Diminished by hunger, man's spirit is diminished as well. His fantasy wanders in quest of bread. His prayer rises toward a bowl of milk.

Thus the shame.

In Hebrew, the word hunger is linked to shame. The prophet Ezekiel speaks about "Kherpat raav," the shame of hunger. Of all the diseases, of all the natural diseases and catastrophes, the only one that is linked to shame in Scripture is hunger—the shame of hunger. Shame is associated neither with sickness nor even with death, only with hunger. For man can live with pain, but no man ought to endure hunger.

Hunger means torture, the worst kind of torture. The hungry person is tortured by more than one sadist alone. He or she is tortured, every minute, by all men, by all women. And by all the elements surrounding him or her. The wind. The sun. The stars. By the rustling of trees and the silence of night. The minutes that pass so slowly, so slowly. Can you imagine time, can you image time, when you are hungry?

And to condone hunger means to accept torture, someone else's torture.

Hunger is isolating; it may not and cannot be experienced vicariously. He who never felt hunger can never know its real effects, both tangible and intangible. Hunger defies imagination; it even defies memory. Hunger is felt only in the present.

There is a story about the great French-Jewish composer Daniel Halevy who met a poor poet: "Is it true," he asked, "that you endured hunger in your youth?" "Yes," said the poet. "I envy you," said the composer. "I never felt hunger."

And Gaston Bachelard, the famous philosopher, voiced his view on the matter, saying, "My prayer to heaven is not, "Oh God, give us our daily bread, but give us our daily hunger."

I don't find these anecdotes funny. These anecdotes were told about and by people who were not hungry. There is no romanticism in hunger, there is no beauty in hunger, no creativity in hunger. There is no inspiration in hunger. Only shame. And solitude. Hunger creates its own prison walls; it is impossible to demolish them, to avoid them, to ignore them.

Thus, if hunger inspires anything at all, it is, and must be, only the war against hunger.

Hunger is not a matter of choice. Of course, you may say, but what about the hunger striker? Haven't they chosen to deprive themselves of nourishment, aren't they hungry? Yes, but not the same way. First, they alone suffer, those around them do not. Second, they are given the possibility to stop any time they so choose, any time they win, any time their cause is attained. Not so [with] the people in Africa. Not so [with] the people in Asia. Their hunger is irrevocable. And last, hunger strikers confer a meaning, a purpose, upon their ordeal. Not so [with] the victims in Ethiopia or Sudan. Their hunger is senseless. And implacable.

The worst stage in hunger is to see its reflection in one's brother, one's father, one's child. Hunger renders powerless those who suffer its consequences. Can you imagine a mother unable, helpless, to alleviate her child's agony? There is the abyss in shame. There, suffering and hunger and shame multiply.

In times of hunger, family relations break down. The father is impotent, his authority gone, the mother is desperate, and the children, the children, under the weight of accumulated suffering and hunger, grow older and older, and soon, they will be older than their grandparents.

But then, on the other hand, perhaps of all of the woes that threaten and plague the human condition, hunger alone can be curtailed, attenuated, appeased, and ultimately vanquished, not by destiny, nor by the heavens, but by human beings. We cannot fight earthquakes, but we can fight hunger. Hence our responsibility for its victims. Responsibility is the key word. Our tradition emphasizes the question, rather than the answer. For there is a "quest" in question, but there is "response" in responsibility. And this responsibility is what makes us human, or the lack of it, inhuman.

Hunger differs from other cataclysms such as floods in that it can be prevented or stopped so easily. One gesture of generosity, one act of humanity, may put an end to it, at least for one person. A piece of bread, a bowl of rice or soup makes a difference. And I wonder, what would happen, just imagine, what would happen, if every nation, every industrialized or non-industrialized nation, would simply decide to sell one aircraft, and for the money, feed the hungry. Why shouldn't they? Why shouldn't the next economic summit, which includes the wealthiest, most powerful, the richest nations in the world, why shouldn't they decide that since there are so many aircrafts, why shouldn't they say, "Let's sell just one, just one, to take care of the shame and the hunger and the suffering of millions of people."

So the prophet's expression, "the shame of hunger," must be understood differently. When we speak of our responsibility for the hungry, we must go to the next step and say that the expression "shame of hunger" does not apply to the hungry. It applies to those who refuse to help the hungry. Shame on those who could feed the hungry, but are too busy to do so.

Millions of human beings constantly are threatened in Africa and Asia, and even in our own country, the homeless and the hungry. Many are going to die of starvation, and it will be our fault. For we could save them, and if we do not, we had better have a good reason why we don't.

If we could airlift food and sustenance and toothpaste to Berlin in 1948, surely we could do as much for all the countries, Ethiopia and Sudan and Mozambique and Bangladesh, in the year 1990. Nations capable of sending and retrieving vehicles in space must be able to save human lives on earth.

Let our country, and then other countries, see in hunger an emergency that must be dealt with *right now*. Others, our allies, will follow. Private relief often has been mobilized in the past: Jews and Christians, Moslems and Buddhists have responded to dramatic appeals from the African desert. One of my most rewarding moments was when I went to the Cambodian border 10 years ago and saw there the misery, the weakness, the despair, the resignation, of the victims.

But I also saw the extraordinary international community motivated by global solidarity to help them. And who were they?

They represented humankind at its best: there were Jews and Christians and Moslems and Buddhists from all over the world. And if ever I felt proud of the human condition, it was then. It is possible to help, but private help is insufficient. Government-organized help is required; only governments can really help solve this tragedy that has cosmic repercussions.

We must save the victims of hunger simply because they *can* be saved. We look therefore at the horror-filled pictures, when we dare to look, day after day. And I cannot help but remember those who had surrounded us elsewhere, years and years ago. Oh, I do not wish to make comparisons. I never do. But I do have the right to invoke the past, not as a point of analogy, but as a term of reference. I refuse to draw analogies with the Jewish tragedy during the era of darkness; I still believe and will always believe that no event ought to be compared to that event. But I do believe that human tragedies, all human tragedies, are and must be related to it. In other words, it is because one people has been singled out for extinction that others were marked for slavery. It is because entire communities were wiped out then that others were condemned to die later in other parts of the planet. All events are intertwined.

And it is because we have known hunger that we now must eliminate hunger. It is because we have been subjected to shame that we must now oppose shame. It is because we have witnessed humanity at its worst that we now must appeal to humanity at its best.

REFUGEES IN THE 1990s[1]
Princeton N. Lyman[2]

The Church World Service is a division of the National Council of Churches of Christ in the U.S.A. devoted to providing worldwide aid to the needy. It engages in works of mercy, relief, technical assistance, reconstruction, and interchurch aid, ministering to the victims of war, famine, flood, and other emergencies. Founded in 1946, the service supports

[1] Delivered to the annual meeting of the World Church Service/Immigration and Refugee Program at 10:00 A.M., February 12, 1991, in Washington, D. C.

[2] For biographical note, see Appendix.

or is directly responsible for self-help development projects in more than 70 countries and has resettled between 500,000 and 600,000 refugees in the United States in the last 40 years.

On February 12, 1991, Princeton N. Lyman, director of the Bureau for Refugee programs of the United States Department of State delivered the keynote address to the annual national staff conference of the Church World Service's Immigration and Refugee Program. A career diplomat, Dr. Lyman has spent most of his public life serving on or directing aid programs and missions throughout the world. He has been honored for his work with awards from the Agency for International Development, the Department of State, and the President of the United States.

In his address, Ambassador Lyman noted:

> Those of us in government have an important role to play. We must develop proposals, ceilings, and budgets which determine just how many and from what countries refugees can come to the United States. But it is you and your affiliates—your volunteers and many families which become involved—which make the program concrete and make it successful. We deal with numbers and abstractions, you deal with the people involved. You make each refugee welcome; you give them their start, their first real taste of America. You give the program its heart.

Inserting the address in the *Congressional Record*, Senator Edward M. Kennedy emphasized the importance of Lyman's topic, "Refugees in the 1990s," saying,

> . . . the international community is faced today with the challenge of an unprecedented movement of refugees—from Indochina to the Soviet Union to Liberia. In fact, the number of refugees around the world has doubled in recent years, while the resources which we contribute to their care has diminished. This is a time which invites vision and insight, and a debate is now occuring within the international community as to how to respond to existing demands and future trends. (March 5, 1991, S2598).

Ambassador Lyman delivered his address to an audience of 119 staff, committee members, and volunteers in the Immigration and Refugee Program at 10:00 A.M.

Princeton Lyman's speech: I appreciate your invitation to make the keynote address for your annual meeting in 1991. We are at the beginning of the final decade of the twentieth century and the question hangs over us whether this is the transition to a new cen-

tury of world peace and cooperation or the beginning of a new
era of uncertainty and instability. Certainly the prospects for this
decade have changed dramatically in just the past few months.

Before addressing the future as it concerns refugees, let me
take this opportunity to express the appreciation of all of us in the
government who work on refugee affairs for the extraordinary
dedication and conscientiousness which each of you and your local organizations devote to refugees coming to the U. S. Those
of us in government have an important role to play. We must develop proposals, ceilings, and budgets which determine just how
many and from what countries refugees can come to the U. S. But
it is you and your families which become involved, which make
the program concrete and make it successful. We deal with the
people involved. You make each refugee welcome; you give them
their start, their first taste of America. You give the program its
heart.

When Dale de Haan asked me to make this talk about the issues we will face in the 1990s, I thought of it as a speculative look
into the future. Then it occurred to me that we are in the 1990s.
The issues we will face are already largely defined for us. We will
be fortunate to solve those already on our plate.

But there are also trends and problems on the horizon rapidly
coming to the fore. We must prepare for these, lest they overwhelm us.

The situation today, and which will define much of our task
in the years ahead, is one that is not encouraging. There are some
15 million refugees in the world today, twice the number of a decade ago. Thirteen million of these are under U. N. care. Many
of these, it is important to note, are the result of long-standing
conflicts, conflicts which today may have even lost some of their
original meaning, but which linger nevertheless. They are a lesson that the legacies of one era stay with us for years, indeed decades thereafter.

Look at the major sources of refugees today. One third of the
world's refugees are Afghans. The conflict in Afghanistan was
triggered by the Soviet invasion in 1979, an invasion from which
the Soviet Union has long since withdrawn its troops, but the
struggle continues. Or look at the conflict in Mozambique, one
which has its origins in a relationship between Mozambique and
the Soviet Union that no longer pertains and from a South African policy that is rapidly changing; the internal sources of the

conflict are also disappearing with the transition to a multi-party system of government and an open economy. Still, the conflict continues, easier to begin than to end. Mozambique accounts for one million refugees. And there is Cambodia, whose internal wars hark back to the Vietnam war, the Cold War, and the rivalry between China and Vietnam, all of which contributed to tearing Cambodian society apart. Even with most of the external powers now agreed on the desirability and indeed the outlines of a settlement, it remains out of reach. Bringing just these three conflicts to an end would allow half the world's refugees under U. N. care to return home.

The positive side to this is that, as the origins of these conflicts are mitigated, active efforts to resolve them are under way. In all of the conflicts I have mentioned, intensive negotiation processes are in train, offering the hope that in the 1990s, these three major refugee problems can be finally resolved.

If that does happen, we can rejoice. But the challenge then will be to pay for these settlements. In each of the cases I have mentioned, the countries in question have been devastated, mined, people dispossessed while others have taken their land, infrastructure destroyed, education and training virtually brought to a standstill. The bill for each of these settlements—for peacekeeping forces, for repatriation of the refugees, and for redevelopment of the countries—thus runs in the billions. Are the resources there? After the tremendous efforts to finance not only the war in the Gulf but the economic damage for front line and other vulnerable states affected by it, after major efforts to assist the new democracies in Eastern Europe and to stave off disaster in the Soviet Union, will the will and resources be there to pay for these solutions? This indeed is one of the great challenges of the 1990s: to pay both for the "sins" of the past and the new problems of the 1990s.

The Gulf war may also exacerbate another old problem, one which has been with us for forty years: the Palestinian refugees. There are presently some two million Palestinian refugees living in Jordan, the Occupied Territories [The West Bank area, Gaza Strip, and Golan Heights] Syria and Lebanon. U.N. assistance to them has been able in recent years to focus on education and health, because basic food and shelter did not have to be provided; many refugees were working, in the Occupied Territories, in the Gulf and sending back remittances, in Israel. But the future of Palestinian workers in the Gulf is uncertain. Already the invasion and occupation of Kuwait has deprived tens of thousands of them of their income and life savings; they are returning not as providers but as people needing assistance themselves. The current situation has also led Israel to impose strict curfews on the refugee camps and other Palestinian living areas in the Occupied Territories, thus depriving many of their livelihood. Already, the U.N.—through UNRWA [United Nations Relief and Works Agency]—has had to begin extending emergency food assistance to both refugees and non-refugees in the Occupied Territories. And Jordan has asked how it can be expected to accommodate the perhaps hundreds of thousands of Palestinians with Jordanian travel documents who might return from the Gulf if they are no longer welcome there after the war. Jordan already claims to have received two hundred thousand Palestinians since the invasion of Kuwait. Thus an old problem may become even worse in the 1990s.

Even as these legacies of past decades carry into the 1990s, new issues are arising. None has perhaps begun to grab the attention of our friends in Europe, and in a different way in Asia, as the spectre of mass migration.

It is seemingly the changes in Eastern Europe that have brought this issue to the forefront. As societies in Eastern Europe—and one hopes in the Soviet Union—become more open, the movement of people takes on a different meaning. When Eastern Europe was under Communist control, we and our European allies treated people fleeing those regimes as refugees for the most part, even when as in some cases their individual experiences did not meet the test of persecution. But with democratic regimes in place, the presence of Poles, Romanians, and prospectively Russians take on new meaning. All over Europe, in more conferences and seminars that we can keep up with, the issue of migration is being discussed, new mechanisms of both cooperation and control are being fashioned and debated, and old systems are being reevaluated.

The source of this concern in Europe is easy to see. In the 1970s, the average annual number of asylum requests for all of Europe and North America was 25,000. In 1980, it jumped to 160,000 but then dropped to 70,000 by 1983. However, in 1990 the number went up to an extraordinary 550,000. Many are from Eastern Europe but at least half are from the Third World. So while much of the recent attention has focused on the Soviet Union and Eastern Europe, the roots of the problem are also in the Third World. Asylum systems in Europe and Canada (and indeed in the U.S.) have been overwhelmed by this rise in numbers. And as the systems have proved incapable of handling these large numbers, the problem has been addressed by inaction rather than action. What I mean is this: some 80% of asylum applications in Western Europe are rejected, yet 85% of the applicants never go back home. At the same time, Europe and North America spend—are you ready?—at least five billion dollars a year on the processing and care of asylum applicants. That is ten times the UNHCR[[United Nations High Commissioner for Refugees] budget for the 13 million refugees under its care. These are some of the factors creating concern.

The other cause for concern is that it is assumed that most of these applicants today are coming more for economic than political reasons. Europe has less of a clear immigration system than Canada, Australia, or of the U.S., so asylum application becomes in most cases the means of entry. But clearly this will not be adequate or appropriate for the 1990s.

These are many challenges for the 1990s that arise from this concern over migration.

One is protecting the principle of asylum for refugees—people fleeing persecution—as nations institute new means of control over their borders. In the backlash against rising numbers of migrants, countries sometime lean toward actions which threaten that principle. We have seen a most disturbing example of that type of action when Yugoslavia recently forced more than 300 Albanians back across the border.

Because of our concern over this issue, the U.S. has entered actively into the debate in Europe. One of our objectives is to protect the right to asylum. For example, we have encouraged and will help fund training in Eastern Europe so that those countries can manage any large influx of people and know how to obtain international help. We have urged the inclusion of the principle of asylum in the various documents coming out of these many fora.

A second challenge, however, is to define ways to protect those who are fleeing oppressive regimes for a complex set of reasons that do not fit within our traditional definition of refugees, but which also is not simply the desire for a better job. We are on tricky ground here. If the definition of refugees, i.e., someone with a well-founded fear of persecution, is broadened too far, we risk losing the sympathy and cooperation of potential first asylum countries in the face of large-scale or even moderate movement of people.

We face this problem already in Southeast Asia with the Vietnamese boat people. By 1989, neither first-asylum nor many of the other resettlement countries were prepared any longer to accept all Vietnamese boat people as refugees. For our part, we could not countenance any of them being forced back to Vietnam, even if they were not individual victims of persecution. An international agreement known as the Comprehensive Plan of Action [CPA] sought to mediate this conflict of views. The CPA provides for screening the asylum seekers to determine those who meet the refugee definition, but also provides a safe means of return for those who do not. But even this effort to extend, if you will, a modicum of international protection to the non-refugees, has been difficult. The UNHCR, by extending its activities to the process of encouraging repatriation of the screened out, has been criticized by some for abandoning its concern for refugees and asylum. On the other hand, first-asylum countries continue to balk at the special protection given to the screened-out, wanting to assure that they will return. We may see in the CPA, even with its special circumstances, a microcosm of the problems we will face in Europe in the 1990's.

The third challenge arising from this concern over migration is that of international responsibility. How should we share the tasks? At a conference I attended recently on the prospects of Soviet migration, the representatives of the newly democratic countries of East Europe said they would gladly fulfill their responsibilities of providing first asylum, assuming, of course, that the West would quickly aid them by letting the refugees pass on through to the western countries, an assumption that did not necessarily sit well with the West Europeans. And what of our responsibilities: how much of European migration should be seen as a European problem, to be addressed at least in the first instance by Europe, or how much an international problem to be shared out equally? How does one find the right balance that does indeed represent equity? In the CPA, with a shared set of responsibilities, we have agreed to resettle at least half the Vietnamese and Lao found to be refugees. Does that entitle us to ask European nations to do more for migrants coming to Europe? Will we be able to exercise sufficient influence in protection issues if we take that stand?

I began the discussion of the issues of the 1990s with old conflicts. Let me conclude this discussion of new challenges on the international front with that of new conflicts, conflicts which do not have their roots in the Cold War or other previous international rivalries, but which are arising from deep internal rifts: ethnic conflict in Liberia, ethnic and sub-regional conflict affecting Rwanda, and perhaps the same phenomena in Eastern Europe. Will we be able to mobilize the international attention and assistance to these new sources of refugees?

Or will they, less directly related to our international positions, be far from our attention and therefore our input? We have so far addressed the Liberian crisis with minimally acceptable responses, but as we see trouble in Rwanda, and growing problems in southern Senegal, and continuing civil way in Sri Lanka, our humanitarian and political impulses will be tested.

The challenges of the 1990s will also raise new issues with regard to our admissions problem. As in other refugee matters, the refugee admissions program today still addresses in large part legacies of past decades. Some 45% of our admissions come from Southeast Asia. We continue to focus on Vietnamese and Laos as a by-product of the war, the dislocations, and the continuing oppression in that region, matters in which we were so heavily involved in the past. It is a responsibility that continues and which we cannot ignore.

Another one-third of our admissions come from the Soviet Union, with special efforts in regard to religious minorities. The roots of that program go back not just to the Cold War but indeed to World War II and the Holocaust. This too is a responsibility from which we cannot turn away.

But in a few years, these clear cases of "special humanitarian concerns", will gradually decline or move gradually into the stream of regular immigration. Already our ODP [Office of Displaced Persons] in Vietnam will bring in twice as many regular immigrants as refugees in FY 91. If the present trend of migration to Israel and the U.S. continues, nearly all the Jews in the Soviet Union will have departed by the end of 1995. What will be the people of "special humanitarian concern" after these? How will we define our interests? Or will we reduce our admissions back to those of an earlier period?

Clearly the 1990s will not be dull, not lacking in challenges. We will be in transition, from addressing several old problems, on which we cannot turn our back, while beginning to see new ones emerging. We need to keep up. And we need to remember the basic purposes of our refugee program: to help those who are victims of persecution. That need unfortunately, will continue to be with us in the 1990s. The sources of persecution, and the nuances of the problems around them, will, however change and challenge us all.

GLOBAL AIDS:
REVOLUTION, PARADIGM AND SOLIDARITY[1]
JONATHAN MANN[2]

The Sixth International Conference on AIDS was held in San Francisco on June 21–24, 1990. In a welcoming message, Chancellor Julius R. Krevans of the University of California, San Francisco, explained the purpose of the meeting:

> This annual conference provides a critical venue to examine where we are, and where we are going. Its theme this year, "From Science to Policy," emphasizes the primacy of new scientific knowledge in the formulation of rational public policy.

Co-sponsors with the University of California, San Francisco, were the World Health Organization, the American Foundation of AIDS Research, the International AIDS Society, and the city and county of San Francisco.

Among the speakers at the conference was Dr. Jonathan Mann, professor at the Harvard School of Public Health, director of the International AIDS Center at Harvard, and former director of the World Health Organization's Global Program on AIDS. Dr. Mann addressed a plenary session in Room A of the Moscone Convention Center on the morning of June 23, 1990 at approximately 10:00 A.M. Mann was the last of six speakers from around the world who spoke for about twenty minutes each.

---

[1]Delivered at a plenary session of the Sixth International Conference on AIDS in room A of the Moscone Convention Center in San Francisco, California, at 10:00 A.M. on June 23, 1990.

[2]For biographical note, see Appendix.

Mann opened his speech with a statement that was alarming:

> Today . . . in 1990, we can see AIDS as a revolution in health, a dramatic, historic break with the past, an upheaval which affects our individual and collective lives, and from which there is no turning back. For no other disease or epidemic in the world's history has challenged the status quo as AIDS has done. Never before, even in the time of the great European plagues, has a health problem catalyzed such a broad rethinking of the health of individuals and society—and, therefore, also of our social and political systems.

Following this dramatic opening, Mann organized his speech in a problem-solution method, discussing the origins of the problem, its history, and current status. He then turned to the future, suggested solutions, and concluded with an appeal for solidarity.

Mann's audience consisted of some 4,000 conference delegates, including M.D.s, Ph.D.s, health professionals, behavioral scientists, people with AIDS, activists, and representatives of the press.

Mann received a prolonged standing ovation at the end of his speech. The stirring reception, according to Dr. Robert M. Wachter, the conference's program director, was also evidence of the gratitude of the AIDS community for his accomplishments as director of the World Health Organization's Global Program on AIDS, which he had headed until two months earlier.

Jonathan Mann's speech: Today, in San Francisco in 1990, we can see AIDS as a revolution in health, a dramatic, historic break with the past, an upheaval which affects our individual and collective lives, and from which there is no turning back. For no other disease or epidemic in the world's history has challenged the status quo as AIDS has done. Never before, even in the time of the great European plagues, has a health problem catalyzed such a broad rethinking of the health of individuals and society, and therefore also of our social and political systems.

Each year, we have met at the International AIDS Conference, and seen how, along with the epidemic, our individual and collective vision has evolved. Each year we have moved forward in our understanding of the pandemic and of ourselves, for each remarkable year has carried the intellectual weight and emotional power of a decade.

Today, in 1990, we know more; we are more experienced; yet we are also more troubled. For the pace of change has been rapid and the collision with our past assumptions sometimes violent.

To appreciate how much has been accomplished, to understand how AIDS has become the crucible in which the future of health is being forged, we must again step back from the specific issues of the day, examine the broad shape of the pandemic, and consider how the sum total of a decade's work has challenged, and started to change, the system of belief and the institutions of the past.

The most important feature of the HIV pandemic is that it is still at a relatively early stage of its development. This has three consequences: first, the pandemic remains volatile and dynamic; second, its major impact has yet to be felt; and third, there is still great potential to influence its future course.

HIV infection is continuing to spread, increasing rapidly in some already affected populations, especially in Africa, Latin America, and the Caribbean, and reaching ever deeper into newly affected areas such as Eastern Europe, the Middle East, and Southeast Asia. Last year, the epidemic in Thailand symbolized the pandemic's growing threat; today, we must draw attention to India, where heterosexual transmission has fueled a rapidly expanding epidemic, already larger than the Thai epidemic. This new wave of HIV infection has serious implications for the future of Asia.

HIV is now part of the global environment and the global potential for HIV spread remains vast. At most 20 percent of the world's 5 million or more injecting drug users have thus far been infected with HIV; the rest are highly vulnerable to explosive HIV spread. A new front in the HIV/injecting drug-user epidemic has opened in Southeast Asia, involving eastern-most India, Myanmar [formerly Burma], Thailand, and parts of Southern China, all linked with the "Golden Triangle". In addition, the well over 100 million new cases of sexually transmitted diseases in the world each year dramatically illustrate the existing, enormous potential for sexual dissemination of HIV.

Since the HIV epidemic is relatively recent, its major impact still lies ahead. Health and social systems are already straining to meet today's needs for care of HIV-infected and ill people, yet the number of people developing AIDS is expected to increase tenfold during the 1990s. The impact of the global epidemic which started in the 1970s will likely continue to grow, even into the first decade of the 21st century.

Finally, the pandemic's short history also means that the potential to influence its future course remains high. There is no country and no population in which AIDS is a "lost cause," unless it is abandoned. Many countries are just now entering a critical opening phase of their HIV epidemic: in Asia, in Eastern Europe, in Central and South America. The final shape of the global pandemic is not yet clear; ultimately, it is here—in prevention of new infections—that the greatest impact on global health will be felt.

What then is the status of the worldwide effort against AIDS? In a few short, remarkable years, the foundation has been built for increasing control of this new global threat to health. Yet today, the pace and growing impact of the pandemic threatens to overwhelm current capacity to prevent infection and care for the infected and ill.

For the epidemics in Africa, Latin America, the Caribbean, and Southeast Asia are not coming under control; they are expanding. The hard-learned lessons from San Francisco, Amsterdam, Sydney, and Nairobi are not being systematically applied: in many communities, information still remains inadequate, inaccurate, or frankly misleading; for many people, needed health and social services still do not exist; in many places, discriminatory and punitive attitudes fester; and thus in all these settings, prevention is simply not being given a real chance.

The gap between rich and poor, among countries and within countries, is widening. Nearly two-thirds of the world's AIDS cases to date and three-fourths of HIV-infected people are in developing countries. Yet the cost of drugs and care means that "early intervention" is still a meaningless concept in developing countries; AZT remains too expensive for most of the people who need it. The industrialized world's total annual contributions to AIDS in the developing world is estimated at $200 million or less; last year, total expenditure for AIDS prevention and care in New York state alone was five times greater. The total budget of the average national AIDS program in the developing world today is less than the cost of caring for only 15 people with AIDS in the United States.

This is the pandemic today: the 700,000 people who have thus far developed AIDS, the roughly eight million people already infected, a young pandemic which is still gaining momentum. We know that a world with an expanding AIDS epidemic cannot be a safe world. Yet more than ever before, complacency,

indifference, denial, and a "business as usual" approach threaten
the success of the struggle with AIDS. Either we build upon and
strengthen and expand what has already been accomplished, or
in the years to come we will fall further and further behind the
pace of the worldwide epidemic.

In the 1980s, in confronting AIDS, no one set out to make
a revolution. Rather, people have only tried, as best they could,
to do the work of preventing HIV infection, caring for the infected and ill, and linking national and international efforts. Yet,
in carrying forward this work, the deficiencies of our health and
social systems have been so starkly and painfully revealed that the
pre-AIDS era paradigm of health, its philosophy and practices,
have been challenged and found to be desperately inadequate
and, therefore, fatally obsolete.

What is this paradigm of health which AIDS has called so
forcefully into question? What events, what deeds, what ideas
were, in retrospect, revolutionary? What are the creative themes
of a new paradigm of health which AIDS is calling into being?

The paradigm we inherited focused on discovering the external agents of disease, disability, and premature death. Inevitably,
the emphasis was medical and technological, involving experts
and engineers; for certain purposes, this approach was quite effective. However, the social views embodied in this paradigm en-
visioned a fundamental dichotomy between individual and social
interests; accordingly, and in concert with the spirit of the age,
governments were called upon to mediate, and to prevent disease
through laws and the work of bureaucracies. Attention to behavioral, social, and societal considerations was often rudimentary
and naive. Coercion was frequently favored; many public health
systems sought efficacy through increasing power to compel, and
human rights were infrequently mentioned, except in the limited
context of reaction against officialdom's abuses of power.

During the past decade and more, the limited capacity of this
paradigm to cope with the health problems of the modern world
was becoming increasingly evident. The critical role of individual
and collective behavior was recognized; for despite cheap and ex-
cellent childhood vaccines, only about half of the world's children
were immunized; we understood that women could not say "no"
to unwanted or unprotected sex, unless they also had the social,
economic, and political power to mean "no"; we discovered that
nuclear power plants cannot be engineered into absolute safety,

for there was, and will always be the so-called "human factor" of Three Mile Island or Chernobyl.

Then, suddenly AIDS emerged, and its impact on the old structure of thought, institutions, and practice was as remarkable, as unexpected, yet somehow as inevitable as the crumbling of an outdated political regime or the collapse of the Berlin Wall.

Let us consider just several of the revolutionary ideas and acts of the past decade.

First, as neither drug nor vaccine was available, behavior was immediately accorded central importance in the fight against AIDS. The major behavior of concern was sexual, about which every society rapidly discovered itself to be profoundly ignorant. The general neglect of behavior in the prevailing philosophy and practice of health became shockingly obvious.

Then, health and social needs for prevention and for care of HIV-infected people and people with AIDS shattered complacency about our health and social systems. AIDS stripped away the veils which had covered deficiencies and inequities in the way health care and social services are organized and delivered in the neglect of groups within society in the low priority accorded to health. HIV-infected people and people with AIDs also articulated human needs with a clarity and in a manner for which the existing structures and services were often fundamentally unprepared.

Next, people infected with HIV, people with AIDS, and those labelled as members of "high risk groups" declared their firm intent to participate in, rather than simply submit to, the processes of prevention, care, and research. The shockwaves from this courageous determination to participate have not subsided; it has challenged clinical research and shaken deeply held assumptions about the role of infected and ill people.

Participation broadened even further as thousands of community, grass-roots organizations responded to often desperate needs for prevention and care services. The prevailing view of government as the major actor in protecting health was challenged by the realities of community action and activism.

Then, somewhat unexpectedly, we found ourselves speaking in the language of human rights and dignity. For in what other health area, at what other time, have we heard such talk of "rights" and "social justice"? Invoking the concepts of human rights, of nondiscriminating, equity and justice, it is not only the content of policy and institutional action which has been challenged, but also the process through which policies and institutional action has been challenged, but also the process through which policies and decisions have been reached.

These acts and many others—the understanding of AIDS as a global problem, the holding of these conferences, the Names Project quilt and other expressions of love—have altered the way we think about health, individuals and society. Towards what new vision, with what insight and power to promote health and prevent disease, is AIDS leading us today?

The key to the new paradigm is the recognition that behavior, individual and collective, is the major public health challenge of the future. In shifting the emphasis to behavior, in its social, economic and political context, the new paradigm will replace coercion with support, discrimination with tolerance for diversity. It will be necessary to develop new ways of thinking about personal and social identities and interactions. In the future, the concepts of incorporation, adaption, and symbiosis may be more relevant and useful than old dichotomies of external versus internal, or individual versus collective. Just as AIDS blurs distinctions between the role of pathogens and the role of immunity in personal health, the next paradigm of health must embody a new understanding of the meaning of "internal" and "external"—and a new definition of what is the "self" and what is the "other".

Using our current vocabulary, for new words may be required, solidarity describes a central concept in this emerging perspective on health, individuals, and society. The AIDS pandemic has taught us a great deal about solidarity. We had a lot to learn, so it has taken time.

The bases of solidarity is tolerance and non-discrimination, a refusal to separate the condition of the few from the fate of the many. Solidarity arises when people realize that excessive differences among people make the entire system unstable. Charity is individual; solidarity is inherently social, concerned with social justice, and therefore also economic and political.

AIDS had helped us to recognize that solidarity is in part a consequence of the objective conditions of the late 20th century. For example, travel and movement are part of the human condition, but never before have so many travelled so far and so frequently as today; since 1950, the officially reported number of international travelers has increased over 15-fold. As the barriers of geographical and cultural distance diminish, the system in which we live—from the products we consume to the air we breathe to the viral pathogens in our environment—reflect an increasingly global linkage and dependence. This also offers infectious agents an unparalleled opportunity for rapid pandemic spread; HIV may be the first virus to take full advantage of this situation, but it is unlikely to be the last. Fortunately, we are also beginning to understand and respond to the consequences of this globalism; global solidarity, imperfect, struggling, yet nevertheless real, can be felt in the creation of the United Nations, in the concern about nuclear war, in growing worldwide resolve to protect the environment, and in the global fight against AIDS.

Yet solidarity can only exist when interdependence is real and felt to be so. Feeling is important; experience with AIDS is a powerful stimulus to greater tolerance and human understanding. AIDS demonstrates the paradox that for an issue to become truly global, it must also become extremely personal. We may well need political innovations to help express new impulses of solidarity—and to develop new bridges between individuals, their local community, and the world.

AIDs has also improved our understanding of solidarity by revealing deficiencies inherent in two of its alternatives: coercion and discrimination.

We all have personal experience with coercion. It has been used on us and we have used it in an effort to influence behavior. But it is essential to ask a basic question: "Does coercion really work, and, if so, to what extent and for how long?"

Available international experience with AIDS leads us to be skeptical of coercion, for there is little if any evidence that coercion has a positive influence on behavior. Nevertheless, we still hear people say that infected people should be "punished", including imposition of isolation and quarantine. There is a persistent myth that quarantine is actually the most potent public health tool we have, perhaps because it is most coercive. However, on closer examination, quarantine is seen to be of quite limited applicability or usefulness, it has high social and economic costs—which have often been ignored—and its impact on an AIDS prevention program is almost certain to be strongly counter productive.

Finally, from experience in many national settings, we learned that in order to have an effective HIV prevention program, discrimination against HIV-infected people had to be avoided. For this reason, protection of rights and dignity is a central issue for AIDS programs. Discrimination reduces participation in HIV prevention activities—thereby diminishing effectiveness—and a discrimination is also a "risk factor" for HIV infection. Vulnerability to HIV infection increases whenever people are discriminated against or socially marginalized for several reasons: their access to information and preventive services is decreased; they have less influence on design of prevention strategies; and, most importantly they have less power and capacity to take necessary steps to protect themselves.

Therefore, while measures to protect human rights will not, of themselves, guarantee an effective AIDS program, denial of human rights is clearly incompatible with effective AIDS prevention and control.

Thus, through AIDS, we have started to shed old, outworn assumptions, we have challenged social myth with social realities, and we are asking again the simple, basic, terrible questions about our personal and collective lives. Our experience has brought us to this point, to discover and recognize solidarity based on human rights, as the touchstone, the central insight, of a new era.

How can we now strengthen, through our work, this solidarity which responds to the objective conditions and aspirations of our time?

First, we must recognize our power. Individuals and small groups can express and catalyze the aspirations of entire peoples.

Next, we must work to broaden the participation of people in decisions which affect them, whoever they may be.

In the process, we must also learn more about human rights. The requirement to observe and respect human rights is contained in the United Nations Charter and the Universal Declaration of Human Rights. As a result, the obligation to respect and protect human rights is universal. All states are bound to them, regardless of the details of each political system. For the first time in history, we have a written, collectively agreed to basis for promotion of human rights, and governments can be held accountable for the way they treat their people. Our goal should be not only to prevent abuses of human rights but to help generate the conditions for the promotion of human rights and dignity, and this requires deliberate, active and steady work.

As part of our responsibility, we should include human rights assessments in the review of AIDS programs at the community, nation, and international level. Not asking about AIDS and human rights issues is a form of neglect, which only serves to reinforce discrimination.

This also means we must define our responses to human rights violations association with AIDS sanatoria of Cuba, in mandatory screening and exclusion of infected foreigners from Saudia Arabia or China, we must speak out.

Finally, we must have the courage to look deeply into our own communities. For the hardest problems of all are closer still to home: problems of work, health care, insurance, schooling, and discrimination in daily life.

Only ten years ago—it seems a century—who could have predicted what we have experienced, who could have imagined the particular forms of courage and creativity we have witnessed—and who would have had the audacity to think that AIDS would not only mirror, but would also help to shape, the history of our time?

To the historian of the future, many issues of current concern will be invisible and the paradigm we are reaching towards will be —in retrospect—self-evident. Yet when this history is written, the discovery of the inextricable linkage between human rights and AIDS, and more broadly, between human rights and health, will rank among the major discoveries and advances in the history of health and society. For the importance of the AIDS revolution reaches far beyond AIDS alone. Solidarity based on human rights expands the levels of tolerance each society grants to its own members and to others; this is vital for AIDS, for health more broadly, and for the future of our political institutions.

This historian of the future will see that we have had the privilege of being present at, and participating in, the creation of new worlds of thought and action—a revolution based on the right to health.

Now, in San Francisco, we face the uncertain years to come. Our solidarity must not desert us now. Here, in the city where the United Nations charter was signed—in this city of special honor in the global struggle against AIDS—we recognize and thank those who have taught us, in their lives and in their deaths, about the power of their love; here we honor those who have guided us as we seek to understand and express the kind of love we call solidarity.

For beyond today, beyond us, we recognize the magnitude of the revolution in thinking which AIDS has catalyzed and how the integrity and wholeness of our work is linked with an instinctive striving—a visceral need—to express our human solidarity. For ours is part of a larger revolution which carries hope, not despair: hope for ourselves, hope for the fight against AIDS, and hope for the world's future.

ISSUES OF RIGHTS AND RESPONSIBILITY

MAJORITIES VERSUS THE FIRST AMENDMENT: RATIONALITY ON TRIAL[1]
Franklyn S. Haiman[2]

A distinguished scholar and leading authority on freedom of speech, Dr. Franklyn S. Haiman delivered the keynote address to the Speech Communication Association's 76th annual convention in Chicago on November 2, 1990. Haiman was a well known and respected member of the organization he addressed. The author of several books on speech communication, his *Speech and Law in a Free Society* had been given the SCA Golden Anniversary book award in 1981. In addition, he had been the recipient of the Winans-Whichelns award for distinguished scholarship in rhetoric and public address and the American Bar Association's Silver Gavel award. He twice was recognized by the SCA for outstanding journal articles.

At the time he delivered his address, Haiman was John Evans Professor of Communication Studies at Northwestern University, where he had taught for 43 years, and was Vice-President of the Americal Civil Liberties Union. He has also served as visiting lecturer at the University of Paris, in France, and the University of Denmark, in Copenhagen.

Haiman's audience for the address was between 400 and 500 members attending the convention of the Speech Communication Association, an organization of teachers, scholars, students, and others interested in spoken communication in its many forms. He delivered the speech 10:00 A.M. November 2, 1990, in the Grand Ballroom of the Chicago Hilton Hotel.

Noting that his speech coincided with the bicentennial of the Bill of Rights, the first ten amendments to the Constitution, Professor Haiman reminded his audience that enactment of the Bill of Rights, the method devised for appointing Supreme Court justices, and the two-thirds rule for constitutional amendments approved by the Founding Fathers indicates that "our democracy is not simply a system of majority rule."

"Unfortunately, this is not well understood by many people," Haiman observed. "Too many of our sister and fellow citizens are prone to believe that *their* values, their ways of living and expressing themselves are, or should be, universal." Haiman then proceeded to discuss three major freedom-of-speech controversies that had "been raging across the land

[1]Keynote speech to a general session of the Speech Communication Association at its annual convention delivered in the Grand Ballroom of the Chicago Hilton Hotel at 10:00 A.M, November 2, 1990, to an audience of 400 to 500 members.

[2]For biographical note, see Appendix.

for the past two years": the flag-burning issue, alleged obscenity and government funding of the arts, and finally, racist, sexist, and homophobic expression on college and university campuses.

Franklyn S. Haiman's speech: Four years ago, on the eve of the Bicentennial anniversary of the U.S. Constitution, I had the privilege, I am again enjoying today, of delivering the keynote address to this organization's annual convention. My repeat appearance occurs on the eve of another national Bicentennial year, that of the first ten amendments to the Constitution, the Bill of Rights. But we have had an unusual kind of prelude in 1990 to our impending observance of the 200th anniversary of the First Amendment, and instead of celebrating its birth we might well have been attending its funeral. The President of the United States, along with a majority of both houses of the Congress, were ready to make that happen by urging and enacting the first amendment to the First Amendment in our history, all for the purpose of ensuring that one particular mode of symbolic behavior that was said to threaten the very foundations of the republic, the so-called desecration of an American flag, would be banished from the marketplace of ideas. Happily, it takes more than a majority of the Congress to amend our Constitution, and a little more than a third of our senators and representatives found the unaccustomed political courage to beat back this surge of allegedly patriotic passion.

The two-thirds rule for amending our Constitution is not the only anti-majoritarian element of our democratic system, nor even the strongest. The Bill of Rights itself is a counter-majoritarian document of the toughest fiber, confirming the view of John Stuart Mill that "If all mankind minus one, were of one opinion, and only one person were of the contrary opinion, mankind would be no more justified in silencing that one person, than he, if he had the power, would be justified in silencing mankind." And the justices of the Supreme Court of the United States are not chosen by a majority of the people nor subject to being voted out of office, but are appointed from an elite corps of judges and lawyers who serve life terms as presumptive guardians of individual liberty against encroachments by the two elected branches of government.

We have heard a lot of talk in recent weeks about Supreme Court justices who, in fulfilling that function, are not supposed to "legislate from the bench," as Chief Justice Warren and Justice Brennan allegedly did, but only to "interpret" the words that our Founding Fathers wrote in the Constitution, as Chief Justice Rehnquist and Justice Scalia allegedly do. Count Alfred Korzybski, Irving Lee, Wendell Johnson and Stuart Chase must turn over in their graves every time that assertion is made, though S. I. Hayakawa, not yet in the grave, may have forgotten what he once would have said about such semantic folderol. Did the Founding Fathers have sit-com television in mind when they wrote the freedom-of-speech clause of the First Amendment, or helicopter surveillance of a marijuana plot in a back yard when they penned the "unreasonable searches and seizures" clause of the Fourth Amendment? It seems unlikely. So, are justices "legislating" or "interpreting" when they write those phenomena into or out of the Constitution? Justice Scalia thinks that flags are protected speech; Chief Justice Rehnquist and almost-Justice Robert Bork think otherwise. Which of these stalwarts of the originalist, literal interpretation, school of thought have defected from the true faith and which have not? Or are they *all* fallible human beings like the rest of us, endowing words with some mixture of what others *seem* to have meant by them at the time they were uttered, what they might have meant by them if they were uttered today, and what we *want* them to mean for today and tomorrow.

I must not pursue this by-way into general semantics and Supreme Court jurisprudence any further, but return to my original point that the Supreme Court, the Bill of Rights, and the two-thirds rule for constitutional amendments are all testimony to the fact that our democracy is not simply a system of majority rule, but a society in which *some* important areas of life are preserved for individual autonomy, and *some* fundamental decisions require, if not unanimity, at least a closer approach to it than 51% of those present and voting.

Unfortunately, this is not well understood by many people—at least not until their own ox is gored—and too many of our sister and fellow citizens are prone to believe that *their* values, their beliefs, their ways of living and expressing themselves, are or should be universal. Although we are a long way from anything that might fairly be characterized as a tyranny of the majority, I would like to suggest here today that we are heading too much in that direction and, what is more troubling, are being offered intellectual justifications for that course which are most sophisticated, more persuasive, and supported by more political power than has been true in the past. Gathering under the banner of what is being called "communitarianism," and no doubt reacting against what is perceived as individualism run amok, we are seeing and hearing a flood of appeals in speeches, columns, books, and prestigious law journal articles for greater "civility" in our discourse, more deference to the sensibilities of the so-called "community," more rationality—as these advocates define that term—in public debate.

Let me illustrate this thesis with three freedom-of-speech controversies that have been raging across the land for the past two years. I will begin with the one that has generated the most heat and least light, the flag-burning issue; proceed to the latest battles over alleged obscenity and government funding of the arts; and end with an issue that has evoked both deep passion and serious intellectual analysis on college and university campuses all over the nation—that of how to deal with the incidents of racist, sexist and homophobic expression that have been erupting in that arena.

The idea that the nation's flag is a symbol so sacred to the American people—or perhaps, more accurately, to about 85% of them—that it must not be defaced or mutilated in public, did not originate with George Bush and his 1988 presidential campaign. Such behavior, if engaged in to communicate contempt for the flag or what it represents, has been outlawed by *state* governments for about as long as this association has existed and was made a *federal* crime as well, in 1968, in response to protests against the Vietnam War. Nor is the idea a new one that such laws should be considered violative of the First Amendment because they prohibit symbolic behavior, and nothing more, on the basis of its political offensiveness, and not because they protect against any substantive evil which a legislature has the right to prevent. Justice Brennan said just that in 1981 in dissenting from a decision of the Supreme Court not to review the conviction of two protesters who had burned a flag on a sidewalk in front of the federal building in Greensboro, North Carolina. It took eight more years for Justice Brennan to persuade a majority of his colleagues, including Justices Scalia and Kennedy, that he was right; and in June of 1989 the decision was handed down in *Texas v. Johnson* that unleashed the barrage of jingoism which demanded a constitutional amendment to undo this dastardly deed. The tone for that campaign was set by the Chief Justice's dissenting opinion, which did not even pretend to be in the realm of rational discourse, starting out as it did with the unabashed assertion that "a page of history is worth a volume of logic." He then proceeded to invoke every image of the flag fluttering through wartime that he could muster, from the marines hoisting it to the top of Mount Suribachi on Iwojima to quoting in their entirety the words of the Star Spangled Banner and of John Greenleaf Whittier's poem, "Barbara Frietchie." Even the moderate and normally reasonable Justice Stevens was swept along in this tide of chauvinism, commenting that "a country's flag is more than a symbol of 'nationhood and national unity' . . . It is a symbol of freedom, of equal opportunity, of religious tolerance . . . The value of the flag as a symbol cannot be measured . . . sanctioning the public desecration of the flag will tarnish its value."

Cooler heads in the Congress managed, in the summer of 1989, to stave off the stampede by offering their colleagues a face-saving, if politically cynical, alternative to amending the First Amendment—a new federal statute which would remedy the most glaring defect in the 1968 law with a viewpoint-neutral ban against *all* public mutilation of the flag, not just against those who do it to express contempt. But the five-person majority of *Texas v. Johnson* courageously—and some thought recklessly, since they had to know they were inviting a renewed effort to amend the Constitution—held their ground and struck down the new law on June 11th of this year, finding it still an intrusion, without justification, on purely symbolic behavior that is protected by the First Amendment. Predictably, the proposed amendment to the Constitution was back on the floor of Congress virtually overnight, and now our representatives and senators had nowhere to hide. Threatened by Republican Senate leader Robert Dole with the retribution of 30-second TV campaign spots fo any who dared to vote as they knew they should, a substantial enough minority of them, with crucial backing from the Democratic leaders of both houses, banded together in mutual support to successfully defend the First Amendment from this majoritarian assault. They will surely survive this act of principle come next Tuesday, majority passions being the fickle and fleeting phenomena they so often are and other issues having moved to forefront of public attention.

The criminal prosecutions this year for exhibiting the photographs of Robert Mapplethorpe in Cincinnati, Ohio, and for selling and performing 2 Live Crews' "As Nasty as They Wanna Be" in Broward County, Florida, following on the heels of the struggle over restrictions on grants by the National Endowment for the Arts, have re-awakened public interest in another perennial free-speech issue: that of obscenity. But there are new twists that make the problem considerably more difficult for those of us who, along with former Supreme Court Justices Black and Douglas, believe that so-called obscene speech and images are as much entitled to protection by the First Amendment as other kinds of communication.

The first complication is the entirely valid point made by Senator Helms and his supporters that there is a difference between criminal punishment by the government of communicative activities of private citizens, on the one hand, and affirmative government support, with the taxpayers' money, of those same acts of communication, on the other hand. Where the First Amendment may prohibit the former, it surely does not require the latter. From this undeniable premise it is then argued that while offensiveness to majority sensibilities may not be a sufficient justification for government suppression of words and pictures, it is certainly a reasonable basis for government refusal to pay for their production and dissemination. But this is a classic non-sequitur. Offensiveness to the sensibilities of others, be they a majority of 90% or a minority of 10%, is no more appropriate a criterion for decision-making about government grants to the arts, humanities, and sciences than it is for the county sheriff to raid a local bookstore. Once the government decides, on an admittedly discretionary basis, that it will fund certain categories of intellectual or cultural activities—be they public schools, libraries, museums, symphonies, dance troupes, or individual artists— there must, of course, be criteria established for selecting who will benefit from the finite amount of money that is available and who will not. Qualitative judgments by peers and professionals, free insofar as humanly possible of ideological bias, are one such appropriate set of criteria. Geographical and cultural diversity, development of new talent, and maintenance of those with established records of accomplishment, may be among some other legitimate considerations. And the exclusion of illegal activity is certainly appropriate, *so long as* the determination of what constitutes illegality is left to the judicial system, where it belongs. The flaw in the 1989 Helms amendment, even as it was watered down by its opponents who still felt some need to throw Jesse a bone, was not that it went beyond the present state of the law in declaring obscenity to be beyond the pale of acceptable public communication, but that it imposed an obligation to make the decision as to what is and is not obscene on the National Endowment for the Arts, on an *a priori* basis, rather than in a court of law, with full due process safeguards.

Whether or not so-called obscene material *should* be illegal in the first place is a question that goes far beyond Jesse Helms and the National Endowment for the Arts dispute. It is a question that has been seriously debated at least since 1957, when the Supreme Court definitively took the position that obscenity is not protected by the First Amendment, if not since 1873, when Anthony Comstock, leader of the Committee for the Suppression of Vice, persuaded the Congress to enact our first federal law against sending obscene literature through the U.S. mail. But that debate has taken on new complexity in the recent past, for it is now not only the prudes and Philistines who think that the Robert Mapplethorpes and 2 Live Crews of this world have gone too far, but calm and thoughtful legal scholars who invoke a facially reasonable communitarian point of view to justify restraints on words or images that violate the community's standards of decency.

One such scholar, political scientist Richard Randall, in a provocative 1989 volume entitled *Freedom and Taboo: Pornography and the Politics of a Self Divided*, proposed that the Supreme Court should abandon its requirement that before something can be found obscene it must be lacking in serious literary, artistic, political or scientific value, and should rely solely on the criterion of "patent offensiveness" to contemporary local community standards. To the critic's response that offensiveness is an immeasurably subjective standard, entirely in the eye of the individual beholder, Randall replies that patent offensiveness *to a community* is objectively measurable. "We are not speaking here of public opinion polls," he says.

More to the point are actual communications. The chief evidence of existing community standards on any matter is what has actually been done or practiced and what the community's response has been to departures from the customary. What sorts of sexual material have been openly available? . . . Was there protest or complaint, indifference, or approval? If so, by whom and in what numbers.

What Randall fails to appreciate is that what he has suggested be added together in an objective way are subjective judgments to begin with. Adding zero to zero still makes zero.

Randall's preference for community standards of decency as the only boundary line for sexually oriented speech is largely a pragmatic one. "Liberty as an absolute value," he argues, "negates the legitimacy and prudence of all opposing interests. . . . Individual liberties," he says,

must co-exist with the equality principle and its operating agent, majority rule . . . In theory, a free speech society works because its members are wise enough, mature enough, or simply self-controlled enough to check their natural inclination to silence troubling views and disagreeable expression . . . Yet few members of any society can consistently reach such heights of political wisdom and temperance . . . The question is not whether freedom of speech should submit to popular preferences and majority will . . . but whether the inevitable and continuing conflict between these two vital elements of liberal democracy has been managed as well as it might be . . . protecting necessary freedom and preventing unnecessary reaction.

I assume from this that Professor Randall would applaud the senators who threw Jesse Helms his bone last year, and look at the year of agony that brought us.

But there is much more than mere pragmatism lurking in Randall's assertion that "liberty as an absolute value negates the legitimacy of all opposing interests" and "must co-exist with the equality principle and its operating agent, majority rule." Although he may not have contemplated this extrapolation, I would point out that the very same principle he has enunciated with respect to obscenity has been the bedrock on which the advocates of campus restrictions on racist, sexist and homophobic expression have built their case. Equality of educational opportunity *versus* freedom of speech, that is the either-or choice they have been offering us for the past two or three years.

Equality of opportunity, they have argued, is denied by a concept of freedom of speech which includes the utterance of racially or sexually derogatory remarks or the display of symbols which denigrate their targets on the basis of their race, religion, sex, or sexual orientation. A 1988 *Harvard Law Review* article explains the rationale as follows:

From the communitarian perspective, permitting group vilification causes significant harm both to individuals and to the political community as a whole. Toleration of group vilification injures individuals because it fails to respect fully the personhood of its targets . . . [It] harms the political community as a whole because it denigrates the idea of equality . . . den[ying] the targets of such expression equal membership in the political community.

As to the old-fashioned notion of John Stuart Mill that error of opinion must be tolerated and countered with more speech in a free marketplace of ideas, Law Professor Mari Matsuda, in an emotionally powerful 1989 *Michigan Law Review* article, which relies on the new narrative style of legal argument and is entitled "Public Response to Racist Speech: Considering the Victim's Story, " offers this Marcusian answer:

What is argued here . . . is that we accept certain principles as the shared historical legacy of the world community. Racial supremacy is one of the ideas we have collectively and internationally considered and rejected.

It would be insensitive, unfair, even arrogant of me to imply that Professor Matsuda and other reputable leaders of the movement for restrictions on racist speech, such as Professor Charles Lawrence of the Stanford Law School, Professor Richard Delgado of the University of Wisconsin Law School, and Dean Mark Yudof of the University of Texas Law School, have abandoned rationality on this issue in the same way as have the proponents of a flag-burning amendment to the Constitution or the prosecutors of the Mapplethorpe exhibit. There *is* a serious problem of racism and sexism on our college campuses; it *does* cause emotional pain and suffering to its targets; and it may indeed hinder their academic performance and opportunities. The narratives that are told of harassment and victimization cannot be dismissed as lacking in authenticity, nor is the point without merit that intelligent women and men regard racist and sexist ideas as anathema to a civilized society. Where reason breaks down is in the leap to the conclusion that it is freedom of *speech* which is in conflict with equality, rather than the racist and sexist *behaviors* and *practices* that underlie the verbal expression of racial and sexual bigotry.

Freedom of speech and equality of opportunity are, and always have been, allies, not enemies. We must not allow them to be divided and conquered. What equality we have achieved in this country—for women, for racial and religious minorities, for gays and lesbians, and for the physically handicapped—has been significantly advanced by the exercise of freedom of speech; and freedom of speech, in turn, has been strengthened and enriched by the increased empowerment of previously disempowered groups. The truly serious problems in our system of freedom of expression today—problems such as access to the mass media of communication and competitiveness in our political campaigns— stem primarily from gross inequalities in the distribution of wealth rather than from excesses of speech, and would be ameliorated by a more equitable economy rather than by limitations on expression.

It is also misleading to suggest, as some do, that the voices of minorities have been silenced, and equality thereby denied, as a result of racist speech, or that the voices of women have been silenced, and equality thereby denied, as a result of violent pornography. That some are intimidated, I do not doubt. But that most are driven into a state of submissive quiescence is simply contrary to the observable facts. Happily the free-speech system works in this respect as it is theoretically supposed to work: people who are insulted and denigrated find the strength within themselves, or in concert with others, to talk back, to insist on being respected, to demand their rights. If they fail it is not because their oppressors have too many words, but because they have too much power. Shutting up those oppressors will not solve the problem; sharing their power will.

One of the ironies of the new communitarianism is the pride it takes in its reasonableness—reasonable in its deference to the standards of decency of the so-called community, reasonable in its recognition of the supposed limits of human tolerance, reasonable in its willingness to exclude from the marketplace of ideas the rhetoric of grunts and groans—such as flag burnings, pornographic images, and racial slurs, a rhetoric which allegedly makes no contribution to rational discourse.

I say this is ironic because it is a corruption of rationality. What is a community if not a composite of *all* of its members, not 51% nor 2/3 nor 95%, but everyone. What, therefore, is a so-called community standard of decency if 5%, a third, or 49% of that community do not share it? It is a *majority* standard, perhaps even the standard of an overwhelming majority, but let us not pretend that it is unanimous and try to pass it off as that of the entire community. The substitution in recent discourse of the word "communitarianism" for "majoritarianism" is a bit of verbal legerdemain, intentional or not, which masks the fact that a community and a majority are not identical. Not that there is anything wrong with majority standards for some purposes, and that they cannot or should not be used as a basis for the outlawing of murder, rape and robbery, even if the murderers, rapists, and robbers do not agree. But we must not be taken in by the fallacy that because such standards are justifiably invoked for murder, rape and robbery they are similarly justified as a basis for the banning of words, pictures, or other symbols of which the majority does not approve. Rather let us hold to the time-tested premise of Thomas Jefferson that "It is time enough for the rightful purposes of civil government of its officers to interfere when principles break out into overt acts against peace and good order."

As to the supposed limits of human tolerance, I would maintain that people learn to tolerate what they have to tolerate. If they are taught from an early age that people and ideas they find disagreeable can be made to go away, they will try to make them go away, and with each success they will be emboldened to go farther the next time. But if they learn, through moral suasion and the steady hand of the law, that they should not and will not be allowed to try to rid the world of whatever they may find offensive, they will accept that, even if grudgingly, and may even grow to appreciate that such a policy is in their own enlightened self-interest, since they, too, may someday be deviants.

Finally, we confront the claim that what I have facetiously called the rhetoric of grunts and groans makes no useful contribution to a marketplace of ideas, that, indeed, it undermines the processes of rational discourse. That notion is not original with the new majoritarians. The U.S. Supreme Court itself, almost half a century ago, held that there are certain categories of speech—for example, the obscene, the libellous, and fighting words—which are of "such slight social value as a step to truth that any benefit that may be derived from them is clearly outweighed by the social interest in order and morality." That ruling, significantly, was in unanimous affirmation of the fighting words conviction of a Jehovah's Witness by the name of Chaplinksy for calling a police officer a "damned Fascist" and a "god damned racketeer." There were no important ideas in this utterance of Chaplinsky? No insight into his feelings? No expression of a political or religious ideology? A rather cramped view, I would suggest, of what constitutes rather discourse or a useful contribution to the search for truth.

Justice John Marshall Harlan (the claimed role model, incidentally, of our new Supreme Court Justice, David Souter) had it much straighter in 1971 when he said, on behalf of a more clear-headed majority of the Court:

Surely the state has no right to cleanse public debate to the point where it is grammatically palatable to the most squeamish among us. . . . Words are often chosen as much for their emotive as their cognitive force. We cannot sanction the view that the Constitution, while solicitous of the cognitive content of individual speech, has little or no regard for that emotive function which, practically speaking, may often be the more important element of the overall message sought to be communicated.

As one who has been concerned and written about ethics and rationality in communication for a long time, even before I became a First Amendment junkie, I do not stand here today to urge you to rush to your next session and call everyone a "son of a bitch" or pull out a pocketful of dirty pictures, and I do not plan to go out in front of this hotel on Michigan Avenue, burn on an American flag, and chant, as they did on this very spot 22 years ago, that "The Whole World is Watching." I am only saying that if anyone should *choose* to engage in those symbolic acts I would hesitate, before knowing a great deal about the social and political context, to label the behavior irrational, and I would certainly not want anyone to call the Chicago cops.

I would like to conclude on a somewhat parochial and personal note. Forty-four years ago, as a graduate student at Northwestern University, I had the great good fortune, for one summer session, of coming under the influence of a visiting professor by the name of James M. O'Neil, a key figure in the renaissance of the classical rhetorical discipline in 20th century America, the prime mover in the founding of this association, its first president, and, for four years, the first editor of its journal. At the time our paths crossed some thirty years after those events, Professor O'Neil was serving extra-curricularly as chairman of the Academic Freedom Committee of the American Civil Liberties Union, a unique role in those days for a prominent lay leader of the Roman Catholic church and self-appointed respondent to the attacks on the political power exercised by the Catholic church in America written by Paul Blanshard, among others. But just as James M. O'Neil was stalwart in the defense of his church, so was he uncompromising in his defense of freedom of expression and vigorous in his advocacy of the central responsibility of teachers and scholars of speech to be engaged in that defense.

He viewed the functions of teacher of speech and guardian of the First Amendment as virtually synonymous. Indeed, it was from him that I first learned about the American Civil Liberties Union, was motivated to become a card-carrying member, and when the opportunity arose a dozen years later, to become even more deeply involved in its work. But it is not my intention here to become a recruiter for the ACLU (although that result would not disappoint me) nor even to engage in boosterism for the Speech Communication Association (which I assume to be superfluous in this setting). It *is* my purpose to propose that the women and men who are seated in this room, like Professor O'Neil, constitute one of the elites of our nation, and let us not blink from the label, whose mission, by virtue of training and position, is to stand up and do battle whenever the tides of majoritarianism threaten to drown out the voices of dissent. We cannot depend on the Supreme Court of the United States to do that job for us; the struggle will be won or lost in the court of public opinion where we will surely be out-numbered but hopefully not out-smarted nor out-talked. True rationality is indeed on trial as we enter the third century of the First Amendment. I hope that you will be in the courtroom to testify.

OUR JUSTICE SYSTEM, SO-CALLED[1]
Donald P. Lay[2]

More people, per capita, are in jail in the United States than in any other country on earth. This was the finding in a 1991 report from Sentencing Project, a Washington research group. In a 1979 landmark study, the National Council on Crime and Delinquency found that South Africa and the Soviet Union kept more of their citizens in jail than did the United States. Now, however, the U.S. heads the list. For every 100,000 people in the U.S., 426 are sentenced to prison or are being held in pre-trial detention. (Cameron Barr, *Christian Science Monitor*, March 7, 1991, p. 12).

In a speech to the National Association of Pretrial Service Agencies,

[1]Keynote address at the annual conference of the National Association of Pretrial Services Agencies presented at 6:00 P.M. in the ballroom of the Radisson University Hotel on September 23, 1990 to an audience of approximately 300.

[2]For biographical sketch, see Appendix.

Donald P. Lay, chief judge of the Eighth Circuit Court of Appeals, addressed this problem. Lay, who has been a federal appellate judge for 26 years, said:

> In an effort to fight crime, we aimlessly set goals of putting more and more people into jails and prisons, regardless of consequential costs of the complete denigration of dignity and resulting human sacrifice. . . . The criminal justice system is a disgrace to a civilized nation that prides itself on decency and the belief in the intrinsic worth of every individual. The system is a complete failure." (*New York Times*, October 22, 1990).

The National Association of Pretrial Services Agencies is an organization whose goals are to educate both practitioners and the general public about pretrial services; to promote and disseminate research and act as a forum for new ideas; to provide technical assistance to pretrial programs; and to encourage establishment of statewide pretrial organizations. The association, which has approximately 350 members, including practitioners, judges, and sheriffs, publishes a quarterly newsletter.

Judge Lay delivered the keynote address at the association's annual conference in Minneapolis on September 23, 1990. He spoke to an audience of approximately 300 members of the association and other conference attendees at 6:00 P.M. in the ballroom of the Raddison University Hotel.

An adapted portion of the speech was printed on the editorial page of the *New York Times* of October 22, 1990.

Judge Lay's speech: In the 1940s the Supreme Court affirmed the incarceration of thousands of American citizens who were of Japanese descent because of a hysterical concern over national security. Now some 45 years later Congress has granted reparations to Japanese families who were shamefully victimized by such detention.

In the 1990s we are guilty of a similar hysterical concern. In an effort to fight crime we aimlessly set goals of putting more and more people into jails and prisons, regardless of consequential costs or the complete denigration of human dignity and resulting human sacrifice. As a nation we countenance, without apparent concern, increasing episodes of temporary banishment of individuals to horrific and indecent environs in our jails and prisons, and falsely assume on their return to society that they will become useful citizens bearing no resentment.

The criminal justice system in America is a disgrace to a civilized nation that prides itself on decency and the belief in the intrinsic worth of every individual.

The criminal justice system in America today is a complete failure. The financial waste incurred by local communities, cities, states, and the federal government is unbelievable. The crimes committed against those who are victimized by the system are intolerable.

The human waste caused by the warehousing of prisoners is unconscionable. The reverberation to our society is found in an increasing crime rate, due to the failure of the criminal justice system to adequately rehabilitate rather than show contempt for prisoners. This cause and effect relationship is totally ignored.

As was recently reported in the *New York Times*, violence erupted in August at Riker's prison complex in New York. A total of 135 individuals, 92 of them inmates, were injured in a nine-jail complex. It is now admitted that officers routinely beat inmates with clubs. In 1980, the Riker's prison population was less than 6,000, with a correction force of 4,500. Today the prison population is close to 14,000 with a correction force of 11,000. The New York Correction Department's budget, which totalled $146 million a decade ago, is now reported at $765 million.

Let me share with you some other interesting statistics:

Charles B. DeWitt, President Bush's nominee to head the National Institute of Justice, has recently observed that the nation's prison and jail population recently passed the 1 million mark and is rising at a 13% annual rate. Maintaining that rate of growth would cost at least $100 million per week for construction of new facilities alone.

For the year ending June 30, 1985, federal detention costs totalled approximately $9 million dollars. Of this $9 million, approximately $7 million was spent on *pre*-adjudication detention. In 1988, total detention costs were approximately $28 million. Approximately $20 million of this was for pre-adjudication detention. During the same period, the total number of cases closed did not quite double, going from 12,397 in 1985 to 21,952 in 1988.

Overall, approximately 29% of all federal defendants remain incarcerated until their trial. About 80% of all federal defendants are detained for reasons of risk of flight or danger to the community (not inability to raise bail). In 1988, 48.6% of the total jail population were pretrial detainees.

There were 343,569 total inmates in the jail population in 1988. Local jail occupancy rate in 1989 was 108% of capacity; in 1988 it was 101%; in 1983 it was 85%. According to the *Jail Population Statistics*, Bureau of Justice Statistics Survey, June 30, 1989, 26% of jails were under federal or state court order or consent decree to limit number of inmates. 51% of jails sampled held prisoners due to overcrowding in other institutions. This figure was 29% in 1988 and 17% in 1983. 395,553 persons were held in U.S. jails (state and federal) (1 out of 469 U.S. adult residents) in 1989. This is a 15% increase over 1988. According to Bureau of Justice statistics, in 1978 there were a total of 3,693 jails in operation, but by 1988 that number had decreased to 3,316, a 5% reduction. From 1983 to 1988, there was a 51% increase in the total jail population.

Judge Edward Becker, Chairman of the United States Judicial Conference Committee on Probation and Criminal Law, recently testified before a congressional committee. He observed: The U.S. Bureau of Prisons presently is holding approximately 3,600 pretrial detainees on any given day. The cost of confinement in these facilities exceeds $11,000 per year per defendant.

The Marshals Service has increasingly come to rely on the Bureau of Prisons to absorb the growing number of pretrial detainees. This has negatively affected the federal judiciary. The Marshals often must travel substantial distances on a daily basis to transport pretrial detainees to court. This problem is exacerbated by a requirement that all travel be completed during daylight hours. In some instances this has limited available court time to 3-4 hours per day. Delays also have resulted because of the inability of defense attorneys to meet with their clients who are detained in facilities distant from their offices. Local jail space is so short in some cities that pretrial detainees must be transported long distances. For example, pretrial detainees from Philadelphia, Pennsylvania, and Providence, Rhode Island, are housed in Otisville, New York. Some defendants in Los Angeles are detained in the San Francisco area.

Federal pretrial detainees in Minnesota are held in four surrounding states. This situation causes: (1) exorbitant transportation costs; (2) difficulties for counsel and the courts in preparing and processing the defendant's case for trial; and (3) hardship on families of pretrial detainees.

The atrocities that take place within jails and prisons, in the name of the state, are commonplace. A few years ago I visited a correctional institution in a southern state. On the weekend I arrived, a 19-year-old farm boy had just been sentenced to jail for one year for possession of marijuana. He was received in their central processing unit, which was designed to hold 120 prisoners. At that time there were 465 prisoners incarcerated in small cells in a 4-level building that afforded little ventilation and no recreational area. On Monday the young man was sent to a psychological evaluation unit. After two hours they picked up his exam papers and he had written only two words: "Help me, help me." Upon questioning, officials discovered that he had been put in a small cell block containing 4 beds with 11 other inmates who had sexually assaulted him for 48 hours, every hour on the hour.

In another instance, a 19-year-old prisoner at the Missouri Training Center, who was the victim of a number of homosexual rapes, was given three alternatives by a prison official: submit, fight back, or escape. He chose the last alternative. The Missouri Supreme Court affirmed his conviction for the escape charge, concluding that conditions of confinement do not justify escape and are not a defense. Dissenting, Justice Seiler wrote:

[The] defendant had already been told by a high prison official that he had three alternatives: submit, defend himself, or escape. The majority opinion does not recommend submission, and as a practical matter, self defense was impossible. All that was left was escape, and under these circumstances, the coercion and necessity were not remote in time, but present and impending. Escape or submission (and I do not believe defendant was unreasonable in not being willing to submit to five-fold sodomy) were literally all this defendant had left. . . .

The evidence shows [the] defendant was confronted with a horrific dilemma, not of his making. No one, I am sure, wants to force a prisoner to live under conditions where he must either become a "punk" and debase himself, or a "snitch" at the risk of his life, but nevertheless this is the effect of our decision, until and unless the state improves the conditions in the prisons.

The public has every right to deeply resent those who commit crime. However, I respectfully submit that the "knee-jerk" reactions by angry executives, politically conscious legislatures, and vindictive judicial officers is taking us down a primrose path with little success in combating crime. The resulting approach is accomplishing nothing more than exorbitantly wasting tax dollars, creating a warehouse of human degradation, and in the long run breeding societal resentment that causes more crime.

In the federal system, the commitment to double the size of our prisons by 1995, to increase mandatory minimum sentences, and to sentence by the crime and not by the individual, is simply a corollary to this societal attitude. Unfortunately, this blind reaction has brought about diminution of basic individual rights in the pretrial detention of more and more individuals accused of crime. This fact once again has led to amazing inefficiency and cost in our criminal justice system.

Preservation of basic human rights is an area in which pretrial service officers should be acutely interested.

In *United States v. Salerno* (1987) in which the Supreme Court found the 1984 Bail Reform Act constitutional, Chief Justice Rehnquist stated: "In our society liberty is the norm, and detention prior to trial or without trial is the carefully limited exception." I respectfully submit that when you consider some of the statistics, you will become convinced that few judicial officers, state or federal, adhere to this constitutional principle.

I respectfully suggest that at least under the language of the Bail Reform Act, when proper supervision of pretrial release is provided, there should be relatively few or no pretrial commitments. If this was the practice, as it should be, consider the resulting benefits: the easing of overcrowded jails, the reduced financial burden to the state and federal governments, and the increased efficiency of the courts to operate on schedule without the wasteful time and expense for transportation by marshals and sheriffs. Consider as well the preservation of the rights to liberty, the presumption of innocence, the ability of defendants to assist counsel in preparing their case, the continuation of employment, and the reduced domestic upheaval achieved by allowing the accused to remain at home.

Few today recognize that the Bail Reform Act of 1984 was not created to cause greater pretrial detention (as it has) but to do away with the need for money bail. Along with the PreTrial Service Officers Act, the Bail Act also seeks to create alternatives to detention under the supervision of government officers rather than private bounty hunters. It is absurd for headline seeking judges to set excessively high bail for white collar defendants. If there exists a high degree of risk that an accused person will flee, he or she can be denied release. Money should have nothing to do with it. On the other hand, with modern surveillance techniques, detention of an accused, other than ones who have committed violent crimes, should be the exception rather than the rule. The recidivism rate of defendants who are given pretrial release is less than two percent.

Space does not permit discussion of another failure of our criminal justice system: the cost of the useless incarceration of persons convicted of nonviolent offenses. There exists a crying need to develop a nationwide system of intermediate sanctions for those who are convicted of nonviolent felonies. Our penology system needs to develop work release programs, community service programs, schooling, vocational training, and other forms of supervised productivity in lieu of wasteful expenditures of tax dollars and wholesale warehousing of individuals.

Punishment is one thing, but our current incarceration policies are wasteful and should be changed. Present policies breed further crime, dehumanize individuals, and require gross expenditures of tax dollars needed for other purposes. With our nation facing both societal and fiscal crises of unrivaled proportions, we must move quickly and forcefully to overhaul the current system.

COMMUNICATIONS IN MEDICINE[1]
NEWTON N. MINOW[2]

In his address, "Communications in Medicine," Newton Minow raised the question of whether doctors and lawyers know how to listen. His speech was the ninth James C. Hemphill lecture. His qualifications to discuss problems of communication include the fact that he is director of The Annenberg Washington Program in Communications Policy Studies, a professor at Northwestern University, a former chairman of the Federal Communications Commission, and an attorney.

Minow's address was part of a series of annual lectures sponsored by the Rehabilitation Institute of Chicago. His audience consisted of approximately 200 doctors, lawyers, rehabilitation professionals, educators, and the institute's board of directors and women's board members. He delivered the lecture at 4:00 P.M. on October 16, 1990, in the auditorium of the Northwestern University Law School in Evanston, Illinois. A recep-

---

[1]The speech was given as part of an annual lecture series sponsored by the Rehabilitation Institute of Chicago at 4:00 P.M., October 16, 1990, in the Northwestern University Law School auditorium, Evanston, Illinois, to an audience of approximately 200.

[2]For biographical note, see Appendix.

tion and the presentation of a certificate of appreciation to Minow preceded the address. Even if they knew little about Minow's career, many listeners were probably familiar with his famous description of television as a "vast wasteland," a remark made while he was F.C.C. chairman thirty years earlier.

The organization of Minow's speech was somewhat unusual. He began the lecture with detailed descriptions of three tragic examples of what he called "the ultimate failure in doctor-patient relationships," and then asked the questions: Why did they happen? Why did they happen now and not in the past? Could they have been avoided? and, Is there a better way to resolve life and death issues? As part of his answer, he said:

I believe the two most significant features of medicine today are the explosive growth in the capabilities and use of new technology and the pervasive need for better, more effective communications.

The remainder of the lecture consisted of an analysis of the problems created by the explosion in medical technology and the pervasive need for better communication to cope with these developments.

His lecture was reprinted in *Vital Speeches of the Day*.

Newton Minow's speech: On the night of January 11, 1983, Nancy Cruzan, a healthy, 25-year-old woman, lost control of her car while driving in Jasper County, Missouri. As the car overturned, Nancy was thrown into a ditch. Paramedics found her with no detectable breathing or heartbeat. Today Nancy lies in a Missouri state hospital, in what is described all too neatly as a "persistent vegetative state." In reality, she lies in a bed, horribly contorted with irreversible muscular and tendon damage, her hands bent so far over that her fingernails press into her wrists. She stares with unseeing eyes, oblivious to her environment, unable to drink or eat. She is fed through a tube in her side; another tube carries away waste. Her brain is atrophying, replaced by a pool of cerebrospinal fluid. Yet she may "live"—if it may be called "living"—in this condition for as long as 30 years.

Prior to her accident, Nancy had twice said, on the occasion of relatives' deaths, that she would never want to be kept alive "to just lay in a bed and not be able to move because you can't do anything for yourself." Her family and friends without exception had testified that "Nancy would be horrified at the state she is in."

The Missouri Supreme Court, however, held that life-support could not be withdrawn from Nancy despite the respectful requests of loving, deeply caring parents. The court could not find "clear and convincing" evidence that she would want it so. Finding that Nancy's prior statements did not meet that standard, the court refused to permit anyone to make the decision on Nancy's behalf. As you know, the U.S. Supreme Court ruled this summer that no right of Nancy's or her family's could compel the Missouri court to deviate from its decision.

While the Supreme Court was handing down its decision in *Cruzan*, the District of Columbia Court of Appeals was deliberating only blocks away in a case, in which our law firm participated, that also involved health care-related decision-making. Angela Cardur had first been diagnosed with cancer at the age of 13. After 14 years of radiation therapy, chemotherapy and repeated major surgery, Angela married and shortly thereafter became pregnant. Angela was delighted about her pregnancy and very much wanted to have the child. On June 9, 1987, when Angela was approximately 25 weeks pregnant, doctors at George Washington University Hospital's high-risk pregnancy clinic discovered an inoperable tumor which nearly filled her right lung. The doctors admitted Angela to the hospital on June 11 and three days later told her that her condition was terminal.

Angela agreed to a course of palliative treatment which, although it offered no hope of recovery and posed some risks to the fetus, was designed to help keep her comfortable long enough to allow the fetus to reach 28 weeks, at which time its chances of a healthy life were significantly greater. Angela, her husband, mother and physicians considered the possibility of providing her with radiation therapy and chemotherapy in order to further relieve her pain and continue her pregnancy.

Angela's condition deteriorated rapidly during the night of June 15th and intubation was necessary to maintain her breathing. The following morning, her physicians concluded that more intrusive treatment was inappropriate because the mother's death was imminent and the unborn child was unlikely to survive. The hospital administration appealed to the local court for directions as to how to balance the interests of the fetus against those of the mother. The court record describes an emotional hearing at the hospital. Angela's overwrought husband was unable to speak. Her physicians advised that Angela was certain to die within 24 hours, but that the baby stood a 50-60 percent chance of being saved if extracted immediately by caesarean section—a procedure which might hasten Angela's death. Angela lay in the room next door, heavily sedated, occasionally responsive but seldom coherent. Her doctors testified that forcing her to confront the decision about whether to undergo a caesarean might very well end her life.

The court, while unable to determine what Angela would have wanted with regard to the unborn child, concluded that the fetus was viable and the District of Columbia had an interest in protecting the potential life of the fetus. The judge ordered the caesarean section and a doctor went to tell Angela:

I explained to her essentially what was going on. . . . I said it's been deemed we should intervene on behalf of the baby by caesarean section and it would give it the only possible chance of living. Would you agree to this procedure. *She said yes*. And I repeated the two questions to her again [and] asked her did she understand. *She said yes*.

But moments later, Angela, unable to speak because of the tube in her trachea, mouthed the words several times, "*I don't want it done. I don't want it done.*"

The judge determined that it was "still not clear" what Angela wanted and ordered the caesarean section performed in order to attempt to save the fetus. The baby lived for only a few hours; Angela Cardur survived the procedure and died two days later.

The District of Columbia Court of Appeals held that the judge had erred, first, by not ascertaining whether Angela Cardur had the capacity to consent and whether she did in fact consent to the procedure; and, second, if she lacked capacity, by not determining what *her* decision would have been had she had the capacity to decide. The court focused on the legal requirement that when a patient is incapable of giving informed consent to any medical procedure, "the court must make a substitute judgment. This means," the appellate court wrote, "that the court must ascertain as best it can what the *patient* would do if faced with the particular treatment decision."

We are all familiar with the tragic case of Sidney Greenspan decided only two weeks ago here in Chicago. Greenspan suffered a stroke in 1984 which left him comatose, his body, like that of Nancy Cruzan, grotesquely stiffened into a fetal position while machines supplied him with nourishment and hydration. Greenspan's wife of 56 years, Belle, went to court in 1988 asking that the feeding tube be removed. She testified that her husband had once said, "You shoot me and I'll shoot you if we ever have to be put in nursing homes." But the court refused, reasoning that since Greenspan could "live" with the feeding tube, he was not terminally ill.

The Illinois Supreme Court overturned that decision and on October 3rd, Cook County Circuit Judge Richard Dowdle authorized Greenspan's doctors to remove the feeding tube. Greenspan's body is expected to follow the course of his brain, and starve to death. But he is still "living" in what his wife called six years of "living hell."

These tragic cases of Nancy Cruzan, Angela Cardur and Sidney Greenspan represent the ultimate failure in doctor-patient communication. Why did they happen now? Why did cases like these not happen in the past? Could the sad results have been avoided? Is there a better way to resolve life and death issues than in the adversarial atmosphere of a courtroom? Why do we think judges and lawyers will reach wiser decisions than families, loved ones, physicians, priests, rabbis and ministers?

I believe the two most significant features of medicine today are the explosive growth in the capabilities and use of new technology and the pervasive need for better, more effective communications. These developments are related. As Dr. Alan Nelson, President of the American Medical Association, has suggested, "enormous and rapid technologic[al] advances" of necessity require that we pay more attention to the humanistic side of medicine.

The same may be said of many, perhaps most, professions today. It is certainly true of law, where many attorneys plunge ahead, armed with high speed computers, laser facsimiles, portable telephones, legal databases, automated time-keeping systems, and far too little regard for the input of their colleagues, or their clients—and far too little listening to the other side.

Today I will concentrate on doctor-patient communication, because it is here that a confluence of three factors has created dramatic needs. These three factors are: (1) as already noted, greater reliance on new medical technologies; (2) increased specialization in medicine and a resulting decline in the long-term, intimate relationship between patient and family doctor; and (3) the medical communities' fear of litigation and liability (both criminal and civil). Together, these three factors have created and repeated communication failures. I address two levels of these failures: communication between physician and patient and communication between the medical and other professions.

We know a great deal about our failings in physician-patient communication, but still too little about how to succeed. Some findings should concern us greatly. One extensive study of more than 800 doctor-patient interactions found that less than five percent of doctors' communication with patients was either personal or friendly; but that the majority of doctors participating reported that they thought they were behaving in a friendly manner.

A second study found that patients described their complaints for an average of only 18 seconds before their physicians interrupted. Only 23 percent of patients studied reported they were able to tell their doctors everything they wanted. Another study found that in 50 percent of all conversations, physicians used technical jargon. The AMA's 1989 survey of public perceptions of physicians found that less than half of those surveyed felt "doctors usually explain things well to their patients." This news is made even worse by the widely held view, confirmed by research, that communication skills deteriorate during medical school.

Dr. Jay Katz writes in *The Silent World of Doctor and Patient*:

We have spared no effort to make better tools, but we have paid little attention to learning how to communicate better with one another."

Norman Cousins, in his book, *Head First—the Biology of Hope*, writes:

Doctors are not entirely to blame for spending so little time directly with their patients. The central fact here is that doctors don't get paid for talking to patients. In a medical economy dominated by third-party paymasters—insurance companies, the government, health plans, etc.—the harsh reality is that doctors get paid mostly for tests and procedures. . . .

An even more basic factor . . . is that physicians are worried about malpractice suits. They have been educated by lawyers to leave no doubt about anything that might happen during the course of an illness. An unequivocal or flat-out method of communicating a diagnosis is regarded by some physicians as a way of protecting themselves against an expensive lawsuit.

Nor is the story one-sided. Doctors appear to be as dissatisfied with their patients' communications skills as are patients with their doctors'. And with good reason. In one study, patients frequently reported that their doctors had not told them things which in fact had been recorded during the taped doctor-patient interview. Another study showed that patients disregarded their physicians' instructions in half of all cases.

Study after study has proven that effective communication between physician and patient is crucial to the health care delivery process. We hardly, however, need in-depth research to tell us this fact, since our own personal experience, confirmed by intuition, show that patients need to communicate symptoms and physicians need to communicate instructions. Effective communication between doctor and patient not only conveys important information, it builds trust and increases confidence, both of which are essential for effective health care.

Moreover, better information, combined with greater rapport, has been shown to actually speed improvement. An early study found that "preoperative encouragement and education by anesthesiologists reduced postoperative pain and resulted in earlier dismissal from the hospital." Postoperative vomiting has been reduced by better preoperative communication between nurse and patient to help prepare the patient for what to expect. Blood sugar control among diabetics has also been improved by more effective doctor-patient communications.

Failures to communicate reduce the effectiveness of the prescribed treatment and impede recovery. Moreover, communication failures have been empirically shown to waste time and money. Finally, many, if not all, malpractice cases involve serious communications failures. Here is the conclusion of a 1985 study:

When the resolution of a dispute involves going to a lawyer, patients have experienced compounded complaints including (a) professional failures in treatment, (b) a lack of communication by the doctor about the nature of diagnosis and (c) some form of insensitivity from the doctor that has been morally upsetting to them [the patients].

A study released this year by the Physician Insurers Association of America found that in 69.2 percent of all malpractice suits arising from delayed diagnosis of breast cancer, the physician initially *ignored* the patient's complaint about a lump in her breast. In 37 percent of these cases, the physician had never taken a family history to learn whether any of the patient's relatives had been diagnosed as having breast cancer.

The vital importance of communications in the physician-patient relationship is well-documented and campaigns for its improvement are already underway in many institutions around the country, especially here at the Rehabilitation Institute of Chicago. The Institute's Leadership Lecture Series introduces all of the physical medicine and rehabilitation residents to a wide variety of communications-related topics, including interviewing skills, meeting with families and dealing with terminally ill patients. The Rehabilitation Institute of Chicago is expanding its doctor-patient communication training program and is a model for improvement in health care communication for the rest of the nation.

Nowhere, however, is communications more important, more lacking or less studied than in the interaction between physicians and their patients, patients' families, medical colleagues, and other professionals about life and death decisions. Technology has given us the ability to extend life, both by moving forward the point at which a fetus may be viable and by prolonging life far beyond the time of independent viability. But the extraordinary achievements of technology pose fundamental questions which physicians, lawyers and judges cannot and should not answer alone.

Shakespeare wrote in *King Lear*, "O! let him pass; he hates him That would upon the rack of this tough world Stretch him out longer." The extent to which each of us shares the Earl of Kent's sentiments is an individual matter, by law to be determined by the individual. In the absence of clear, precise information, however, determinations about treatment for a person who is incapacitated, unconscious or otherwise lacks decisional capacity, are all too frequently resolved in court. Why are these communications failures? Why do they end up in court for resolution? How can we formulate wiser and more humane solutions?

Cruzan, Cardur, Greenspan and cases like them, should make us re-examine ourselves. First, they seem to suggest different applications of ostensibly the same standard for evaluating life and death treatment decisions. Missouri, the District of Columbia and Illinois are deeply concerned about what the patient would have wanted. In Missouri, when a patient's wishes cannot be demonstrated by "clear and convincing evidence"—a very high evidentiary standard—the state *presumes* that the individual would want to continue "living"—even if in a persistent vegetative state. In short, the individual's interests may be subordinated to the state's interest in preserving life at all costs.

In the District of Columbia, on the other hand, the right of the individual to choose is so important that a judge must make every effort to determine what the individual would want. The judge must try to put himself in the place of the patient and make a decision based on whatever evidence exists about how the patient would have made the decision. The judge may not attempt to make an objective determination as to what might be in the best interest of the patient. Rather, in the words of the District of Columbia Court of Appeals, "the court must ascertain as best it can what the *patient* would do if faced with the particular treatment question."

In Illinois, which, like Missouri, requires the same "clear and convincing" evidence of a patient's desires, statements to the family about not wanting to live in a debilitated condition have proven sufficient to meet that standard. We face the unsettling prospect that the physical state of a person's existence may very well turn on the geographic state in which his or her body is lying.

A second, and more compelling reason for concern, is that these two cases highlight our failure—the medical and legal professions'—to *anticipate*, rather than merely react to, critical issues posed by rapidly advancing medical technology. Physicians and attorneys did not need to be clairvoyant to have anticipated the speed of Angela Cardur's decline or the possibility of some tragic occurrence depriving Nancy Cruzan of the ability to indicate her wishes about her own health care. On the contrary, it is precisely because we cannot predict what will happen to whom that we need to communicate better. We need to listen: listen to each other about the health care and legal issues posed by new technologies; listen to legislatures and courts so that we know what the law requires; and listen to our patients and clients, prompting them to make fundamental, even if uncomfortable, decisions and respecting their answers.

Although Angela Cardur's physicians knew she was terminally ill and knew that she was 25 weeks pregnant, they apparently failed to ascertain her wishes at anytime during her care regarding her own treatment and that of the fetus. As her condition rapidly deteriorated, necessitating medication which was likely to inhibit her decisional capacity, no one even then sought Angela's input about the inevitable decisions affecting her care. The process of determining what Angela might have wanted and the indignity and glaring publicity suffered by Angela, her family and her physicians, could have been avoided entirely if someone had only asked, if someone had only listened.

Ann Lander's column last month published a letter which speaks directly to the importance of medical professionals listening to their patients and patients' families. The letter said:

While a patient in the hospital, my husband's heart stopped. An emergency team rushed in and worked feverishly to resuscitate him. They succeeded.

Sounds wonderful? Well, not exactly. The dear man was 86 years old and had terminal cancer. He lived another three days in agony.

By no stretch of the imagination could "saving" his life be called a humanitarian act. He would have been much better off had they just left him alone. Needless to say, so would have I, as well as the other members of our family.

The simple act of *listening* could have saved this family, as well as that of Angela Cardur, additional agony at an already tragic time in their lives.

Although no one expected Nancy Cruzan's or Sidney Greenspan's tragedies, there, too, the pain of the substitute decision-making process could have been avoided. The majority of people in this country will at some point during their lifetimes be unable to participate in medical treatment decisions affecting their own care. Chronic or degenerative ailments have in this century replaced infectious diseases as the primary cause of death in the Western world. According to medical ethicist Joseph Fletcher, 80 percent of Americans who die in hospitals are "likely to meet their end . . . in a sedated or comatose state; betubed nasally, abdominally and intravenously; and far more like manipulated objects than like moral subjects." And a fifth of all adults surviving to age 80 will suffer a progressive dementing disorder prior to death. As the baby-boom generation ages and medical technology continues to develop, more and more people will at some point during their lifetimes be unable to participate in medical treatment decisions affecting their own care. Knowing these facts, it would seem clear, even unavoidable, that every person in the United States should make some provision for decision-making about his or her health care in the likely circumstance that he or she is incapacitated.

There are many possible options. For example, during the past two decades 42 states and the District of Columbia have enacted living will statutes, under which a competent adult may prepare a document authorizing or requiring the withholding or withdrawal of specified medical treatments in the event of a catastrophic illness or condition which renders the person incompetent to make such a decision. Courts in other states, such as New York, have authorized the use of living wills in the absence of statutory provision.

Another provision through which individuals can seek to protect their rights if incapacitated is a durable power of attorney. A general durable power of attorney permits any competent individual to name someone to exercise decision-making authority under specified circumstances on his or her behalf. All states and the District of Columbia have provisions for general durable power of attorney.

A third, new option is the medical directive, a hybrid of the living will and the durable power of attorney. Under a medical directive, an individual, in consultation with his or her physician, as well as relatives or other personal advisors such as an attorney, provides precise instructions for the type of care he or she does or does not want in a number of scenarios. For each scenario, individuals are asked to indicate for each of twelve treatments whether they (1) would want the treatment; (2) would not want the treatment; (3) are undecided; or (4) if appropriate, would want a trial of the treatment to be discontinued if there were no clear improvement. The individual may also use the medical directive to appoint a proxy decision maker to help interpret the application of the specific instructions or fill in unanticipated gaps. The directive would then become part of a patient's permanent medical record. A card indicating the existence of a medical directive might also be carried in a wallet or purse.

Through the use of any of these three instruments—a living will, durable power of attorney, or medical directive—the family, friends and doctors of Nancy Cruzan, Angela Cardur, and Sydney Greenspan would have been spared the past seven years of litigation and emotional turmoil. Nancy Cruzan would not be forced, against her apparent wishes, "to just lay in bed and not be able to move because you can't do anything for yourself."

The medical and legal communities are beginning to deal with the many difficult issues posed by new medical technology. Living wills and durable powers of attorney, while available by law in most states and widely supported by physicians, at least in theory, have thus far been little used. As of 1987 only nine percent of Americans had completed a living will. Few physicians ever ask their patients whether they have a living will; even fewer advise their patients to prepare one. Even for the small percentage of the population that does, living wills seldom seem to be used in clinical practice. Living wills just do not make it in the patient's chart, largely because physicians are never *told* that a living will exists.

Following the *Cruzan* decision, many more people are asking how can they avoid ending up like Nancy. Requests for information on living wills from one New York City organization alone have increased from 20,000 per month to over 150,000 since *Cruzan* was decided this summer. We must make certain, however, that physicians and hospitals know when their patients have completed living wills. And we must assure that these instruments are not limited by vague terms, such as "heroic measures" or "life prolonging procedures," which offer little guidance to physicians and are unlikely to indicate the patient's desires regarding specific treatments in a specific situation in the "clear and convincing" manner, which states like Missouri require.

The medical directive reflects a significant improvement over earlier measures. But its legal force is uncertain, particularly in the eight states whose legislatures have not provided for living wills. In any case, the success of the medical directive depends largely on the willingness of physicians and attorneys to advise its use and then spend the time necessary with each patient or client to complete it. It depends on the willingness and ability of physicians in particular to communicate effectively with patients. Drs. Linda and Ezekiel Emanuel, leading proponents of the medical directive, write that the medical directive places an emphasis on "prior discussion." It provides a context for "extensive exploration of a patient's wishes and how they reflect a particular view of life and the process of dying. It provides a unique opportunity for a physician to educate the patient of life-sustaining technology and how it can fit with the patient's wishes." Discussions about the directive would in some cases "reveal that the patient's wishes seem incompatible with the physician's principles . . . alert[ing] the patient to the possibility of seeking alternative medical care."

The medical directive is proof of what doctors and lawyers can accomplish when we listen to each other and work together. It indicates the importance of communications to medicine and the effort that will be necessary if we are to effectively harness medical technologies in the service of humankind. And it is the type of initiative which is essential if we are to avoid wasting literally *billions* of health care dollars, stay out of the courts, and guarantee the essential right to every individual of the dignity of self-determination.

If we are to keep the health care decisions for generations of Angela Cardurs, Nancy Cruzans, and Sidney Greenspans out of the courtroom, we, doctors and lawyers together, must learn to anticipate, rather than merely react to, critical issues posed by rapidly advancing medical technology. We need to learn to listen better, to each other and to our patients and clients, prompting them to face important, difficult decisions.

Living wills, powers of attorney, and medical directives are three possible routes for protecting the rights of individuals when they are unable to speak for themselves. Knowing what we know about the tragedy of Nancy Cruzan and 10,000 other Americans who lie in a coma today, every person should make some provision for the likely eventuality of being silenced by illness or injury. It is our responsibility to encourage their doing so, not only for those people who can afford to take advantage of our services, but for the tens of millions who cannot, for those patients and clients we see in low-income clinics and for people we seldom see.

The time to discuss a person's desires regarding life-sustaining treatment is before the trauma occurs. Every person upon entering a hospital should be asked as part of the routine admission process, "Have you made any provision for decision-making on your behalf if you are unconscious or incapacitated?" If the answer is "yes," the document should be placed prominently in the patient's chart. If "no," an opportunity should be provided for discussing the various alternatives with a qualified professional.

The same questions should be asked by attorneys when preparing traditional wills for clients; by physicians during the regular office visits of their patients; and certainly by any medical professional whose specialty involves diagnosing and treating life-threatening diseases.

We should take seriously the business of instructing those who will follow us about the urgency of these issues. We are beginning to see a seminar here at Northwestern University and at colleges and universities around the country, in which students from both law and medical schools, led by distinguished physicians, attorneys, judges and ethicists, grapple with the inseparable issues of communications, ethics, and medical decision-making. We need much more. We should be teaching today about the importance of legal instruments which may keep life and death decisions out of the courts and in the hands of patients and their loved ones, where they belong.

We must also create other opportunities and incentives for effective communication between individuals and their families, physicians and other medical professionals, members of the clergy *and* lawyers. These may take the form of public education campaigns in the media, schools, churches and synagogues. They may also include funding and training for members of hospital and medical center staffs, community centers, and nursing homes. And we must work with insurance companies and federal and state governments to address Norman Cousin's apt diagnosis that much of physicians' reluctance to spend adequate time directly with their patients is due to "the harsh reality . . . that doctors get paid mostly for tests and procedures," not for talking with their patients.

But legal instruments, educational programs, and incentives are not the end of the story. Hippocrates said that he "would rather know what sort of person has a disease than what sort of disease a person has." Today we can know both; in fact, we must know both, because knowledge of diseases is useless if we do not understand the people who are afflicted by them. Already strong voices within the medical community are realizing the importance of communications and are working to teach, stimulate, and reward communications skills. The Rehabilitation Institute of Chicago is at the forefront of this movement and Dr. Henry Betts is a powerful advocate.

Another powerful advocate is Norman Cousins, who learned from his own medical crisis the significance of effective doctor-patient communication to physical health, and who has shared that learning with broad public audiences. I leave you this evening with some of his wise words:

There are qualities beyond our medical competence that patients need and look for in doctors. They want reassurance. They want to be looked after and not just looked over. They want to be listened to. They want to feel that it makes a difference to the physician, a very big difference, whether they live or die. They want to feel that they are in the doctor's thoughts. The physician holds the lifeline. The physician's words and not just his prescriptions are attached to that lifeline.

This aspect of medicine has not changed in thousands of years. Not all the king's horses and all the king's men—not all the tomography and the thallium scanners and two-D echocardiograms and medicinal mood modifiers—can preempt the physician's primary role as the keeper of the keys to the body's own healing system.

I pray that you will never allow your knowledge to get in the way of your relationship with your patients. I pray that all the technological marvels at your command will not prevent you from practicing medicine out of a little black bag. I pray that when you go into a patient's room you will recognize that the main distance is not from the door to the bed but from the patient's eyes to your own—and that the shortest distance between those two points is a horizontal straight line—the kind of straight line that works best when the physician bends low to the patient's loneliness and fear and pain and the overwhelming sense of mortality that comes flooding up out of the unknown, and when the physician's hand on the patient's shoulder or arm is a shelter against the darkness.

REPRODUCTIVE FREEDOM: FUNDAMENTAL TO ALL HUMAN RIGHTS[1]
FAYE WATTLETON[2]

For the past 13 years, Faye Wattleton has served as president of the Planned Parenthood Federation of America, the nation's oldest and largest family planning service. When she was appointed to the post in 1978 at the age of 34, she was the first woman, the first black, and the youngest executive ever to serve in that position. A former nurse from Ohio, she vowed to lead the federation in a crusade to guarantee every person's right to decide if and when to have a child, at the same time contending that Planned Parenthood is not pro-abortion, but pro-choice.

Aware of the value of a high public profile, Wattleton also was determined to transform the traditionally low-keyed organization into a visible force. Commenting on her success in attracting publicity, *Business Week* wrote, "In terms of public recognition, Faye Wattleton may be the nonprofit equivalent of Lee Iacocco." (March 26, 1990, p. 69).

Time described her:

Nearly 6 ft. tall, imperially slim, and sleekly dressed, she is usually the cynosure of attention at any gathering. *Harper's Bazaar* named her one of their eight "Over-40 and Sensational" women last sum-

[1]Delivered to an audience of 200–250 employees of Esprit de Corp as part of its "Be Informed" lecture series in the company gymnasium, San Francisco, California, at 12:00 P.M. on December 11, 1990.

[2]For biographical note, see Appendix.

mer, and she is a stunning refutation of the cliché of the dowdy feminist. In an era when non-profit organizations seek out celebrity spokespeople to get their message across, she is the public relations ideal, a spokeswoman who has become a celebrity. (December 11, 1989, p. 82.)

In a profile in the *New York Times Magazine*, Marianne Szegedy-Mosak wrote:

> Tough, single-minded and telegenic, this missionary's daughter and former nurse . . . has emerged, over the last decade, as the most visible and persuasive spokeswoman for abortion rights. . . . She defends her cause coolly, rationally, as though it will triumph through its manifest reasonableness.
>
> It doesn't hurt that the message comes from a woman who looks for all the world like a network anchor—with an extra dash of glamour. Beneath the immaculately tailored, carefully maintained surface, however, is a tough, shrewd operator. (August 6, 1989, p. 18).

Wattleton's high visibility, however, brings out critics as well as admirers. She has had death threats from extremist opponents and is often accompanied by a bodyguard.

Representative of the many speeches Wattleton delivers each year was her address to Esprit de Corp, a national sportswear merchandiser with a commitment to social and environmental issues. Given in San Francisco on December 11, 1990, her address was part of the company's "Be Informed" lecture series. It was delivered to a lunch time audience of between 200 and 250 employees, male and female of various jobs and all ages, in the firm's gymnasium.

Faye Wattleton's speech: I love to visit northern California, everyone here is so health-conscious and outdoorsy. I've heard that's especially true of Esprit people, so I think you'll appreciate a sports tidbit I read recently. *Bicycling* magazine polled its readers and learned that 84% daydream about sex while they're cycling. Somehow I wasn't surprised. But then I read that 20% daydream about cycling while they're having sex!

Well, I won't ask for a show of hands here, but I think it's safe to say that sex is important to most of us! Whatever our age or circumstances, we all make sexual decisions—and we cherish the freedom to make those decisions privately, without meddling or coercion.

The freedom to chart our reproductive destinies is a more recent acquisition than you might think. As late as 1965, contraception was still illegal in most of the U.S. Before then, biology was still destiny. Women were economically deprived and socially dependent. And men suffered too, saddled with children they could not feed or clothe.

In this day and age, control over our reproduction is a given. Women and men can plan our futures because we can plan our child-bearing. This dramatic advance is just one of the many steps forward our nation has made in recent decades, including enormous progress in human rights, women's rights, civil rights, children's rights.

But today we look down the road toward the future and we see warning signs: "Danger ahead!" The danger isn't limited to our reproductive liberty, either; we see threats to our very progress as a democratic, pluralistic society. A tyrannical minority is determined to reverse the changes that were achieved in my generation. They want to tell us which forms of speech are censored, which books we may read, which music and art we may enjoy, even which God to pray to. Armed with Puritanical moralism, they have set out to control everything they view as obscene.

This crackdown on free expression will have a cataclysmic impact on our fundamental rights. This is not the America I know and love!

Around the world, nations are steering toward greater freedom for all citizens, holding our constitutional ideals as their compass—while here at home, we fight not to lose ideals. Is this the America we want to see as we end the 20th century?

The framers of our Constitution established the ideal of fundamental freedoms, freedoms that would endure in an ever-changing society, freedoms far removed from the reach of politicians. The Bill of Rights plainly states that "the enumeration [in] the Constitution of certain rights shall not be construed to deny or disparage others retained by the people." In plain talk, that is, the framers didn't want to spell out every one of our liberties. They didn't want to limit our freedoms to their day and age, with no room for expansion!

Given how different life was in those days, I'm glad! Let's remember that Washington and Jefferson owed slaves! Their wives didn't vote! For all we know, they weren't even convinced the world was really round!

With few exceptions, rights have been expanded for the disenfranchised: women, minorities, children, the disabled. Americans have come to take it for granted that our right to decide when and if to reproduce is as fundamental as our right to free speech or to assemble in this room! Nine out of 10 Americans believe that right is constitutionally guaranteed. For 18 years, since the *Roe v. Wade* decision, we've counted on constitutional protection for our right to control our fertility.

But today, we are fighting to hold onto these most basic freedoms. The Reagan-dominated Supreme Court has thrown these rights into chaos.

First, women's access to abortion was restricted in the case called *Webster*, in July 1989. A year later, the court handed down the *Ohio* and *Hodgson* rulings, which allowed states to require parental notification for teens seeking abortions. All three rulings have created more restrictive standards by which all abortion laws will be judged. And though they target the most vulnerable women, the young and the poor, these rulings threaten all women.

I want to focus briefly on the teen cases, and the dangerous idea of legislating family communication. Parents should be involved in teens' important decisions, and their sexual decisions are no exception. I can personally identify with this. My daughter Felicia and I always discuss sexuality issues openly, only these days, *I'm* the one asking most of the questions! But compulsory communication is no joke. Besides, it doesn't work. It only disrupts families, forces young women to lie, and destroys young lives.

Instead of legislating family behavior, we should spend more time and resources on helping families communicate better. Laws should be aimed at giving our young people greater opportunities, not on treating them like property. If Felicia ever became pregnant and felt she couldn't involve me, I'd be hurt and saddened. But she's lived with me for 15 years. She knows me a little better than government regulators. If she couldn't come to me, the last thing I'd want is the government coming to her!

The government has no business telling any of us what to do with our private lives or our family lives! Teen or adult, rich or poor, black, brown, or white, any female able to become pregnant must be able to prevent pregnancy and to choose whether or not to end pregnancy. The government should stay out of it.

No human right is more basic than our right to reproductive freedom. And no human right is so gravely threatened. The late Supreme Court Justice Louis Brandeis once wrote that "the greatest dangers to liberty lurk in insidious encroachment by men of zeal—well-meaning, but without understanding." When it comes to the anti-choice extremists, that description may be overly charitable!

This isn't really a struggle over abortion. It's over controlling women and controlling our sexuality. Otherwise, why would the extremists be intent on eliminating sexuality education and contraception?

The most damaging evidence of their true agenda is their attack on Title X, the federal family planning program that helps prevent 516,000 abortions each year. This attack comes in the form of a so-called gag rule imposed by President Reagan in 1988. The gag rule says that publicly funded clinics can't give a pregnant woman any information on abortion, even if continuing the pregnancy threatens her health! If one of you were a patient in one of these clinics, the staff wouldn't be able to tell you abortion is an option! They couldn't refer you to someone who would tell you! They couldn't even lend you the "Yellow Pages" so you could look up an abortion provider on your own!

This is bald censorship. The gag rule turns doctors into indoctrinators, and patients into pawns. Planned Parenthood argued against the gag rule in the Supreme Court last month. It remains to be seen if the Court will show common sense and compassion, and overturn this obvious ploy to disrupt family planning programs.

It's frightening that the end of the 20th century so closely resembles the beginning. Seventy-five years ago, the founders of the family planning movement had to battle repressive crusades begun in the 19th century, crusades like that of Anthony Comstock, the one-man vice squad who, in 1873, persuaded Congress to label birth control "obscene." In the first year the Comstock statute was in effect, Comstock himself confiscated 200,000 pictures and photos, 100,000 books, 5,000 decks of playing cards, 30,000 boxes of aphrodisiacs, and more than 60,000 of what were then referred to as "rubber articles." I wonder how he fit all that into his night table drawer!

Today, 120 years after his heyday, Comstock is back to haunt us, in the form of Jesse Helms! In 18 years in the Senate, Mr.

Helms has tried to erode personal privacy almost as the Comstock statute did in 92 years!

The Supreme Court encouraged busybodies like Senator Helms. When it handed down the *Webster* case, the court invited state legislators to make our private decisions for us. The court declared that it doesn't trust women with our own choices.

But legislators soon found themselves facing an angry American majority, who want the government off the backs and out of the wombs of women! And in case some politicians were still missing the point, pro-choice America spelled it out for them last month on election day. Across the country, we remembered who our friends are! We remembered to promote our values by voting our values, the universal values of diversity, pluralism, and independence.

However proud we are of our election day victories, reproductive issues should never make it to the ballot box in the first place. Abortion, contraception, privacy, these are fundamental freedoms that should be off limits to lawmakers. And we, the pro-choice majority, have the power to turn this debate around, to remove it from the political arena. We must renew our determination to fight for permanent protection for our freedoms, whatever it takes, for as long as it takes.

Your activism can help make that goal a reality. In fact, you can be more influential than many people, because you're fortunate enough to work for a company that values activism. I was so impressed to learn about the policy on volunteerism here at Esprit. For an employer to take social change so seriously that they encourage you to be activists on company time, that is truly extraordinary.

So I urge you, become activists on behalf of reproductive freedom, for yourselves, for your loved ones, and for the millions of less fortunate women and men who have no one else to speak on their behalf.

Now is the time to improve family communication about sexuality. Start with your family! Now is the time to call for comprehensive sexuality education in the schools, to help teach young people how to live healthy, responsible lives. Now is the time to improve access to contraception for those who need it most, the young and poor. Now is the time to insist on expanded research for better birth control. The National Academy of Sciences reports that the U.S. lags decades behind other nations in this area, with fewer options available, and no concerted commitment to develop new ones.

About all, now is the time to demand that our government leaders stay out of our private matters. We must not rest until they recognize that the right to make personal reproductive decisions is fundamental, inalienable, and non-negotiable. It is not contingent on age or circumstances or geography. It is not a "single issue." And it is not open to partisan debate!

America's lawmakers must stop meddling in the lives of women and families. Surely they have more important things to do, like housing the homeless, feeding the hungry, and educating the ignorant. Like showing concern and compassion for the children already born. And like waging war on the root causes of abortion, unintended pregnancy.

Reproductive freedom is in crisis. But realistic solutions are within our reach, if we all work together. I know you may sometimes wonder how much difference one person's efforts can make. Consider the phenomenon that meteorologists call the "Butterfly Effect": A single butterfly stirs, deep in a forest. The motion of its wings makes tiny air currents. At just that moment, a passing swirl of air happens to pick up those tiny currents, and they become a puff of breeze. Then a momentary gust picks up that breeze and it becomes a gentle wind—and so on, and so on, until, weeks later, the movement of that one butterfly at that one moment changes the course of a tornado on the other side of the globe!

All of us in the universe are linked, over time, and over distance. One butterfly, one person, can make a difference. A big difference. So take wing, today. And remember what Queen Victoria once said: "We are not interested in the possibilities of defeat!"

ACHIEVING COMMUNITY THROUGH DIVERSITY

IN PRAISE OF CITIES[1]
DAVID N. DINKINS[2]

On November 7, 1989, David N. Dinkins was elected the 106th mayor of New York City. He was the city's first new mayor in twelve years and its first black mayor ever.

Commenting on Dinkins' victory, Sam Roberts wrote:

> Although it was the narrowest victory since 1805, his election was a milestone, a powerful symbol of change in a city where non-Hispanic whites, although they still control the levers of economic power, no longer constitute a majority. Belatedly—New York was the last of America's 10 largest cities to elect a mayor who was black, female, or Hispanic—the city's politics had caught up to its demographics.
>
> Unusually for a large American city, no single racial or ethnic group in New York constitutes a majority. (*New York Times Magazine*, April 7, 1991, p. 28).

In his inaugural address as mayor, Dinkins described his vision of the city:

> I see New York as a gorgeous mosaic of race and religious faith, of national origin and sexual orientation; of individuals whose families arrived yesterday and generations ago, coming through Ellis Island, or Kennedy Airport, or on Greyhound buses bound for the Port Authority.

"In that spirit," he said, "I intend to be the mayor of all the people of New York." (*Representative American Speeches 1989–1990*, p. 149). Throughout his first year in office, Dinkins stressed the mosaic of racial, ethnic, and religious diversity of the city, and urged tolerance and unity.

---

[1]Delivered at a convocation of the University of California at Berkeley in the open-air Hearst Greek Theatre in Berkeley, California, at 10:30 A.M. on September 13, 1990.

[2]For biographical note, see Appendix.

On September 13, 1990, Dinkins reaffirmed his faith in cities, and New York in particular, in an address delivered at a convocation of the University of California at Berkeley marking the school's 118th year of classes. Dinkins presented his speech to an audience of 1,600 people, ranging from freshmen to members of the graduating class of 1922, at the open-air Hearst Greek Theatre on the university campus at 10:30 A.M. The speech and a press conference following it were widely reported in San Francisco and area newspapers, the *New York Times* (September 14, 1990, p. A16) and *Newsday* (September 14, 1990, p. 1).

The *San Francisco Chronicle* reported:

> Although he only made occasional references to Berkeley, Dinkins was warmly received by students, staff members, and faculty who gave him standing ovations at the Hearst Greek Theater. (April Lynch, September 14, 1990, p. 1)

Commenting on Mayor Dinkins's tone of public address, Senator Daniel Patrick Moynihan observed:

> Mayor Dinkins speaks with determined reason against bigotry, ignorance, and hate. He is, with inspiring effort, striving to calm the fears and passions which have ignited into violence, and have infected communities with noxious vigor. We fervently hope that his words find their audience with composing effect. (*Congressional Record*, May 22, 1990, p. S6721).

Mayor Dinkins' speech: Good morning.

I am deeply grateful to former Chancellor Ira Heyman and his successor, Chancellor Chang-Lin Tien, for inviting me to address the distinguished students, faculty, staff, and alumni at this great center of learning, the University of California at Berkeley, a symbol of freedom for universities throughout the world.

To step onto these historic grounds today is to fulfill an American pilgrimage. The most basic human impulse is to communicate; the Free Speech movement rescued the life of the mind of our country, and neither America nor the academy has been the same since.

It was at Berkeley that the academy emerged as America's searing conscience; it was from Berkeley that students spread throughout the Deep South to aid the Negro struggle for civil rights; and it was again at Berkeley that the first Asian-American was appointed to lead a major American university. Congratulations, Dr. Tien.

I am here today to do something that may be as unfashionable in 1990 as the defense of free speech in 1964: to praise cities. But although my voice may seem isolated, I'm in very good historical company, for human beings have sung in praise of cities for thousands of years.

I find the open air of the Hearst Greek Theatre an appropriate forum for my remarks, for the ancient Greeks believed deeply in their cities. Their passion has left its mark on our pattern of thought and on the language we speak.

The very words we use when we refer to cities belong to ancient idioms: "metropolis" comes to us from Athens, "urban" and "civic" from Rome, the twin pedestals upon which Western civilization was erected.

For without the spark provided by cities, the torch of human civilization stands as a dry sheaf. It is not by accident that we call the period between the decline of ancient urban centers and the rise of medieval Western cities "the Dark Ages."

When Athens and Rome collapsed, so did the West; and when cities rose again—Paris and Prague, London and Lyons, Freiburg and Florence—so did the West emerge from rustic feudalism and blossom anew with a million ideas and a bursting ambition to see beyond the horizon.

Medieval Germans used to say that "City air makes man free," and indeed, it was in cities that democracy evolved and from them that it spread throughout the world. From Paris and the French Revolution of 1789 to Prague and the Velvet Revolution of 1989, cities have called their nations forth to the great work of freedom.

In America too, cities have led the way to freedom and democracy; "the shot heard 'round the world" was fired in defense of Boston, and it was followed by barrages in Philadelphia, New York, Trenton, Princeton, Charleston, and Yorktown.

Thomas Jefferson drafted the Declaration of Independence in a room at the corner of Market and Seventh Streets in Philadelphia and sent it to be printed in Baltimore, where the Continental Congress sat in session.

Eleven years later in Philadelphia, George Washington presided over the Constitutional Convention which gave birth to a document so momentous that, 202 years after it was written, it inspired Eastern Europeans to brush aside police states as they reached for its truth.

Cities liberated America, and they have continued to liberate us ever since. They serve as our commercial and intellectual marketplaces, where economics and philosophy, entertainment and art, science and technology, ideas and emotions, flourish and enrich the American experience.

Like a mighty engine, urban America pulls all of America into the future: 77 million Americans, almost one-third of our population, live within the limits of our cities.

And corporate America lives in our cities as well. For all the growth of suburban office parks and rural shopping malls, no self-respecting major bank or insurance company, no major law firm or hospital would be at home outside of our cities.

Our ballet companies and museums, theaters and sports teams, great restaurants and fine hotels, and our great halls of education—Harvard and Berkeley, Chicago and Austin—all depend on urban centers.

Our cities pulse with vitality and diversity. It is there that so much astonishing individual achievement flowers. But it can blossom only in an orderly social system that allows our people to plan for the future and compete for the bounty that surrounds us.

That is a fact. In the areas of housing and child care, in mass transit and public education, in drug enforcement and expanded medical services, the federal government retreats. In New York City ten years ago, federal funds constituted 19.4 percent of our budget; today, that share has shriveled to 9.7 percent.

More than billions of dollars, these figures represent the nutrition that might have saved a low-birth weight baby; they represent hospitals that might have cared for hundreds more AIDS patients; they represent drug treatment slots that might have helped thousands of junkies change from thieves to taxpayers.

Every American mayor has a litany of federal dereliction that has hamstrung our efforts to provide the fundamental services of government.

The national administration has punished urban America by transferring to us enlarged responsibility but denying us expanded resources. Indeed, the change involves more than neglect; it reveals hostility as well.

Yet, as our cities go, so goes America and our unique civilization. Why, then, does my song of praise find no accompaniment in Washington or in our state capitals?

It turns out that condemnation of cities is also a very ancient tradition. In one of the oldest stories in the book, cities are painted as bloody cauldrons of iniquity and despair, in contrast to the crisp virtue of the countryside.

Tension pulses in the relationship between town and country. In exchange for the corn and wheat of the countryside, cities have provided tractors and tools for the harvest as well as markets for rural products. This co-dependence makes the relationship uneasy.

Nations survive only as well as their cities. After New York City overlook London as the financial capital of the world in the 1920s, Great Britain lost its empire.

America had grown greatly in the preceding 50 years: we industrialized and challenged the world.

Huge numbers of immigrants kept the fires of American industry burning. In those years, our rural population doubled, but our urban population grew almost seven-fold.

As cities grew, so did friction with the countryside. An international depression just before the turn of the century threatened to turn that friction into a national schism.

Out of this tension arose populism, a political ideology that interpreted the legitimate grievances of farmers and other rural Americans hit hard by the economic contraction as a classic struggle between good and evil.

The populists felt the honest, hardworking farmer represented the highest good, while the Wall Street financier, more often than not an immigrant Jew, embodied the greatest evil, using such "tricks" as the Gold Standard to squeeze away the wealth of farmers.

The great metaphor of populist demonology belongs to that famous orator and presidential candidate, William Jennings Bryan. In his 1896 speech before the Democratic National Convention, Bryan warned, "You shall not crucify mankind upon a cross of gold."

Populism was an exceptional, ephemeral movement, for it set rural dwellers against urban, and no nation can long survive that sort of division. Progressive nations simply do not shoot themselves in the foot.

But cities survived and prospered, often with the enthusiastic support and cooperation of federal and state governments. In fact, until quite recently, the national administration stood alert as an honor guard at the gates of our cities.

John F. Kennedy spoke forcefully in their behalf: "We will neglect our cities to our peril," he said, "for in neglecting them we neglect the nation."

Lyndon Johnson expanded upon JFK's efforts to assist our cities, which had deteriorated enough by the time of his presidency that Johnson felt compelled to issue this dire warning to Congress:

If we permit our cities to grow without rational design; if we stand passively by, while the center of each becomes a hive of deprivation, crime, and hopelessness; if we devour the countryside as though it were limitless while our ruins, millions of tenement apartments and dilapidated houses, go unredeemed; if we become two people, the suburban affluent and the urban poor, each filled with mistrust and fear one for the other, if this is our desire and policy as a people, then we shall effectively cripple each generation to come.

But with the passing of LBJ from the political stage, the federal government began its gradual abandonment of our cities—a great turning-point in American history.

This new epoch began with "the Southern strategy," a cynical revival of populist sentiments that exploited the tension between cities on the one hand and suburbs and rural areas on the other, a tension already exacerbated by the great postwar migration of African-Americans and Latinos into our cities.

And those same African-Americans and Latinos have particularly suffered since the American presidency departed from the ideal of urban-rural harmony and played to the fears concerning our cities. For the division in our country has been much more than urban-rural, as the Willie Horton ads of 1988 demonstrated all too vividly.

This national cleavage has left our urban centers tattered and bruised, scrambling to fend for themselves in a hostile environment.

In 1975 the *New York Daily News* told it all in a now-famous headline: "Ford to City: Drop Dead."

But New York did not drop dead. It roared back in a way that took the breath out of those who would gladly have presided over its funeral. We shot dozens of towers into the sky and welcomed hundreds of thousands of newcomers from all over the world. We learned to eat streetside souvlaki and to trade stock index futures and barrels of oil made of paper.

In such an environment, New York managed its financial recovery without much help from Washington; but a quieter market was growing at the same time, one that was to change the scenery on the stage of history by the end of the decade. It was a market for a new drug that prodded its users to ever greater acts of violence.

And it appeared as a new president took office who felt that the only answer for America's cities was to neglect them in the hope that they would just go away.

Call it what you will—populism, the southern strategy, the sagebrush rebellion—the politics of anti-urbanism even propelled the current administration into the White House.

Yet, where do Americans go when they have a dream but not the opportunity to fulfill it? Where do Americans go when they have AIDS but no treatment center, or when the local community ostracizes them for their disease? Where do they go when they are down on their luck and need a roof over their heads?

Indeed, where do human beings from throughout the world go in order to escape the iron grip of dictators, to make a brand new start, to seek equality and opportunity? Six million of them arrived in America during the 1980's, and they went to our cities, about one million to New York alone.

And our cities welcome them: the sick, the suffering, the hungry, the homeless. We welcome them with open arms, whether they arrive in a first-class jet or an ambulance, whether they bring along Swiss bank accounts or just the shirts on their backs, whether they speak English or Swahili.

The city nurtures all who enter; we assume that in 5 months or 5 years or 50 years, our guests and their families will have become part of our great family.

Of course this steady stream of new arrivals requires an extraordinary array of services. But we would no more turn them away than a hospital would turn away a patient.

To my great pride, the Statue of Liberty shines its light on New York harbor; yet, the words inscribed on its pedestal belong to every city:

Give me your tired, your poor,
Your huddled masses yearning to breath free,
The wretched refuse of your teeming shore.
Send these, the homeless, tempest-tossed to me.

In the long run, American civilization and all humankind are served well by our cities. Yet the administration in Washington has made a virtue of bashing us and trashing us, so much that even state governments have abandoned their cities under cover of this anti-urban ideology. Our cities have been left to sweat and suffer for the last quarter-century.

If we are to reverse our fortune, we must expose anti-urbanism as a false and insidious ideology. We must demonstrate that, though it may win an election today, turning Americans against their cities will destroy our country tomorrow.

The media, too, have picked up a strain of anti-urbanism; in recent days they have deluged newsstands and airwaves alike with pronouncements and prophecies about our cities, especially New York.

Consciously or unconsciously, a national news magazine of enormous circulation distorted its own poll data to bring them into line with Washington's conclusion that American cities are crumbling around us, particularly our greatest city, New York.

Time magazine reported that 59 percent of New Yorkers would leave the city if they could. The article neglected to mention that its own data showed that 70 percent of our people feel that despite its faults, New York remains the greatest city in the world.

But in this, too, I am an optimist; not only do I hope the media will soon recover, but I also hope they will lead the way to curing our country of the same virulent disease, for none of us, least of all the media, can thrive unless our cities thrive.

My argument applies to all cities, but even more to New York because of its size. In fact, I hope you'll forgive me if I seem to be boosting New York, in defiance of the polls and newspapers. I am, after all, the Mayor.

To put New York's size in perspective: If one were to combine the populations of Los Angeles, San Diego, San Francisco, San Jose, Long Beach, Sacramento, Fresno, Oakland, and Berkeley, the total would still not add up to that of New York, no matter what the Census Bureau says about us. [*Note: based on 1986 Census Bureau figures*] America's cities are its marketplaces, and New York stands as our nation's most important marketplace; in fact, it is the most important market in the world, by almost any measure.

A popular notion has it that with a computer and a FAX machine you can move to Montana and still keep your blood pressure high. Yet as large as our villages have become, we still make our best deals face-to-face over the back fence. And even when we do resort to electronic communication, the words and images flow through our great cities.

A study of American telecommunications earlier this year revealed that more than 35 percent of all international phone calls made from the United States originate in New York City.

An astonishing share of the world's wealth changes hands on Wall Street, whose markets trade more than half of all shares of stock brought and sold the world over, more than London, Tokyo, Brussels, Milan, San Francisco, and Chicago *combined*.

On any given day, financial transactions in New York City represent approximately one-third of the Gross National Product of the United States. That's a trillion and a half dollars *a day*, almost as much as it will cost to bail out the S & L's, at the rate the problem is growing.

And guess where governments go to levy their taxes? Remember Willie Sutton, the safecracker? When asked why he robbed banks, Sutton answered, "Because that's where the money is." Governments follow the same rigorous logic, and they are rewarded so well for their efforts that far from drain the American economy, cities *subsidize* that economy.

Our own analysis in New York suggests that we receive only 77 cents from the federal government for each dollar we send it, even after we account for our share of such national responsibilities as the armed forces.

Thus, when we insist on federal support for housing, transportation, health, and safety, we do *not* ask Washington and our state capitals for a subsidy; we seek only to cut our own subsidy, and that of other American cities, to the federal government. It is they who are the recipients of grants-in-aid from us.

If we could reduce that subsidy by even a fraction, we could cure almost all of our own urban problems with our own solutions.

In the days when New York City did not underwrite the federal and state governments, we built the Brooklyn and Queensborough bridges, the world's most extensive mass transit system, block after block of decent housing, reservoirs, aqueducts, and an extraordinary network of parks, boulevards, and roads, and we still took in the world's homeless and poor.

Our marketplace can meet its own social needs. But the antiurban ideology emanating from Washington over the last 25 years has obscured these glorious achievements by depicting cities as recipients, not givers.

It has pitted cities against suburbs and the countryside. Yet we are not at war with the suburbs, and we have no quarrel with the countryside. We stand as ready as ever to serve as their partners.

For we depend on each other more than we know. The wheat of the farmer in Iowa ends up as bread in a supermarket in Little Rock; the advertising executive from New York buys a home in Fairfield, Connecticut, and sends her children to school there; the corn grown in Indiana is turned into fuel to run buses in Denver; the shrimp trawled by Vietnamese fishermen in Louisiana is flown to restaurants in Detroit, Phoenix, and Omaha.

The result of a quarter-century of antiurbanism is an economy on the verge of collapse, with our cities left to get by on a starvation diet. We are like tenant farmers, from whom the federal government takes so large a share that we cannot feed our own families.

The politics of antiurbanism, the ideological basis for the federal withdrawal from our cities, must be brought to an end. The gorgeous mosaic of America must be brought together again—city and country, black and white, rich and poor—all together.

That is why I have invited the mayors of America's largest cities to join me in an urban summit this fall. It is cities that must lead the way and reunite our divided country, for the future of America resides in its cities.

As I speak, America is undergoing its greatest ethnic and cultural change since the turn of the century. Thirty percent of the population of New York was born in another country: 170 different ethnic groups call our city home, making New York the most complex, diverse city in human history.

And not just New York; more than half of the public school students of Los Angeles are Latinos. Almost 30 percent of freshmen entering the University of California are Asians. Miami has become a Latino city and Milwaukee has seen a revival of its Polish neighborhoods. It is this great mixture of ethnic identities learning to live together that makes cities the nurseries of freedom and democracy.

To win our cause, and to halt the destruction of our cities, urban leaders must band together into the largest lobbying effort Washington has ever seen. And we must make our voices heard not only in Washington but in state capitals and throughout the country.

For unless our great cities prosper, the American civilization that inspired a whole world to freedom will itself not survive.

We must bring urban affairs back to the top of the list of priorities of both our state and federal governments, and to its rightful place in the curricula of America's great centers of academic excellence.

At the same time, we must realize that cities alone cannot effect the changes we seek. The political boundaries of New York City, for example, were fashioned well before it was evident that northwestern New Jersey, southern New York State, and eastern Connecticut would someday be drawn into our city's dynamic economy.

Thus when I speak of New York, I speak not only of our 8 million residents, I speak of the 25 million who comprise the metropolitan area. The same hold true for every metropolis: our suburbs are the most important partners in our day-to-day lives.

If we are to succeed in reordering our nation's priorities, we must begin by building coalitions with our suburban neighbors.

For all the simplistic talk of Democratic-liberal cities and Republican-conservative suburbs, this alliance is a natural one, for when our cities prosper, so do our suburbs. And when our cities suffer and decay, suburban dwellers also feel an encroaching sense of insecurity.

Nevertheless, some still ask: Can we really achieve an urban-suburban alliance? What are our chances?

And I answer: What were the chances that a Haitian immigrant would become a leading student at one of America's finest law schools and at the same time be chosen Miss America? What were the chances that an African-American would be elected Mayor of the greatest city in the world, a city of whose population only one-fourth is African-American.

The challenges of our cities are the challenges of America. They must be met by all Americans. Together, all together, we will carry our message to Washington.

But even if we succeed in reducing our subsidy to the federal government—and I know we will succeed—even if we do, we will still require a final ingredient, and that is you, the young people of this great nation, soon to be our educators and our lawyers, our leaders in politics and business, our writers and our doctors.

Cities are the racing heart of our civilization, the home of our greatest ideas. Cities are where the problems of America are worked out. Cities are the soul of America, but good citizens are the soul of our cities.

The ancient Greeks fervently believed that human beings were political creatures, that is, creatures of the "polis" or city. They felt that human beings reached their fullest potential only in the city.

Three thousand years ago, the Greek poet Alcaeus remarked that, "Not houses finely roofed, nor the stones of walls well-built, nor canals and dockyards make the city, but human beings able to use their opportunity."

For your good, and for ours, use your opportunity: bring your talents and your skills, your ideas and your passions, your hopes and your dreams to our cities.

COMMUNITY AND THE ARTS[1]
JOHN E. FROHNMAYER[2]

It is not usual for stories about the arts to make the front page or the evening television news, but that is what happened in the spring of 1989. Art suddenly became newsworthy because of a dispute concerning exhibits of works by two relatively unknown photographers, Andrew Serrano and Robert Mapplethorpe. The Serrano exhibit included a photograph of a plastic crucifix in a bottle of urine, which Serrano said expressed his feelings about contemporary Christianity. The Mapplethorpe show included photographs described as "homoerotic." Discovery that both artists had been partially funded by the National Endowment for the Arts, a government agency, sparked a controversy that would balloon into a national debate over freedom of expression, the role of the artist in the community, and the funding of controversial works by a government agency supported by public taxes.

---

[1]Delivered as the keynote address to the second annual "Corporate Council Celebrates the Arts" luncheon at 1:00 P.M., June 27, 1990, in the Grand Ballroom of the Westin Hotel in Seattle, Washington.
[2]For biographical note, see Appendix.

Although the Mapplethorpe photographs had been exhibited elsewhere without incident, the announcement that they would be shown at the Corcoran Gallery of Art in Washington, prompted 25 senators to introduce a bill to prohibit NEA from funding "obscene" or "indecent" art. The bill didn't pass, and the controversy continued. In March, 1990, President Bush spoke out on the question, saying he was offended by "some of the filth that I see and to which federal money has gone." "Having said that," he continued, "I don't know of anybody in the government or any government agency that should be set up to censor what you write, or what you paint, or how you express yourself." (*Chronicle of Higher Education*, April 4, 1990, p. A21.)

Caught in the middle of the dispute was the National Endowment for the Arts and its director, John E. Frohnmayer. Artists and civil libertarians who strongly opposed any restrictions on freedom of expression confronted conservatives, religious leaders, and organizations such as the Reverend Donald E. Wildmon's American Family Association, which sent a letter to Congressmen pleading against letting "Congress give your hard-earned tax dollars to people who will produce hate-filled, bigoted, anti-Christian and obscene art." Frohnmayer responded to this appeal by embarking on,

> . . . a barnstorming tour of talk shows and public speeches designed to counter Wildmon's campaign as well as publicize his agency's accomplishments. The earnest chairman, who is an elder in the Presbyterian church, repeatedly pointed out that the grants Wildmon opposes represent only a handful of the 85,000 projects the agency has financed during its 25 years. (Bruce Selcraig, "Reverend Wildmon's War on the Arts," *New York Times Magazine*, September 2, 1990, p. 22.)

Among the audiences Frohnmayer addressed on his tour was that assembled for the second annual "Corporate Council Celebrates the Arts" luncheon in Seattle, Washington, on June 27, 1990, an event designed to recognize the contribution of businesses and individuals to the arts community. The speech was delivered at 1:00 P.M. in the Grand Ballroom of the Westin Hotel to approximately 1,000 corporate executives, elected city, county, and state government officials, members of arts organizations' boards, others from the arts community, and the press.

As Frohnmayer rose to speak, some 40 people walked out of the luncheon in protest of remarks he had made earlier in the day in a private meeting with a small group of art professionals. Frohnmayer was reported to have said at the meeting that "certain political realities" made it unlikely that some grants recommended by the endowment's peer panels would receive support. (Barbara Gamarekian, *New York Times*, June 29, 1990, p. B1). Peter Donnelly, president of the Corporate Council of the Arts, sponsor of the event, pointed out "that 940 people didn't walk out—they stood and cheered." Commenting on Frohnmayer's speech, Donnelly said,

He made a wonderful, inspirational speech and laid out very honestly the crisis that faces the N.E.A. It was right from the heart, and the best speech from the head of the endowment I've heard in all the years I've been in this business. (*New York Times*, June 29, 1990, p. B1)

(For additional information on the controversy over government funding of the arts, see speeches by Kitty Carlisle Hart and Isabel Allende in *Representative American Speeches, 1989-1990*.)

John E. Frohnmayer's speech: Mr. Mayor, Chief Executive and distinguished leaders: When I first went to the other Washington, I was sitting in the basement of the Old Post Office having a cup of coffee. I had been in town about ten days, and I noticed this guy next to me kept looking at me and looking, and I thought, "Gee, I've only been here ten days, and I'm already recognized." Finally, he couldn't stand it any longer, and he leaned over and said, "Aren't you Tom Brokow?" Well, that was before I found out that having your picture in the paper isn't such a great deal.

It has been nine months since I left this part of the territory for the other Washington, and during that time, I've felt like the sole oarsman on a scull with seven coxswains all shouting different commands, most of them epithets at me. I think that has something to do with those of us in the arts because we seldom pull together in the same direction; yet, it is necessary as a community who believed in the arts to find direction and pull together in the same direction because the crisis is real and the time is now.

I would like to talk to you today about the focus on the community and the fact that the arts can be, and as you all know are, a leader in our community: to help bring a sense of civilization, a sense of values, a sense of unity to those places which we call home whether they are in our neighborhood or our city or our country or our planet.

The arts are a leader because they identify what it is to be thoroughly human. Because they identify that means of expression which is the most fundamental expression of our humanity, whether it's our agony or our joy. Let me give you one example of the arts as a healer.

In 1980, the National Endowment for the Arts held a competition to receive a design for a Vietnam memorial, the most divisive era that this country has seen in this century. Maya Lin, a 21-year-old student from Yale University, submitted a two page proposal on lined notebook paper which competed against all these tremendous maquettes of sophisticated proposals. On her paper she described a scar in the earth. And as a Vietnam veteran myself, I know you cannot descend into the earth at the Memorial and feel the black marble and see the names of those who died and not come out of the earth and feel healed. It is, I believe, one of the finest examples of art as a healer in our country. Let me give you just one other quick example.

There is a group called YaYa: Young Artists/Young Aspirations in New Orleans. Jana Napoli is an artist with a gallery there, and she was across the street from an industrial school where young, generally directionless, black kids from all over New Orleans came to put in their time, which tended to be more hanging around her gallery than at the school.

So Jana decided to put them to work. She decided that they would learn design and composition and color. She got house paints, half-used cans, which she could salvage for almost nothing, and the kids found discarded wooden furniture on the streets, repaired it and then painted it with fanciful dream-like sequences and designs. Lo and behold, they started to sell their furniture. Not only did they sell it but this group of about a dozen black kids had their pictures in the *National Arts* magazine, the *National Italian* magazine, and *Life* magazine. They are over in Italy, paying their own way through what they have sold for three weeks this summer. And one of those kids named Skip told me, "My goal is to earn enough money that I cannot only take myself to college but so I can take two other people with me."

And that is Jana's dream of community. To use the arts to bring together those skills, that empowerment, that sense of self-determination and self-accomplishment that can be so important to helping people build community.

What we in the arts face today is an unparalleled threat to the existence of the National Endowment for the Arts. There is a substantial campaign, and I mean substantial, to eliminate the National Endowment entirely or to so constrict it that it would not continue to exist in a recognizable form. Now I say to you today that while the threat is very real, we in the arts bear some of the blame for bringing it on ourselves, and I want to give you four reasons why I think that blame is at least partially ours.

The first is that we have let our contacts with Congress grow fallow. We've acted like the spoiled child in a lot of ways. Keep sending money, Mom and Dad, and we'll talk to you about what we're doing with it 10, 15, 20 years from now when we're adults and when we're accountable. But, indeed, accountability is the name of the game, and we must re-establish that trust with Congress which we have allowed to slip away over the past 10 or 15 years.

And we bear some blame for our own situation, secondly, because we have allowed the commitment of the American people at large in the worth of the arts to slip away. We have suggested that the Arts Endowment is something different from them. The word that I keep hearing is that the Arts Endowment only funds that which is for the elite. Little do they know about the Japanese American Cultural Center in Los Angeles, El Teatro Campesino, or the Dance Theater of Harlem or any of those other groups who are so integral to the preservation of our culture from all areas of our society. But it is our fault for not letting them know the accomplishments, not letting them know about those 85,000 grants which have been so significant, not just in Seattle and King County, but throughout every county in the land.

And the third thing we have failed to do is that we have assumed that the average person will understand modern art without explanation and when they don't, it's their fault, not ours. Again, it's an educational failure, one I hope and intend that the Endowment's focus in the next years will help rectify. The situation's a little bit like Oscar Wilde's comment after the premiere of *Lady Windemere's Fan* in London; he said, "The play was a great success, but the audience was a total failure." We must communicate because if the arts don't communicate, the arts fail, not the public. Communication is the stock and trade of what the arts are all about.

And finally, and I think most importantly, we tend to forget whose endowment it is. It's not the endowment for sculptors, and it's not the endowment for dancers, and it's not the endowment for writers or photographers or playwrights. It is the endowment to bring arts to the American people. It is the bridge that exists between the arts and the people, and on that bridge there must be two-way traffic.

I'm often asked by those who attack us, "Why should the government of the United States support artists?" And my answer is,

"It shouldn't." Let me give you an analogy. The United States government does not support doctors. The United States government has determined that the American people are entitled to a minimal level of health care, and therefore we have a national health system. Likewise, the American government has, I believe, in its wisdom, decided that it is important for the soul and spirit of our country that we have some involvement of the government in the arts, and that is why we have a National Endowment for the Arts. And that is the message which we must convey in order to make sure that the business leaders and the mayors, the councilpersons and the truck drivers, the leaders of the Girl Scouts and the nurses and schoolteachers, and indeed every American citizen appreciates that the arts can make all of our lives more worth living, more expressive, more fulfilling.

Our enabling legislation, which I believe to be one of the finest pieces of legislation that Congress has ever written, says the following:

Democracy demands wisdom and vision in its citizens and it must therefore foster and support a form of education, and access to the arts and humanities, designed to make people of all backgrounds and wherever located masters of their technology and not its unthinking servant.

And that is, indeed, what we must do in this technological age. We must prepare our schools to help our children understand and appreciate the aesthetic dimension of our lives. We must be prepared to use creativity not as an adjunct to our education but as the central component of our education because creativity will be the currency of the 21st century. And if we are going to compete in industrial design, in the making of airplanes or cars, clothing or software, we must have people who know that it's all right, and indeed it is a part of being human to express yourself even if that expression is different from what others express. And indeed the creative genius, from early education through all our lifetime, must be prized among all other things in our society.

I want to give you just two quick examples of creativity which has been supported by the Arts Endowment, some of these 85,000 grants that you're not hearing about these days:

310 million people (that's more than the population of the country) saw the eight media series we helped put on public television last year. Shows like *Great Performances* including *Dance in America*, *AmericanPlayhouse*, *American Masters*, *Alive from Off Center*, *Metropolitan Opera Presents*, *Live From Lincoln Center*, *Point of View*, and *Wonderworks*. $4.6 million of NEA

money was matched by $35 million in private funds to help these shows air. For a penny and a half per viewer, *you* were able to watch quality arts performances, films and dramatic series.

That's on the large scale, but on the smaller scale, the results are equally dramatic and indeed moving. The Tears of Joy Theatre out of Vancouver, Washington has a festival every year at which over 25,000 children are exposed to the arts first-hand. Susan Hamilton, a teacher in the Evergreen School District, said, "It is organizations like Tears of Joy Theatre that help make Vancouver a wonderful place to live." But there is an effect beyond that. Last year, an autistic child was observed conversing with a puppet at the Festival. It was the first time the child had ever spoken.

I know the investment of the arts in this community. My figures for endowment investment in the Seattle community was $2.3 million for 71 grants last year. And the astounding statistic is that in 1988, the endowment gave $119 million worth of grants across the nation; to complete those projects, the private sector contributed $1.35 billion, over a 10 to1 leverage.

I would suggest to you, ladies and gentlemen of the business and arts community, that's the way our government ought to work. That kind of incentive, that kind of leverage, is indeed what I believe government is all about. And yet if you look at the current *Newsweek*, you will see that only 42 percent of the people polled feel the government has a role in support of the arts. State that conversely, and 58 percent of the people in this country do not appreciate the role that the arts play.

Let me call to your attention, if you haven't seen one other piece of communication, this is a full page ad to the Congress of the United States signed by Pat Robertson of the Christian Coalition. It says that the NEA has used funds to promote naked men engaged in intercourse, little children with exposed genitals, Jesus Christ in urine, and so forth. It lists six items and then the ad says: "Vote for the NEA appropriation just like Pat Williams, John Frohnmayer and the gay and lesbian task force want and make my day."

I would tell you, ladies and gentlemen, that this kind of reduction to the soundbite is exactly what we face. And I admit to you to being a political neophyte. I don't know about spin or positioning and hardball and soundbites, but I do know that some parts of our government have not only worked well, they have worked brilliantly. And the question is: "Will this kind of publicity kill the Arts Endowment, or will the good and decent people of this country, be they Christians or Jews, religious or non-religious, Republicans or Democrats, or any other stripe, be heard?" Because if you are not, ladies and gentlemen, what will carry the day is what is loudest, and what is loudest right now is "make my day."

We need to decide whether there will be a federal presence or whether government will slide farther and farther toward anonymity, toward providing us with less than the basics and with nothing for the soul. The question is: dare we hope for a better society? Dare we let our opinions be known? Dare we risk offense lest those opinions be stated publicly and on the open record? Will these 20 pictures that you must judge dismantle 25 years of solid demonstrable progress toward a more human and complete society? It's really up to us: to use the arts and their tremendous power of healing to make the case for the arts, but most importantly not to hurl epithet for epithet but rather to use dignity, use truth, to use wisdom and to use the power that is the arts to promote the cause of the arts. True art has great power, and that is, I believe, our greatest strength in this debate. Not just for today, and not just for two weeks from now when Congress votes, or next month, or maybe even next year, because this is an ongoing educational process to infuse this debate with facts, with logic, with reason, which has always been the strength of the American populace.

And so I leave you now with the words of the poet, Samuel Hazo:

I wish you what I wish myself:
Hard questions and the nights to answer them,
and the grace of disappointment,
and the right to seem the fool
for justice, that's enough.
Cowards might ask for more,
Heroes have died for less.

COMMENCEMENT ADDRESSES: MAKING A DIFFERENCE

THE LESSONS OF LIFE[1]
MARIAN WRIGHT EDELMAN[2]

In a profile on CBS television's popular "60 Minutes" on October 22, 1989, Ed Bradley began,

> Her name is Marian Wright Edelman, Yale Law School, Class of '83, the first black woman admitted to the Bar in the state of Mississippi. Active in liberal Democratic politics, but admired by one of the Senate's most conservative Republicans, who says she fights more effectively for children than anybody else in our society, Marian Wright Edelman is the founder of the Children's Defense Fund. Her constituents are America's 73 million children. They may not vote and they may not have money to contribute to election campaigns, but they have relatives who vote and contribute to campaigns. And she told Harry Reasoner she never lets the men and women she lobbies up on Capitol Hill forget that.

In another profile, Robert Coles, the child psychiatrist, said,

> She has built up a major American institution that is *sui generis*. . . . Of course, this country has always been fascinated by children, because of its own youthfulness and hopefulness. But she educates us about them. She organizes a body of knowledge —statistical, investigative, observational, and analytic—and she puts it together in astonishing ways. (Calvin Tompkins, *The New Yorker*, March 27, 1989, p. 48.)

Senator Edward Kennedy noted,

> . . . it is a rare individual whose visionary and tireless efforts make a difference in the lives of others and the life of the country. One

---

[1]Delivered at the Yale University Class Day exercises on the Old Campus, Yale University, New Haven, Connecticut, at 3:30 P.M., May 27, 1990.

[2]For biographical note, see Appendix.

such American is Marian Wright Edelman, president of the Children's Defense Fund. (*Congressional Record*, April 5, 1989, S3305).

For her leadership, determination, and eloquence, Mrs. Edelman has received many awards, honorary degrees, and speaking invitations. She regularly is invited to deliver commencement and other addresses at colleges and universities throughout the country, and accepts as many as she can. One such address was her speech at Yale University's Class Day exercises in New Haven, Connecticut, on May 27, 1990.

The annual Class Day activities took place a day before Yale's commencement exercises. Mrs. Edelman delivered her address under sunny skies at approximately 3:30 P.M. to 1,272 graduating seniors, their families and friends on the Old Campus. Many of the seniors, who were clad in their caps and gowns, wore placards marked with the symbol for women in celebration of the 20th anniversary of co-education at Yale College. During the festivities, they shouted greetings to each other and waved white balloons. The Class Day activities began at 2:30. Before Mrs. Edelman's speech, students read a Class of 1990 history, read the traditional Ivy Code, and Yale College Dean Donald Kagan presented awards to outstanding seniors. An estimated 10,000 people attended the exercises. (*Yale Weekly Bulletin and Calendar*, June 4-11, 1990, p. 2)

In her address, Mrs. Edelman reflected on her childhood as a black child in a segregated society, provided information on the condition of children in America today, and sought to inspire the graduates to commit themselves to improving the future of our children. Her speech presentation, if typical, probably was rapid-fire and urgent. Calvin Tompkins notes:

> Friends and well-wishers often tell Marian Wright Edelman that she talks too fast. Addressing an audience, she will start off fairly deliberately, making an effort to pace herself and to remember about pauses, but sooner or later the urgency of her subject gets the upperhand, and the words come pouring out—facts, statistics, and moral imperatives mixed together in an eloquent barrage that leaves her listeners feeling somewhat overwhelmed. Reporters have a hard time keeping up with her. Her message is always clear, however, and the rapid-fire delivery has never seemed to interfere with her effectiveness. (*The New Yorker*, March 27, 1989, p. 48).

Marian Wright Edelman's speech: It is a great honor to share this day of accomplishment, celebration, and transition with the graduates of 1990 and your families. I am pleased that more than 80 of you applied to and 40 of you are going to participate in Teach for America which sends graduates to serve in teacher-shortage areas. I hope many more of you will wander off the beaten career path and help redefine what success is in the America of the 1990s.

When I was growing up, service was as essential a part of my upbringing as eating and sleeping and going to school. Caring black adults were buffers against the segregated prison of the outside world that told black children we weren't important. But we didn't believe it because our parents said it wasn't so. Our teachers said it wasn't so. And our preachers said it wasn't so. The childhood message I internalized was that as God's child, no man or woman could look down on me and I could look down on no man or woman.

We couldn't play in segregated public playgrounds or sit at drugstore lunch counters so my daddy, a Baptist minister, built a playground and canteen behind the church. Whenever he saw a need, he tried to respond. There were no Black homes for the aged so my parents began one across the street and our whole family helped out. I didn't like it a lot at the time, but that's how I learned it was my responsibility to take care of elderly family members and neighbors and that everyone was my neighbor.

I went everywhere with my parents and members of the congregation and community were my watchful extended parents. They reported on me when I did wrong and applauded when I did well. Doing well meant being considerate towards others, achieving in school, and reading. The only time my daddy wouldn't give me a chore was when I was reading. So I read a lot!

Children were taught that nothing was too lowly to do and that the work of our heads and hands were both valuable. As a young child I was sent with an older brother to help clean the bed and bed sores of a poor, sick woman and learned just how much even the smallest helping hands can mean to a lonely person in need.

Black adults in our families, churches, and community made children feel valued and important. They spent time with us and struggled to keep us busy. And while life was often hard and resources scarce, we always knew who we were and that the measure of our worth was inside our heads and hearts and not outside in material possessions or personal ambition. Like Walker Percy, my elders knew instinctively that you could get all A's and still flunk life.

I was taught that the world had a lot of problems; that Black people had an extra lot of problems, but that I should face up to and was obligated to struggle and change them; that extra intellectual and material gifts brought with them the privilege and responsibility of sharing with others less fortunate; and that service is the rent each of us pays for living, the very purpose of life and not something you do in your spare time or after you have reached your personal goals.

I'm grateful for these childhood legacies: a living faith reflected in daily service; the discipline of hard work and stick-to-it-ness; and a capacity to struggle in the face of adversity. Giving up was not part of my elders' lexicon: You got up every morning and did what you had to do and you got up every time you fell down and tried as many times as you had to until you got it done right. They had grit. They valued family life and family rituals, and tried to be and expose us to good role models. And role models were those who achieved in the outside world, like my namesake Marian Anderson, and those who lacked formal education or money but who taught us by the special grace of their lives Christ's and Gandhi's and Heschel's message that the kingdom of God is within. And every day I still try to be half as good as those ordinary people of grace who were kind and patient with children and who shared whatever they had with others.

I was 14 years old the night my daddy died. He had holes in his shoes but two children out of college, one in college, another in divinity school, and a vision he was able to convey to me dying in an ambulance that I, a young black girl, could be and do anything , that race and gender are shadows, and that character, self-discipline, determination, attitude, and service are the substance of life.

I want to convey that same vision to you today as you graduate into an ethically polluted nation where instant sex without responsibility, instant gratification without effort, instant solutions without sacrifice, getting rather than giving, and hoarding rather than sharing are the too-frequent signals of our mass media, popular culture, and political life.

The standard for success for too many Americans has become personal greed rather than common good. The standard for striving and achievement has become getting by rather than making an extra effort or service to others. Truth telling and moral example have become devalued commodities. Nowhere is the paralysis of public or private conscience more evident than in the neglect and abandonment of millions of children of all races and classes whose futures we adults hold in trust. Their futures will shape the ability of our nation to compete morally and economically as much as yours as children of privilege.

Yet:

Every 8 seconds of the school day, an American child drops out (500,000 a year);

Every 26 seconds of the day, an American child runs away from home (1.2 million a year);

Every 47 seconds, an American child is abused or neglected (675,000 a year);

Every 67 seconds, an American teenager has a baby (472,000 a year);

Every 7 minutes, an American child is arrested for a drug offense;

Every 30 minutes an American child is arrested for drunken driving;

Every 53 minutes an American child dies from poverty in the wealthiest nation on earth (9,855 a year);

The 1990s will be an era of struggle for the American conscience and future. The battles will not be as dramatic as Gettysburg or Vietnam, but they will shape our place in the twenty-first century world. The bombs poised to blow up the American dream and shred America's social fabric emanate from no enemies without. They are ticking away within ourselves, our families, our neighborhoods, and cities, and in our loss of national purpose and direction.

We have lost our sense of what is important as a people. And too many young people, white, black, brown, rich, and poor, are growing up unable to handle life in hard places, without hope, and without steady compasses to navigate the morally polluted seas they must face in adulthood.

Since I believe it is the responsibility of every adult—parent, teacher, preacher, and professional—to make sure that children and young people hear what we have learned from the lessons of life, hear what we think matters, hear over and over that we love you, that you are never alone, and that you should never believe that life is not worth living or cheap, your own or anybody else's, at home or abroad, I want to share a few lessons with you today to take along as you leave Yale. You can take them or leave them, but you can't say you were never told. Too many of us who are parents have been so busy today making sure our children had all the things we didn't that we may not have shared the things we did have that enabled us to survive and succeed.

At Yale, you got your lesssons from your teachers first and then got examined on how well you learned them. In life the test and consequences come before the lessons. And in an era of AIDS and potentially lethal drugs, the consequences can be fatal.

Lesson one: Don't feel entitled to anything you don't sweat and struggle for. And help our nation understand that it is not entitled to world leadership based on the past or on what we say rather than how well we perform and meet changing world needs. For those black and other racial minority graduates among you, I want you to remember that you can never take anything for granted in America, even with a Yale degree and even if too many whites still feel "entitled" solely by the accident of birth. And you had better not start now as racial intolerance resurges all over our land. It may be wrapped up in new euphemisms and better etiquette, but as Frederick Douglass warned us earlier, it's the same old snake.

Douglass also reminded all of us that "men may not get all they pay for in this world, but they must certainly pay for all they get."

So I hope you will struggle to achieve. Don't think for a moment that you've got it made with your Yale degree and are entitled to move up the career ladder. It may get you in the door, but it won't get you to the top or keep you there. You've got to work your way up, hard and continuously. Don't be lazy. Do your homework. Pay attention to detail. Take care and pride in your work. Few of us are gifted enough to get by on first drafts. People who are sloppy in little things tend to be sloppy in big things. Be reliable. Take the initiative in creating your own opportunity and don't wait around for other people to discover you or do you a favor. Don't assume a door is closed; push on it. Don't assume if it was closed yesterday, it's closed today. An don't any of you ever stop learning and improving your mind and spirit. If you do, you and America are going to be left behind.

You have come of age in a political era when too many political leaders and voters are looking for a free lunch. As a people we seem unable or unwilling to juggle difficult competing demands or to make hard choices and sacrifices to rebuild family and community for the good of the nation. Many whites favor racial justice as long as things remain the same. Many voters hate

Congress, but love their own Congressman as long as s/he takes care of their special interests. Many husbands are happier to share their wives added income than the housework and child care. Many Americans decry the growing gap between the rich and the poor and middle class and escalating child suffering as long as somebody else's taxes are raised and somebody's else's program is cut. We have got to grow beyond our national adolescence!

Lesson two: Set goals and work quietly and systematically toward them. Too many of us talk big and act small. So often we get bogged down in our ego needs and lose sight of broader community and national goals. It's alright to want to feel important as long as it is not at the expense of *doing* important deeds, even if we don't get the credit. You can get a lot achieved in life if you don't mind doing the work and letting other people get the credit. You know what you do and the Lord knows what you do and that's all that matters.

Lesson three: Assign yourself. My daddy used to ask us whether the teacher gave us any homework. If we said no, he'd say "well assign yourself". Don't wait around for your boss or your friend or your spouse to direct you to do what you are able to figure out and do for yourself. Don't do just as little as you can to get by as so many Americans are doing today in our political and economic life. If you see a need, don't ask why doesn't somebody do something, ask why don't I do something. Don't wait around to be told what to do. There is nothing more wearing than people who have to be asked or reminded to do things repeatedly. Hard work, initiative, and persistence are still the non-magic carpets to success for most of us. Help teach the rest of the country how to achieve again by your example.

Lesson four: Use your political and economic power for the community. Vote and hold those you vote for accountable. Less than half the young people under 25 registered and only 36 percent voted in the 1988 election. Run for political office and enter government service. And don't think that you or your reelection or job are the only point once you do: strenthening families and communities and protecting American ideals are the point of gaining power. Don't confuse social and political charm with decency or sound policy. It's wonderful to go to the White House or Congress for a chat or a meal but words and sociability alone will not meet children's or the nation's needs. Political leadership and different budget priorities will. Speak truth to power. And put your own money and leadership behind rhetoric about concern for families and children in your own homes, in your own law firms, and corporations and in whatever areas you decide to pursue.

Lesson five: Never work just for money. Money alone won't save your soul or build a decent family or help you sleep at night. We are the richest nation on earth with one of the highest incarceration, drug addiction, and child poverty rates in the world. Don't confuse wealth or fame with character. And don't tolerate or condone moral corruption whether it's found in high places or low places or is white, brown or black. It is not okay to push or use drugs even if every person in America is doing it. It is not okay to cheat or lie even if every Millken, Boesky, North, Secord, or public official does. Be honest. And demand that those who represent you be honest. Don't confuse morality with legality. Dr. King noted that everything Hitler did in Nazi Germany was legal. Don't give anyone the proxy for your conscience. And don't spend every dollar you earn. Save a dime and share a dime.

Lesson six: Don't be afraid of taking risks or of being criticized. If you don't want to be criticized then don't say anything, do anything, or be anything. Don't be afraid of failing. It's the way you learn to do things right. It doesn't matter how many times you fall down. All that matters is how many times you keep getting up. "It's not failure," former Morehouse College president Dr. Benjamin Mays said it's "a sin", it's "low aim." And don't wait for everybody to come along to get something done. It's always a few people who get things done and keep things going. This country needs more shepherds and fewer sheep.

Lesson seven: Take parenting and family life seriously. And insist that those you work for and who represent you do so. As a nation, we mouth family values we do not practice. Seventy nations provide medical care and financial assistance to all pregnant women; we are not one of them. Seventeen industrialized nations have paid maternity/paternity leave programs: we are not one of them and our Yalie President of the United States is threatening to veto an unpaid parental leave bill. Today, over half of mothers of infants are in the labor force and 62 percent of the net growth in the 1990s labor force will be women. We still don't have a safe, affordable, quality child care system. And the men in Congress are still bickering rather than completing action on child care bills passed by both Houses and the White House, despite President Bush's frequent photo opportunities and promises at child care centers during the 1988 presidential campaign, threatens still another veto.

It is time for the mothers of this nation to tell the men of this nation to get with it and stop the political hypocrisy so that parents can have a real choice about whether to remain at home or choose to work outside the home without worrying about the well-being of their children.

What a dilemma parents, especially women face today in a society that supports neither the option to care for children at home without falling into poverty or of going into the labor force with adequate, affordable child care. On the twentieth anniversary of the admission of women to Yale, I fear these critical issues will not be given the priority they demand until more women are in decision-making roles. Abigail Adams gave the charge in 1779 when she wrote John Adams to:

Remember all Men would be tyrants if they could. If perticuliar care and attention is not paid to the Ladies we are determined to foment a Rebellion, and will not hold ourselves bound by any laws in which we have no voice, or Representation.

I hope your generation will raise your sons to be fair to other people's daughters and to *share*, not just help with, parenting and family responsibilities. I hope you will help strengthen the American tradition of family by stressing family rituals: prayers if you are religious, and if not, regular family meals and gatherings. Be moral examples for your children. If you cut corners, they will too. If you lie, they will too. If you spend all your money on yourself and tithe no portion it for our colleges, churches, synagogues, and civic causes, they won't either. And if you snicker at racial and gender jokes, another generation will pass on the poison my generation still did not have the will to snuff out.

Lesson eight: Remember and help America remember that the fellowship of human beings is more important than the fellowship of race and class and gender in a decent, democratic society. Be decent and fair and insist that others be so in your presence. Don't tell, laugh, smile at or acquiesce in racial, ethnic, religious or gender jokes, or any practices intended to demean rather than enhance another human being. Stare them down. Walk away from them. Make them unacceptable in your homes, religious congregations, and clubs. Counter through daily moral consciousness the proliferating voices of racial and ethnic and religious division which are gaining respectability over the land, including college campuses. Let's face up to rather than ignore our ongoing racial problems which are both America's historic and future Achilles heel. White folks did not create black folks. Men did not create women. Christians did not create Jews. So who gives anybody the right to feel entitled to diminish another?

How many more potential Martin Kings, Colin Powells, Frederick Gregorys, Sally Rides, and Barbara McClintocks is our nation going to waste before it wakes up and recognizes that its ability to compete in the new century is as inextricably intertwined with its poor and minority children as with its white and privileged ones, with its girls as well as its boys?

Let's not spend more time, whites or blacks, pinning and denying blame rather than remedying the problem. Rabbi Abraham Heschel put it aptly: "we are not all equally guilty but we are all equally responsible" for building a decent and just America.

Lesson nine: Listen for the sound of the genuine within yourself. "Small," Einstein said, "is the number of them that see with their own eyes and feel with their own hearts." Try to be one of them. The black theologian Howard Thurman, told the young ladies of my alma mater Spelman College, that there is "something in every one of you that waits and listens for the sound of the genuine in yourself which "is the only true guide you'll ever have. And if you cannot hear it, you will all of your life spend your days on the ends of strings that somebody else pulls." There are so many noises and pulls in our lives, so many competing demands and signals that many of us never find out who we are. Learn to be quiet enough to hear the sound of the genuine within yourself so that you might then hear it in other people.

Lesson ten: Be confident that you can make a difference. Don't get overwhelmed. Sometimes I get frantic about all I have to do and spin my wheels. I then recall Carlyle's words that: "Our main business is not to see what lies dimly at a distance, but to do what lies closely at hand." Try to take each day and each task as they come, breaking them own into manageable pieces for action while struggling to see the whole. And don't think you have to "win" immediately or even at all to make a difference. Sometimes it's important to lose for things that matter.

I frequently end speeches with the words of Sojourner Truth, an illiterate slave woman, who could neither read nor write but was full of moral energy against slavery and second class treatment of women. One day during an anti-slavery speech she was heckled by an old white man. "Old woman, do you think that your talk about slavery does any good? Why I don't care any more for your talk than I do for the bite of a flea." "Perhaps not, but the Lord willing, I'll keep you scratching, " she replied.

A lot of people think they have to be big dogs to make a difference. That's not true. You just need to be a flea for justice bent on building a decent America. Enough fleas biting strategically can make even the biggest dog uncomfortable and transform even the biggest nation. Bite so that we can transform America together in the 1990s.

Nathan Hale, facing the firing squad in 1776, said: "I regret that I have only one life to give to my country." You have only one life to live for your country. Live it creatively and well, and ensure that America's ideals are strengthened because you held them high for generations to come.

CHOICES AND CHANGE[1]
Barbara Bush[2]

Unquestionably the most highly publicized commencement address of 1990 was Barbara Bush's speech to Wellesley College's 112th graduating class on June 1, 1990. Interest in the speech was so widespread that Wellesley compiled a scrapbook of the more than 7,000 news stories, editorials, letters to the editor, and political cartoons that poured into Wellesley following the announcement of Mrs. Bush's selection as the graduation speaker. Commencement 1990 at Wellesley was one of the year's big stories.

The story behind the story began on March 15, 1990, when 150 graduating seniors issued a petition protesting the selection of Mrs. Bush as commencement speaker. They wrote:

---

[1]Commencement address at Wellesley College in Wellesley, Massachusetts, delivered on June 1, 1990, at approximately 11:00 A.M.
[2]For biographical note, see Appendix.

. . . We are outraged by this choice and feel it is important to make
ourselves heard immediately. Wellesley teaches us that we will be rewarded on the basis of our own work, not on that of a spouse. To
honor Barbara Bush as a commencement speaker is to honor a woman who has gained recognition through the achievements of her husband, which contradicts what we have been taught over the last four
years at Wellesley. Regardless of her political affiliation, we feel that
she does not successfully exemplify the qualities that Wellesley seeks
to instill in us.

We realize that retracting our offer to Mrs. Bush at this time
would be discourteous. Therefore, we propose extending an invitation to an additional speaker who would more aptly reflect the self-
affirming qualities of a Wellesley graduate.

Opposition to the invitation was based partly on the fact that Mrs. Bush
had dropped out of Smith College after a year to marry George Bush. Actually, Mrs. Bush had not been the first choice of the selection committee.
The first choice had been Alice Walker, black author, single mother, and
Pulitzer Prize winner for *The Color Purple*, who declined.

In spite of all the advance publicity, no serious disruption occurred
on the day of the commencement exercises. Miles Benson wrote, "It was
the gentlest of confrontations." (New Orleans *Times Picayune*, June 2,
1990, p. 1). Mrs. Bush and Wellesley College had invited Raisa Gorbachev, wife of the Soviet President Mikhail Gorbachev, who was in the
country to meet with President Bush, to participate in the exercises and
address the graduates. John Robinson, of the *Boston Globe*, described the
occasion as follows:

From the moment she arrived on the idyllic campus, Bush and her
guest, Raisa Gorbachev, wife of Soviet President Mikhail S. Gorbachev, received a tumultuous welcome, a greeting that belied the early opposition to the choice of Bush to address the graduates. (June
2, 1990, p. 1).

Michele N.K. Collison reported in the *Chronicle of Higher Education*,

Mrs. Bush heard no shouts of protest. Indeed, many students waved
at the white-haired grandmother and even said they admired her.
Others held banners that read "I love Babs." Mrs. Bush was greeted
with thunderous clapping and cheering when she made a humorous
reference to the controversy her visit had sparked. She said,
"Somewhere out in this audience may even be someone who will follow in my footsteps and preside over the White House as the President's spouse." She paused, then added, "And I wish him well." (June

13, 1990, A25)

Miles Benson observed,

> . . . Barbara Bush, with Raisa Gorbachev at her side, faced feminist critics at Wellesley College and gave them warmth, humor, and a commencement address about family values to go along with their career ambitions. She left them cheering. Some even raised their hands in a clenched fist salute to Bush. (New Orleans *Times Picayune*, June 2, 1990, p. 1)

Abigail McCarthy, in *Commentary* (July 13, 1990, p. 408) said, "The First Lady's response on graduation day added to her enormous popularity. Her *joie de vivre*, her confidence, her humor and common sense won the day." Margaret Carlson, in *Time*, noted, "Barbara Bush, who was once so shy she cried over having to speak to the Houston Garden Club, delivered the speech of her life." (June 11, 1990)

Response to the speech, however, was not entirely favorable. "Although Mrs. Bush clearly wowed many at the commencement ceremony," Michele Collison reports, "over a third of the students wore purple arm bands 'to celebrate the unknown women who have dedicated their lives to others." (*Chronicle of Higher Education*, June 13, 1990, p. A25). Some students reported they were embarrassed by the notoriety that came from the widespread publicity over the protest and blamed the news media.

The ceremonies preceding Mrs. Bush's address began at 10:30 A.M. with a processional from Severance Green to large white tent where the exercises took place in front of an audience of 5,500. Following the national anthems of the USSR and the United States, came a welcome speech by Wellesley President Nannette C. Keohane, a student address, and then speeches by Mrs. Bush and Mrs. Gorbachev. The ceremonies concluded with the conferring of degrees, a benediction, and a recessional.

Barbara Bush's speech: Thank you President Keohane, Mrs. Gorbachev, trustees, faculty, parents, Julie Porer, Christine Bicknell, and the class of 1990. I am thrilled to be with you today, and very excited, as I know you must all be, that Mrs. Gorbachev could join us.

More than ten years ago when I was invited here to talk about our experiences in the People's Republic of China, I was struck by both the natrual beauty of your campus and the spirit of this place. Wellesley, you see, is not just a place, but an idea, an experiment in excellence in which diversity is not just tolerated, but is embraced.

The essence of this spirit was captured in a moving speech about tolerance given last year by the student body president of one of your sister colleges. She related the story by Robert Fulghum about a young pastor who, finding himself in charge of some very energetic children, hit upon a game called "Giants, Wizards, and Dwarfs." "You have to decide now," the pastor instructed the children, "Which you are: a giant, a wizard, or a dwarf? At that, a small girl tugging on his pants leg, asked, "But where do the mermaids stand?"

The pastor told her there are no mermaids. "Oh yes there are," she said. "I am a mermaid."

This little girl knew what she was and she was not about to give up on either her identity or the game. She intended to take her place wherever mermaids fit into the scheme of things. Where do the mermaids stand, all those who are different, those who do not fit the boxes and the pigeonholes? "Answer that question," wrote Fulghum, "and you can build a school, a nation, or a whole world on it."

As that very wise young woman said, "Diversity, like anything worth having requires *effort*." Effort to learn about and respect difference, to be compassionate with one another, and to cherish our own identity, and to accept unconditionally the same in all others.

You should all be very proud that this is the Wellesley spirit. Now I know your first choice for today was Alice Walker, known for *The Color Purple*. Instead you got me, known for the color of my hair! Of course, Alice Walker's book has a special resonance here. At Wellesley, each class is known by a special color, and for four years the class of '90 has worn the color purple. Today you meet on Severance Green to say goodbye to all that, to begin a new and very personal journey, a search for your own true colors.

In the world that awaits you beyond the shores of Lake Waban, no one can say what your true colors will be. But this I know: You have a first-class education from a first-class school. And so you need not, probably cannot, live a "paint-by-numbers" life. Decisions are not irrevocable. Choices do come back. As you set off from Wellesley, I hope that many of you will consider making three very special choices.

The first is to believe in something larger than yourself, to get involved in some of the big ideas of your time. I chose literacy because I honestly believe that if more people could read, write, and comprehend, we would be that much closer to solving so many of the problems plaguing our society.

Early on I made another choice which I hope you will make as well. Whether you are talking about education, career, or service, you are talking about life, and life must have joy. It's supposed to be fun!

One of the reasons I made the most important decision of my life, to marry George Bush, is because he made me laugh. It's true, sometimes we've laughed through our tears, but that shared laughter has been one of our strongest bonds. Find the joy in life, because as Ferris Bueller said on his day off, "Life moves pretty fast. Ya don't stop and look around once in a while, ya gonna miss it!"

The third choice that must not be missed is to cherish your human connection, your relationships with friends and family. For several years, you've had impressed upon you the importance to your career of dedication and hard work. This is true, but as important as your obligations as a doctor, lawyer, or business leader will be, you are a human being first and those human connections, with spouses, with children, with friends, are the most important investments you will ever make.

At the end of your life, you will never regret not having passed one more test, not winning one more verdict, or not closing one more deal. You will regret time not spent with a husband, a friend, a child, or a parent.

We are in a transitional period right now, fascinating and exhilarating times, learning to adjust to the changes and the choices we, men and women, are facing. I remember what a friend said, on hearing her husband lament to his buddies that he had to babysit. Quickly setting him straight, my friend told her husband that when it's your own kids, it's not called babysitting.

Maybe we should adjust faster, maybe slower. But whatever the era, whatever the times, one thing will never change: fathers and mothers. If you have children, they must come first. Your success as a family, our success as a society, depends not on what happens at the White House, but on what happens inside your house.

For over fifty years, it was said that the winner of Wellesley's annual hoop race would be the first to get married. Now they say the winner will be the first to become a C.E.O. Both of these stereotypes show too little tolerance for those who want to know where the mermaids stand. So I offer you today a new legend: the winner of the hoop race will be the first to realize her dream, not society's dream, her own personal dream. And who knows, somewhere out in this audience may even be someone who will one day follow in my footsteps, and preside over the White House as the president's spouse? I wish him well.

The controversy ends here. But our conversation is only beginning, and a worthwhile conversation it is. So as you leave Wellesley today, take with you deep thanks for the courtesy and honor you have shared with Mrs. Gorbachev and me. Thank you. God bless you. And may your future be worthy of your dreams.

NEW DIRECTIONS IN HIGHER EDUCATION

E. PLURIBUS UNUM[1]
Donald Kagan[2]

At campuses across the country students and faculty have become increasingly involved in debate over cultural pluralism, the demand for greater diversity in the courses offered and in the professors hired to teach them. Leaders of the movement sometimes called the "rainbow coalition" seek a broader representation of non-European cultures in the basic university curriculum and a greater recognition of the contribution of women to Western civilization.

The debate spilled over from the campus into the popular press in 1990-1991, with newspapers and magazines carrying articles and editorials concerning the traditional curriculum. Mary Niederberger described the controversy:

> In ivory towers across the nation, scholars are railing against the "dead white males." And some of the living guys aren't getting high marks either. They are the targets of a movement that seeks to end the traditional makeup of a university curriculum, as well as who teaches it and who learns it.
>
> Instead of the longstanding Western culture courses—dominated by such dead white males as Aristotle, Freud, Plato, and Shakespeare—advocates of this new "diversity" promote the study of works of women, gays, blacks, and other minorities and cultures. In addition, the movement, known also as "multiculturism," "deconstruction" and "postculturalism", seeks to interpret classics in new ways. (Baton Rouge *State-Times*. May 10, 1991, p. 6A)

A leading spokesman for curriculum revision to reflect greater diversity is Henry Louis Gates, Jr., W.E.B. DuBois professor of humanities at Harvard. Gates refutes those who contend that we must "master our own culture" before learning others by asking the question:

> What gets to count as "our" culture? What has passed as "common culture" has been an anglo-American regional culture, masking itself

[1] Address to the Class of 1994 of Yale College, delivered at 4:00 P.M. on September 1, 1990, in Woolsey Hall, Yale University, New Haven, Connecticut.

[2] For biographical note, see Appendix.

as universal. Significantly different cultures sought refuge under-
ground. . . . It's only when we're free to explore the complexities
of our hyphenated culture that we can discover what a genuinely
common American culture might look like.

Is multiculturalism un-American? Herman Melville didn't think
so. As he wrote, "We are not a narrow tribute. . . . We are not a nation, so much as a world." We're all ethnics; the challenge of transcending ethnic chauvinism is one we all face. (*New York Times*, May
4, 1991, p. 15).

For a more detailed discussion of his position, see Gates's speech,
"Cultural Pluralisms," in *Representative American Speeches, 1989–1990.* p.
163.)

On September 1, 1990, at 4:00 P.M. Donald Kagan, dean of Yale College, the undergraduate portion of the university, discussed this issue in
a speech to 1,400 entering freshmen in the class of 1994, along with parents, friends, and faculty in Woolsey Hall. The audience of 3,000 was
gathered to open the school year. In his address, which had the title "E
Pluribus Unum," Kagan acknowledged the diversity in America, saying
"Americans do not share a common ancestry and a common blood," but
contended that what we do "have in common is a system of laws and beliefs that shaped the establishment of the country, a system developed
within the context of Western civilization. From these premises, Kagan
argued that "It should be obvious then, that all Americans need to learn
about that civilization to understand our country's origins and share in
its heritage and character." (*New York Times*, May 4, 1991, p. 15)

While Kagan's remarks probably sounded harmless to many, at Yale
and other universities they were denounced by some as "racist," "sexist"
and "obnoxious." (Stephen Goode. "All Opinions Welcome—Except the
Wrong Ones," *Insight into the News*, April 22, 1991, p. 9) The speech received wide coverage at the time of its delivery and later in the national
press.

Donald Kagan's speech: Ladies and gentlemen of the Class of 1994,
parents, and friends, greetings and welcome to Yale. To a greater
degree than ever before this class is made up of a sampling, not
of Connecticut, not of New England, not even of North America,
but of all the continents of the world. As I stood a year ago greeting the Class of 1993 I was thrilled by how much Yale and America have been enriched in the three centuries since its foundation
by the presence and the contribution of the many racial and ethnic groups rarely if ever represented in Yale's early years. The
greater diversity among our faculty and student body, as in the
American people at large, is a source of strength and it should be
a source of pride, as well.

But ethnic and racial diversity is not without its problems. Few governments and societies have been able to combine diversity with internal peace, harmony, freedom, and the unity required to achieve these goals. Perhaps the greatest success in ancient times was achieved by the Roman Empire, which absorbed a wide variety of peoples under a single government, generally tolerated cultural diversity, and gradually granted to all Roman citizenship, the rule of law, and equality before the law. But the Romans had imposed their rule over independent nations by force and maintained peace and order by its threat. From the nations whose cultures they tolerated they did not create a single people; they did not and could not rely on the voluntary and enthusiastic participation in government and society of a unified population, as a modern democratic republic must.

From the Middle Ages until its collapse in 1918 the Hapsburg Empire did a remarkable job of bringing a great variety of different ethnic groups into the main stream of government and society, but it never succeeded in dissolving the distinct identities of the different groups, living together in separate communities, speaking their native languages, competing and quarreling with one another, and finally hostile to the dominant ethnic groups. The destruction of the Hapsburg Empire and its dissolution into smaller units did not end ethnic dissention, which threatens the survival of such successor states as Czechoslovakia and Yugoslavia.

In our time nationalism and ethnicity have emerged as immensely powerful forces, for good, but also for evil. Optimistic hopes for a diminution of differences among peoples and for a movement towards the unity of all mankind have been dashed as national and ethnic hostilities have played a major part in bringing on two terrible world wars. Even today they endanger the integrity of the Soviet Union and threaten peace both in Europe and in Africa. They have brought inter-ethnic slaughter to Nigeria and all but destroyed the beautiful land of Lebanon.

From its origins the United States of America has faced a new challenge and opportunity. Its early settlers from the old world were somewhat diverse but had much in common. Most were British, spoke English, and practiced some form of Protestant Christianity. Before long, however, people of many different ethnic, religious, and national origins arrived with different cultural traditions, speaking various languages. Except for the slaves brought from Africa, most came voluntarily, as families and individuals, usually eager to satisfy desires that could not be met in their former homelands. They swiftly became citizens and, within a generation or so, Americans. In our own time finally, after too long a delay, African-Americans also have achieved freedom, equality before the law, and full citizenship. People of different origins live side by side, often in ethnic communities, but never in enclaves of the country separated from other such enclaves. Although some inherit greater advantages than others, all are equal before the law, which does not recognize ethnic or other groups but only individuals. Each person is free to maintain old cultural practices, abandon them for ones found outside his ethnic group, or to create some mixture or combination.

Our country is not a nation, like most others. "Nation" comes from the Latin word for birth: a nation is a group of people of common ancestry, a breed. Chinese, Frenchman, and Swedes feel a bond that ties them to their compatriates as to a greatly extended family and provides the unity and commitment they need. But Americans do not share a common ancestry and a common blood. They and their forebears come from every corner of the earth. What they have in common and what brings them together is a system of laws and beliefs that shaped the establishment of the country, a system developed within the context of Western Civilization. It should be obvious, then, that all Americans need to learn about that civilization if we are to understand our country's origins, and share in its heritage, purposes, and character.

At present, however, the study of Western civilization in our schools and colleges is under heavy attack. We are told that we should not give a privileged place in the curriculum to the great works of its history and literature. At the extremes of this onslaught the civilization itself, and therefore its study, is attacked because of its history of slavery, imperialism, racial prejudice, addiction to war, its exclusion of women and people not of the white race from its rights and privileges . Some criticize its study as narrow, limiting, arrogant, and discriminatory, asserting that it has little or no value for those of different cultural origins. Others concede the value of the Western heritage but regard it as only one among many, all of which have equal claim to our attention. These attacks are unsound. It is both right and necessary to place Western Civilization and the culture to which it has given rise at the center of our studies, and we fail to do so at the peril of our students, our country, and of the hopes for a democratic, liberal society emerging throughout the world today.

In response to those who claim that Western culture is relevant only to a limited group it is enough to quote W.E.B. Du Bois, the African-American intellectual and political leader, writing at the turn of the century in a Jim Crow America:

I sit with Shakespeare and he winces not. Across the color line I walk arm in arm with Balzac and Dumas, where smiling men and welcoming women glide in gilded halls. From out of the caves of evening that swing between the strong-limbed earth and the tracery of the stars, I summon Aristotle and Aurelius and what soul I will, and they come all graciously with no scorn or condescension. So, wed with Truth, I dwell above the veil.

For him the wisdom of the West's great writers was valuable for all, and he would not allow himself or others to be deprived of it because of the accident of race. Such was and is the view of the millions of people of both genders and every ethnic group who have personally experienced the value and significance of the Western heritage.

The assault on the character of Western civilization badly distorts history. Its flaws are real enough, but they are common to almost all the civilizations known on any continent at any time in human history. What is remarkable about the Western heritage and what makes it essential is the important ways in which it has departed from the common experience. More than any other it has asserted the claims of the individual against those of the state, limiting its power and creating a realm of privacy into which it cannot penetrate. By means of the philosophical, scientific, agricultural, and industrial revolutions that have taken place in the West, human beings have been able to produce and multiply the things needed for life so as to make survival and prosperity possible for ever-increasing numbers, without rapacious wars and at a level that permits dignity and independence. It is the champion of representative democracy as the normal way for human beings to govern themselves, in place of the different varieties of monarchy, oligarchy, and tyranny that have ruled most of the human race throughout history and rule most of the world today. It has produced the theory and practice of the separation of church from state, thereby protecting each from the other and creating a free and safe place for the individual conscience. At its core is a tolerance and respect for diversity unknown in most cultures. One of its most telling characteristics is its encouragement of criticism of itself and its ways. Only in the West can one imagine a movement to neglect the culture's own heritage in favor of some other. The university itself, a specially sheltered place for such self-examination, is a Western phenomenon only partially assimilated in other cultures.

My claim is that most of the sins and errors of Western Civilization are those of the human race. Its special achievements and values, however, are gifts to all humanity and are widely seen as such around the world today, although its authorship is rarely acknowledged. People everywhere envy not only its science and technology but also its freedom and popular government and the institutions that make them possible. The roots are to be found uniquely in the experience and ideas of the West. Western culture and institutions are the most powerful paradigm in the world today. As they increasingly become the objects of emulation by peoples everywhere, their study become essential for those of all nations who wish to understand their nature and origins. How odd that Americans should choose this moment to declare it irrelevant, unnecessary, and even vicious.

There is, in fact, great need to make the Western heritage the central and common study in American schools, colleges and universities today. Happily, student bodies have grown vastly more diverse. Less happily, students are seeing themselves increasingly as parts of groups, distinct from other groups. They often feel pressure to communicate mainly with others like themselves within the group and to pursue intellectual interests that are of particular importance to it. The result that threatens is a series of discrete experiences in college, isolated from one another, segregated, and partial. But a liberal education needs to bring about a challenge to the ideas, habits, and attitudes that students bring with them, so that their vision may be broadened, their knowledge expanded, their understanding deepened. That challenge must come from studies that are unfamiliar, sometimes uncomfortably so, and from a wide variety of fellow-students from many different backgrounds, holding different opinions, expressing them freely to one another, and exploring them together.

If the students are to educate each other in this way some part of their studies must be in common, and their natural subject is the experience of which our country is the heir and of which it remains an important part. There is, after all, a common culture in our society, itself various, changing, rich with contributions of

Americans who come or whose ancestors came from every continent in the world, yet recognizably and unmistakably American. At this moment in history an objective observer would have to say that it derives chiefly from the experience of Western Civilization, and especially from England, whose language and institutions are the most copious springs from which American culture draws its life. I say that without embarrassment, as an immigrant from a tiny country on the fringe of the West, without any connection with the Anglo-Saxon founders of the United States. Our students will be handicapped in their lives after college if they do not have a broad and deep knowledge of the culture in which they live and the roots from which it comes.

There are implications, too, for our public life. Constitutional government and democracy are not natural blessings; they are far from common in the world today, and they have been terribly rare in the history of the human race. They are the product of some peculiar developments in the history of Western civilization, and they, too, need to be thoroughly understood by all our citizens if our way of governing ourselves is to continue and flourish. We must all understand how it works, how it came to be, and how hard it is to sustain.

Our country was invented and has grown strong by achieving unity out of diversity while respecting the importance and integrity of the many elements that make it up. The founders chose as a slogan *e pluribus unum*, which kept a continuing and respected place for the plurality of the various groups that made up the country, but they emphasized the unity which was essential for its well-being. During the revolution that brought us independence Benjamin Franklin addressed his colleagues, different from one another in so many ways, yet dependent on one another for survival and success, using a serious pun to make his point. He told them that they must all hang together or assuredly they would all hang separately. That warning still has meaning for Americans today. As our land becomes ever more diverse the danger of separation, segregation by ethnic group, mutual suspicion and hostility increases and with it the danger to the national unity which, ironically, is essential to the qualities that attracted its many peoples to the country. Our colleges and universities have a great responsibility to communicate and affirm the value of our common heritage, even as they question it and continue to broaden it with rich new elements.

Ladies and gentlemen of the Class of 1994, you, too have important responsibilities. Take pride in your family and in the culture they and your forebears have brought to our shores. Learn as much as you can about that culture and share it with all of us. Learn as much as you can of what the particular cultures of others have to offer. But most important, do not fail to learn the great traditions that are the special gifts of that Western civilization which is the main foundation of our university and our country. Do not let our separate heritages draw us apart and build walls between us, but use them to enrich the whole. In that way they may join with our common heritage to teach us, to bring us together as friends, to unite us into a single people seeking common goals, to make a reality of the ideal inherent in the motto *e pluribus unum*.

CHANGING PERSPECTIVES ON EDUCATION[1]
GEORGE REEDY[2]

On November 16, 1990, retiring Nieman Professor of Journalism George E. Reedy delivered his farewell address at Marquette University. In his lecture, Reedy reflected on his long and varied career as an educator, political advisor, author, and lecturer. His professional activity included serving as a newspaper correspondent and reporter; consultant and staff director for several United States Senate committees; press secretary to President Lyndon B. Johnson; and author of six books and numerous articles on government and politics. From 1972 to 1977, Reedy had served as dean of the College of Journalism at Marquette and from 1977 to 1990 as Nieman Professor at the university.

Reedy discussed the sweeping social revolution caused by technological advances and their effect on our environment. The more obvious changes he cited were in our language itself, our methods of comprehension, a tendency toward greater specialization in higher education, and the need to reconsider skills courses as subjects to be taught in colleges and universities.

Reedy delivered the address to an audience of between 150 and 200 people at 8:00 P.M. in the Monaghan Ballroom of the Alumni Memorial

---

[1]Delivered as The Farewell Nieman Address in Monaghan Ballroom, Alumni Memorial Union, Marquette University, Milwaukee, Wisconsin, 8:00 P.M., November 16, 1990.

[2]For biographical note, see Appendix.

Union on the Marquette University campus in Milwaukee, Wisconsin. The speech in its entirety was reprinted in *Vital Speeches of the Day* and a lengthy excerpt was included in the *Chronicle of Higher Education* (December 19, 1990, B5).

George Reedy's speech: It is a heavy and daunting responsibility to deliver a lecture entitled "The Farewell Nieman Address." There is something Wagnerian about the words in that combination. I have an uneasy feeling that at the conclusion of my remarks, Rhine maidens, engaged by Marquette's Special Events Department, will float into this hall on an air-born swan boat to bear me away to a resting place in Valhalla where Siegried, Barbarossa, and I can be entombed while awaiting our revival for the final conflict. If so, I will see you again at Gotterdammerung.

Of course, my farewell is somewhat qualified and the ultimate burial remains down the road. What I have really retired from is the steady diet of meetings and committees that afflict the modern Groves of Academe. I will continue to teach, although on a limited schedule, and I will continue to write, at least as long as my typewriter holds out and rescues me from the horrors of word processors. I like both teaching and writing too much to quit cold turkey. Meanwhile, however, my retirement will give me an opportunity to practice the delivery of my own funeral elegy and, perhaps, if I get good enough at it, I will be allowed to preside at the obsequies.

When it was first proposed that I give this lecture, I looked back on my life and began to count the years that I have spent in various jobs and professions. It came to me as something of a surprise to find that I have spent more of my adult life teaching than anything else. The passing years have seen me in a variety of positions: journalist, soldier, government official in both the legislative and the executive branches of the government. At times, when I hear them reading a brief biography, my reaction is "What's wrong with that guy? He can't seem to hold down a steady job!" The answer is that I did find a steady job right here Marquette, and it accounts for 40 percent of my working days. It also accounts for the happiest of my working days.

I do not wish to imply that I was unhappy everywhere else. Living is something I have enjoyed as long as it was a process that constantly brought me new problems. What I do mean, however, is that all the other things I did as a reporter, an activist, a political advisor and spokesman for others were really preparation for what I have done here. My life has given me a perspective on the methods and the goals of education and I have applied it in the classroom. What I hope I can do tonight is to share with you that perspective.

You should know where I come from. I am a product of the "New Plan" at the University of Chicago sponsored by Robert Maynard Hutchins. This provided me with one of the most exciting periods of my life. The University of Chicago in the 1930s was a hotbed for intellectual discussion ranging from Leninism at one end of the intellectual spectrum to neo-Thomism at the other. The dormitories rocked with heated discussions of pragmatism versus Marxism. One married couple in the graduate school got a divorce because she was a socialist and he had become a disciple of St. Thomas Aquinas. We still had a football team, but nobody really cared about it and it was dropped for a lack of spectators before I graduated.

At the center of this activity was Hutchins himself, a compelling and arrogant personality. He was a man with a mission: to restore higher education to the medieval ideal. He was responsible for bringing the founder of neo-Thomism, Mortimer Adler, to the university, and had he been able to do it, I am convinced he would have based the entire curriculum on the trivium and the quadrivium. He never said it in so many words but it was clear from his attitude that he regarded Harvard as a trade school for stock salesmen, Yale as an institution dedicated to turning out bond salesmen, and Princeton as an establishment where wealthy people could park their brats when they got out of control. Oxford, of course, could be mentioned with respect as long as it was in slightly patronizing terms. After all, the University of Chicago was *the* center for intellectuals, and we were never allowed to forget it.

The scene was adolescent snobbery at its most egregious complicated by his desire for students who were slightly flaky. He expressed it years later when he was asked for a public comment on a piece I had written sharply critical of the findings presented by his Commission on Press Responsibility. "Just say," he replied, "that George is like all University of Chicago students: very bright but a little odd." Believe it or not, coming from him that was an accolade of the highest order.

We were deliberately encouraged to argue with the faculty and I spent my four years trying to educate a group of singularly uneducable professors. I will never forget Sam Harper who thought he knew more about the Russian revolution than I did just because he had been there when it happened. I never succeeded in convincing him to the contrary. I should add that in later years I developed a sense of awe over the good humor with which he handled an obstreperous youngster. He actually treated me as though I had some sense and, as a result, I eventually settled down and began to think about what he was saying. That may well be the first real lesson I had in what it takes to make a good teacher.

Time, as it does for most people, cured the adolescent snobbery. I learned from the harsh reality of life the meaning of [Ambrose] Bierce's definition of education as that which "discloses to the wise and disguises from the foolish their lack of understanding." I also learned that eccentric as were Hutchins' ideas, he made challenges to thinking an exciting joy. The classroom was a playing field for the exercise of one's wits rather than a cellar where one was forced to undergo a fraternity hazing process. Even more important it was also a ground where students learned how to stand on their own intellectual feet. Every experience of my life has reinforced a conviction that, aside from a certificate, an independence of mind is the important reward of an exposure to a college or university.

I should add that I am not at all convinced that we professors "educate" students. What we do that merits the salaries we receive is to force them to use their minds and stuff things into their heads which they can use to educate themselves. But the process of education itself depends upon each individual. Another professor, whose name I will not disclose, comes to my mind. He had the personality of a box of laundry soap and a voice like a cracked gramophone record. He taught philosophy and to him the subject began and ended with Plato. He could discuss other philosophers knowledgeably, but only as a commentary on the man he regarded as the master thinker of all ages. His voice would quaver when he lectured on the cave scene in the *Republic*, and in the ritual tones of a Tridentine mass he would say: "This is the grrrreatest thing that has everrrrrr been wrrrritten in the whole historrrry of human thought."

Sitting in the class with all the intellectual arrogance of a freshman just past his 17th birthday, I would say to myself: "What in the devil is this old goat talking about. A bunch of jerks sitting in a cave with their heads tied? What kind of nonsense is this."

Of course I remembered it because I had to pass a test. But to say that I understood it would be fakery. That took many years which included police beats, a major war, political campaigns and conventions, at one of which I nearly had my ear chewed off in a fight. Finally, I discovered that the professor had a good case, and I now reread the cave scene at least once a year. But I would never have known it was there if he hadn't planted it in my head.

I have focused so much on my college days because I want what I am going to say next to be based upon the student. There are forces at work which tend to make us lose sight of that perspective. Like every other institution in modern society, we tend to base recognition, rewards, and advancement on quantitative criteria and I am not at all certain that the elements of good teaching are amenable to quantitative analyses. It is relatively simple to count published articles, outside lectures, and hours spent on service committees. But the instruments we have for measuring the ability of instructors to spark intellectual reactions from their pupils are, in my judgment, inadequate. Furthermore, I am highly dubious over the prospect of any statistical method to measure quality.

At this point, I want to be certain that no one does what they call in Texas "chase jackrabbits in the deer season." It would be deadly to separate scholarship from the university process. All I am suggesting is that we review our processes to be certain that our faculties find teaching as much on the cutting edge of their professional consciousness as publication. Teaching and scholarship should go together and will as long as we retain some balance in our judgments on the quality of performance.

Flexibility is of special importance in the period we are now entering. We are being caught up in a social revolution as sweeping as any in history, possibly even more sweeping. Technology is changing our environment at a constantly accelerating rate and there is no indication that it will slow down. There is an old Hegelian principle which holds that quantitative changes result in qualitative changes, and that is what is happening to us right now. The instruments of applied science are going far beyond the goal of making work easier for us as individuals. They are also producing a new society in which our relationships with other people are taking on new forms and in which social institutions must react differently to the world than they have in the past. Education is a social institution.

The more obvious changes are coming in our language itself. Because of the computer and because of television we are virtually eliminating words and introducing new ones into our vocabularies. No one any longer gives "advice" because they are too busy supplying "input." No one "reacts" anymore because they are too busy "providing feedback." Were these merely words to described new objects, their introduction would not be of great moment. But they are more than that. They reflect the thought processes of a machine, to the extent that a machine can have thought processes. They match the binary mathematics upon which computers are based, switches which go on-off, on-off through all eternity. We may not realize it but our intellect is something that is starting to work according to the binary methods. It is a litle scary. I have a son who is a whiz with computers and he tells me that computer language has been devised for a machine with the intellect of a low-grade moron. It bothers me to hear educated men and women using it.

Television is also changing our language and our methods of comprehension. When I first started to teach, nearly 20 years ago, I was baffled by student papers that treated the word "of" as a verb. A typical sentence would read: "I would of gone to Chicago if I had of known that I could of gone half fare." It took me some time to realize that my students had spent so much more time viewing television instead of reading books that they had mistaken the common contraction for "have" for the preposition "of". These same students, by the way, only had one spelling for the word "to" whether it was being used to indicate direction, numerical quantity, or addendum.

If nothing were involved but grammatical lapses, this would not be a serious problem. But there is an underlying reality to this situation which requires some thought. It is that people comprehend a different universe on television than they do when they receive information from either radio or the written word. One example will make my point clear.

In 1960, I travelled with Lyndon B. Johnson during the campaign in which he was John F. Kennedy's running mate. On the weekend of the famous debate between Kennedy and Nixon, we suspended our campaigning and went to the LBJ ranch. There we deliberately split into two parts, half watching the debate on TV and the other half listening on radio. I was with the TV contingent. When the debate was over, the radio people walked in with long faces. They thought Nixon had won hands down. We TV viewers, on the other hand, were elated as we had come to the conclusion that it was a sure fire win for Kennedy.

The trouble is that two weeks later, I got my hands on a transcript of the debate and the radio people were right. Nixon was a formidable debater and he had clearly won by the normal rules of point scoring. I spent several years after that questioning people on whether they had watched the confrontation on TV or heard it on radio and what they remembered of the proceedings. The televiewers recalled Kennedy's shock of hair and his stabbing finger and his air of confidence. They described Nixon as needing a shave and said he had a shifty look. But none of them name the subject of the debate. The radio people, on the other hand, recalled as much as seven years later that the discussion had centered on Quemoy and Matsu. I have found that people still react the same way to the difference between TV and radio and print media.

Up to this point, our reaction in academe has been somewhat limited. We have installed word processors in our academic buildings and we have brought the TV (I include the use of cassettes) into the classroom. We have not, however, gotten down to the basic questions of how we are going to revise our curricula to cope with the new factors in our lives. What are the courses that are required to equip our students for grappling with the real world?

Since World War II, there has been a tendency for higher education to specialize. This was a natural development. The war touched off a technology explosion which produced data far beyond the powers of a human brain to manage. The only way to handle the situation was to produce specialists, men and women who knew everything there was to know about relatively small slices of knowledge. We lacked the mechanism which could permit large scale storage of data subject to instant retrieval when needed. Many universities and colleges went overboard completely in the field of specialization. One of the factors which led me to come to Marquette in 1972 was the discovery that it had resisted the temptation and still required its students to broaden their intellectual horizons while they were here.

We now have the mechanisms that *do* permit the storage of data in staggering amounts and their retrieval upon demand. And one of the by-products is the approaching end of the age of specialization. The doom of the specialist draws closer every time someone punches the keys on a word processor. Of course, we will still need doctors, lawyers, plumbers and electricians. But will there still be a brisk market for all the specialties we have fostered in the economic and social fields? I doubt it. The future will belong to those who know how to handle the combinations of information that come out of the computer, what we used to call the "generalist". The day of the generalist is just over the horizon and we had better be ready for it.

There is another aspect which we must consider. It is the problem of the so-called "skills" courses, so beloved by our students. Will they be viable in the age of technology? I think we had better take another look. Skills courses are usually taught by instructors who have not exercised the skill in the real world for a number of years. During those years, the skills have certainly changed. The word no longer stands still. I have as much practical experience as any journalism professor you can name. But if I were to enter a newspaper office today, I would be bewildered. I would catch up in a couple of weeks because I understand journalism and can figure out any new tools given a little time. But that certainly doesn't qualify me to teach the skills, which is why I have limited myself to teaching courses in ethics and other areas where there are basic principles that do not change.

The point here is that I believe we must reconsider skills courses as subjects to be taught in universities. Obviously, we will still need them for what we once called "the learned professions." But are we really performing a service for students by teaching them "how" to do things by methods which may be obsolete by the time they graduate? The learned professions, of course, can continue as they have in the past because they are in the field of graduate studies. But how about some of the specialties we have developed in business, journalism, and the health sciences? Are there other ways of going about such training in such areas?

One alternative to what we are now doing would be to turn skills training over to private industry. Actually, many corporations in the United States are doing that already. They prefer college graduates who have a wealth of general information and do not have to be "untaught" methods. The training they receive in industry will always be in step with contemporary reality. In England, they have gone even further. There journalists are trained by newspapers themselves. They are "hired" under a status known as "cadet" where they follow real reporters around until they have proven themselves. If we were to inaugurate something similar in the United States, we could send prospective journalists to schools of communications where they would learn communications principles, ethics, history, law, and other types of intellectual discipline which would give them the solid base upon which to stand while pursuing their chosen profession.

Let us not dwell on this point too long. I believe we are going to proceed to skill training as an arm of industry whether we consciously plan it or not. The more important point is what do we do in our efforts to prepare students for the world into which they will step. There is no simple solution. Merely defining the problem is a task of horrendous difficulty. Finding an answer for it is going to take many minds working over a long period of time.

Let us begin by describing the type of student we wish to produce. In the first place, he or she must be thoroughly familiar with the varieties of human knowledge without having their mental processes clogged by too much factual data in any of them. In the second place, they must know what questions to ask when confronted with a problem of life. In the third place, they must have the capacity to combine bits and pieces from all the intellectual disciplines that lead to answers. Finally, they must have a solid moral and ethical base which they can use in establishing priorities for action.

What I am describing may sound fairly simple. But to do anything about it will require massive overhauls of curricula and different perspectives by both faculty and students. An example of the latter is the realization than an education should prepare one for life and that a career is only a part of life—not the whole. We must also erect safeguards against the elevation of the computer to godlike proportions. It is very easy to fall into the error of thinking of the machine as an intelligent being and people who use it constantly tend to regard it in such terms. I wince when somebody says: "The computer is asking me whether to hyphenate this word or skip to the next line," and it has not been too long since I heard an air travel agent cussing out his machine because it wouldn't give him the route he wanted.

People who can exercise an independent intellect will not let the computer do their thinking for them. They will treat the gadget for what it is—a descendant of the abacus, the adding machine, quiepas, and every other gadget in history which has enabled human beings to count and to keep records. It cannot substitute for human mentality.

It is time to start now a nationwide reexamination of undergraduate curricula. We should take such subjects as philosophy and theology from the dust bin to which they have all too often been consigned and restore them to central positions. At the same time, we should insist that students who, up to now, have been specializing in the humanities and the social sciences, learn the basic principles of the physical and biological sciences. I should add that no one should be exempted from mastering the fundamentals of mathematics. We express most of our public debates in the world today through arithmetical symbols. We had better know what those symbols mean.

Fortunately, here at Marquette we have gone a long way to those goals already. We have even converted a number of communication specialties into a college of communication which will force us to concentrate on general principles. No one leaves here with a BA or a BS without some exposure to the intellectual disciplines that are essential to human beings. But we have a long way to go.

The ultimate end will be an undergraduate degree which indicates an educated, rather than a trained, mind. Am I trying to recreate the famed Renaissance Man? The answer is yes, as long as you interpret the word "man" in a generic, rather than sexual, sense. But the point is that the computer has made this a practical proposition for the first time since the Renaissance. We now have a tool with which we can release the human soul from slavery to limitations on facts. Let us use it to master our destiny rather than let the tool become our master.

And now I expect the swan boat is on its way and I must say goodbye, with a cautionary note to my students that I will see all of you next Tuesday. I hope I have given some of you intellectual food for chewing and digestion. And I close by saying how grateful I am to Marquette—where I really found my home. Thank you for coming tonight.

IN MEMORY AND CELEBRATION

DWIGHT D. EISENHOWER:
A REMEMBRANCE AND REDEDICATION[1]
GERALD R. FORD[2]

The year 1990 marked the 100th anniversary of the birth of Dwight D. Eisenhower, commander of the allied forces in Europe in World War II and 34th President of the United States. The year-long celebration began on March 27 with a joint session of the House of Representatives and Senate and a White House commemorative ceremony addressed by President George Bush.

Two major observances took place on the weekend of the centennial anniversary of Eisenhower's birthday (October 14, 1890). The first was a two-day series of events entitled "In Celebration of Ike" on October 13 and 14 in Abilene, Kansas, where the former president had grown up. The second was a five-day symposium, "The Eisenhower Centennial Celebration: A Retrospective View," sponsored by Gettysburg College and the Dwight D. Eisenhower Society on October 10-14.

Participants and speakers at the two events included historians, politicians, political scientists, reporters, members of the Eisenhower administration, and others who had known him. Among those taking part were Senator Robert Dole, Clark Clifford, Walter Cronkite, Winston Churchill III, Bob Hope, son John Eisenhower and grandson David Eisenhower, Julie Nixon Eisenhower, the Reverend Billy Graham, and former President Gerald Ford.

Gerald Ford, speaking on the final day of the symposium at Gettysburg College presented his tribute to an audience of 2,500 gathered on the lawn near the house that Eisenhower used as his retirement office at 10:30 A.M.

The events of the day also included a dinner, inauguration of the Eisenhower Leadership Prize, panel discussions, symposia, and an exhibition of Eisenhower's paintings and papers. The celebration and Ford's speech received wide coverage in both the electronic and print media.

Gerald Ford's speech: It's wonderful to be back in Gettysburg on such a significant occasion. I came here several times during

---

[1]Delivered at the Eisenhower Centennial Celebration to an audience of 2,500 on the lawn of Gettysburg College, Gettysburg, Pennsylvania at 10:30 A.M. on October 14, 1990.

[2]For biographical note, see Appendix.

Dwight Eisenhower's presidency and retirement, where I enjoyed seeing the farm and Ike's obvious joy in Pennsylvania, his ancestral home. Over the years as I returned to honor Ike, I have learned to appreciate this historic ground as much as Ike did. I am most pleased that Gettysburg College and the Eisenhower Society have used this centennial celebration to confirm Eisenhower's status as one of Gettysburg's two favorite adoptive sons, the other being Abraham Lincoln.

I have been asked about my recollections of General Eisenhower. The first was when I joined with 18 other members of the House and Senate in a letter urging him to be the Republican candidate for President in 1952. I knew him mainly by reputation. I'd spent World War II in the Navy in the South Pacific, where we had our hands full and simply expected Ike would take care of things on the other side of the world. Frankly, we upstart Republican Congressmen greatly annoyed our Republican elders by backing Ike so early. I don't think we were the decisive factor in the General's decision, but I like to brag about my splendid powers of perception at an early age in my Washington political career.

I had two powerful reasons for jumping early on the Eisenhower bandwagon: first, I had been impressed by his performance in putting NATO together and his broad vision of economic as well as military cooperation in the postwar era. Whether we were privates, lieutenants or five-star generals, those who served in the Second World War were determined to prevent a third. That is why so many of us got involved in politics: the old and comfortable notion of American isolationism just wouldn't wash.

Secondly, we had learned the hard way that working together, as nations as well as individuals, is the way to win. So we liked Ike's ideas and we liked his style. We worked our hearts out for him in 1952. I remember Betty and me riding the Eisenhower whistle-stop train in my Congressional district in Michigan, but I doubt if Ike and Mamie remembered our names much beyond Grand Rapids.

One of the best things about the Eisenhower landslide was that it put me in the majority party in the House of Representatives for the first and (I regret to say) only time. This made a place for me on the Appropriations Committee and as Chairman of its Army Subcommittee. In that role, I learned a lot about our defense spending and came to appreciate how much more President Eisenhower knew about this critical issue.

On the steamy August day in 1974 when I suddenly found myself President of the United States, I was asked which of my predecessors I admired the most. This urgent decision was necessary, I was told, because of the traditional rearrangement of Presidential portraits on the White House walls. Never mind about George Washington, they said he stays above the fireplace here in the Oval Office whether you like him or not.

But my three favorite Presidents would hang in the adjacent Cabinet room to brood silently over our deliberations during my term of office. This was not a matter I had done a lot of soul-searching about, but it was my first instant Presidential decision. "Put Lincoln and Harry Truman over there," I said, "but General Ike will stay right here on my right hand."

My three choices surprised some people: except for coming from humble beginnings, they were as different as can be. Two qualities of President Eisenhower impressed me very vividly: his commonsense and devotion to duty, and, although 24 years my senior, his youthfulness of mind and spirit. He was genuinely interested in the younger men and women in government; never too busy to listen attentively to our problems and opinions. I have tried to follow his example; remembering a saying he often repeated: "You don't ever learn anything while you're doing all the talking."

As I was wondering what I might say about President Eisenhower that hasn't been said a hundred times over, the idea that kept coming to mind was how much I wish Ike could have witnessed the astonishing events of the past year: the Berlin Wall coming down, the rebirth of freedom in Eastern Europe, the Soviet Union standing with the United States and its allies to condemn naked aggression in the Middle East. All the things he started, open borders and people-to-people contacts, relaxing of East-West tensions, real progress in curbing their arsenals of mass destruction, consultation instead of confrontation between Moscow and Washington, all seem to be coming to pass before our eyes.

In this second crusade for freedom and decency in a peaceful world, no American deserves a higher place than Dwight David Eisenhower. Yet what he did was not for glory, but for duty, honor, country; in the conviction that America is not good because it is great, but that America is great because it is good. Dwight Eisenhower knew America as more than her great cities, her productive factories, even her abundant harvests. He said it all in a single line: "The greatness of America lies in the goodness of America."

Because America gave Ike Eisenhower a chance, he gave America all that he had. It was in her name that he went off to West Point in the summer of 1911. It was for her sake that he rallied the greatest fighting force ever assembled to crush the Nazi menace and keep the lights from going out all over the world. It was for her security that he assumed the highest office a grateful nation could bestow, then used his power and prestige to resist Communist aggression so that future Americans could enjoy the opportunity he had known in Abilene.

The plain truth is that security is planned, not blindly bought," said President Eisenhower in 1953. It is the product of thought, and work, and our ability and readiness to bear our military burden for however long the threat to freedom persists.

We would do well to remember those words in the post-Cold War era. For this world remains a dangerous place. We may wish every nation was left free to develop its resources in peace with its neighbors. We may hope that the international rule of law will be everywhere observed, so that American military forces need never again be sent to challenge ruthless aggression.

But wishes are no substitute for national will. And wishful thinking only invites aggression from madman tyrants who would hold the civilized world hostage to their misplaced delusions of grandeur.

In recent days Americans have stood up for their legitimate national interest, and we have stood up to those who seek to undermine regional peace and western economies. We have done what we had to do, not because we desired confrontation with any power, but because it was right. And though no one harbors any illusions that our policy is without risk, we all recognize that the greater risk would be to do nothing. America cannot capitulate to black mail.

Dwight Eisenhower understood this better than anyone when he said, "There is in world affairs a steady course to be followed between an assertion of strength that is truculent and a confession of helplessness that is cowardly."

President Bush is pursuing just that steady course. He deserves our support. He has mine. Along with it go our prayers, not only for the President, but for all our men and women in uniform, for their loved ones at home, and for every family whose lives are touched in any way by crisis in the Persian Gulf.

Finding that steady course is the supreme test of leadership, one which Dwight Eisenhower passed with flying colors. Indeed, it is Ike's leadership we celebrate tonight, for he left our nation and the world an enduring legacy of leadership.

It is particularly fitting that as part of the national celebration of Eisenhower's legacy Gettysburg College has established an award which will make a substantial contribution to the development of leadership. I am pleased to announce tonight that the Board of Gettysburg College has founded the Eisenhower Leadership Prize that will be awarded annually to an individual who is assuming progressively more influential positions in national or international affairs.

The Eisenhower Prize, which will be awarded first on October 14, 1991, will recognize leadership in education, scientific research, politics, medicine, and other important fields of human endeavor. I was especially impressed to learn that this award is not reserved exclusively for high-profile leaders, but may be given to individuals who have not won previous public recognition for their activities. We need to understand that leadership manifests itself in many lives and in many ways, not just in the careers of presidents and generals.

We need to make sure that the leaders of today have an opportunity to inspire and encourage the young people who will become the leaders of tomorrow. The Eisenhower Prize will help accomplish this key task by bringing the award winner to campus each year to talk with students, and to pass along to a new generation the critical techniques of leadership.

Dwight Eisenhower would be particularly proud of the prize named in his honor. Ike loved America's young men and women, for he realized that they are the nation's future. By encouraging and nurturing them, we will ensure that Dwight Eisenhower's principles and hopes are so much alive that this centennial of this birth will be not so much a remembrance as a rededication.

Thank you and God bless America.

APPENDIX

BIOGRAPHICAL NOTES

BUSH, BARBARA PIERCE (1925-   ). Born, Rye, New York, Student, Smith College, 1943-44; honory degrees, Stritch College, 1981; Mount Vernon College, 1981; Hood College, 1983; Howard University, 1987; Judson College, 1988; Bennett College, 1989; Smith College, 1989; Morehouse School of Medicine, 1989; Honory chair advisory board Reading Is Fundamental; honorary member Business Council for Effective Literacy; membership advisory council Society of Memorial Sloan-Kettering Cancer Centers; honorary member board of directors Children Oncology Services of Metropolitan Washington; honorary chair national advisory council Literacy Volunteers of America, National School Volunteers Program; sponsor Laubach Literacy International; honorary chair Leukemia Society; honorary member board of trustees Morehouse School of Medicine; honorary national chair National Organ Donor Awareness Week, 1982-86; president, Ladies of the Senate, 1981-88; member, womens committee Smithsonian Associations; honorary chairperson for the National Committee on Literacy and Education United Way, Barbara Bush Foundation for Family Literacy, Washington Parent Group Fund, Girls Clubs of America, 10th Anniversary Harvest National Food Bank Network; honorary chair National Committee for the Prevention of Child Abuse and Childhelp United States; honorary president, Girls Scouts United States; honorary chair National Committee for Adoption; National Outstanding Mother of the Year award, 1984; USO Woman of the Year, 1986; Distinguished Leadership award United Negro College Fund, 1986; Mount Saint Joseph College Distinguished American Woman Award, 1987. (See also *Current Biography*, 1989.)

BUSH, GEORGE HERBERT WALKER (1924-   ). Born, Milton, Massachusetts, B.A., Yale University, 1948; honorary degrees, Adelphi University, Austin College, Northern Michigan University, Franklin Pierce College, Allegheny College, Beaver College; co-founder, director, Zapata Petroleum Corporation, 1953-59; president, Zapata Off Shore Company, 1959-64, chairman of the board, 1964-66; member of 90th-91st U.S. Congresses, 7th district of Texas; U.S. ambassador to the United Nations, 1971-72; chairman, Republican National Committee, 1973-74; chief, U.S. Liaison Office, Peking, People's Republic of China, 1974-75; director of Central Intelligence Agency, 1976-77; vice president of the United States, 1981-89; president of the United States, 1989-   , director, lst International Bank, Ltd., London, 1st International Bank, Houston, Eli Lilley Corporation, Texasgulf, Purolator; chairman, Heart Fund; trustee, Trinity University, Baylor College of Medicine, Phillips Academy; chairman, Republican Party of Harris County, 1963–64; delegate to Republican National Convention, 1964, 1970; served as lieutenant (j.g.), pilot, U.S. Naval Reserve, World War II; decorated, D.F.C., air medals. (See also *Current Biography*, 1983.)

DINKINS, DAVID N. (1927–   ). Born, Trenton, New Jersey, B.S., Howard University, 1950; J.D., Brooklyn Law School, 1956; attorney, Dyett, Alexander, Dinkins, Patterson, Michael, Dinkins, Jones, 1956–75; district leader, New York State Democratic Party, 1967–   , assemblyman, New York State Assembly, 1966; president, board of elections, 1972–73; city clerk, 1975–85; Manhattan borough president, 1986–1990; mayor, New York, 1990–   , member, board of directors, New York State Americans for Democratic Action; member, Urban League; board of directors, 100 Black Men; pioneer of excellence, World Institute of Black Communications, 1986; Righteous Man Award, New York Board of Rabbis, 1986; Man of the Year, Corrections Guardians Association, 1986; Distinguished Service Award, Federation of Negro Civil Service Organization, 1986; Man of the Year Award, National Association of Negro Business and Professional Women's Clubs. (See also *Current Biography* 1990.)

EDELMAN, MARIAN WRIGHT (1930–   ). Born, Bennettsville, South Carolina, Merrill scholar, universities of Paris, Geneva, 1958–59; B.A., Spelman College, 1960; L.L.B., Yale University, 1963; L.L.D., Yale University, Smith College, 1969; honorary degrees from Lowell Technical University, 1975, Williams College, 1978, Columbia University, University of Pennsylvania, Amherst, St. Joseph's, Trinity, Russell Sage, 1978, Syracuse University, 1979, College of New Rochelle, 1978, Swarthmore, 1980, Northeastern University, 1981, Bard, 1982, University of Massachusetts, 1983; staff attorney, NAACP Legal Defense and Education Foundation, Inc., NYC, 1963–64; director, NAACP Legal Defense and Education Foundation, Inc., Jackson, Miss., 1964–68; partner, Washington Research Project of Southern Center for Public Policy, 1968–73; director, Harvard University Center for Law and Education, 1971–73; president, Children's Defense Foundation, 1973–   ; member of executive committee, Student Non-Violent Coordinating Committee, 1961–63; member, Presidential Commission on Missing in Action, 1977, Presidential Commission on International Year of the Child, 1979, Presidential Commission on Agenda for 80s, 1980; member, board of directors, Center for Law and Social Policy, Eleanor Roosevelt Institute, National Office for Rights of the Indigent, NAACP Legal Defense and Educational Foundation; trustee, Chairman of Board, Spelman College; trustee, March of Dimes, People for the American Way, Joint Center for Political Studies; member, Yale University Corporation; trustee, National Council Children and TV, Martin Luther King Memorial Center; honorary fellow, University of Pennsylvania Law School; Outstanding Young Woman of America, 1966; *Mademoiselle* magazine award, 1965; Louise Waterman Wise award, 1970; Whitney M. Young award, 1979; people of year award Black Enterprise, 1979; Leadership award National Women's Political Caucus, 1980; Black Women's Forum award, 1980; medal Columbia Teacher's College, 1984; Hubert Humphrey Civil Rights award, the Leadership Council on Civil Rights; John W. Gardner Leadership award of Independent sector; Service Achievement award, Common Cause, Compostela award Cathedral of St. James, 1987, MacArthur prize fellow, 1985, Albert Schweitzer Humanitarian prize Johns Hopkins University, 1987, Hubert Humphrey Civil Rights Award, Fordham Stein prize, Radcliff University medal, 1989, many others.

FORD, GERALD RUDOLPH, JR. (1913–). Born, Omaha, Nebraska; B.A., University of Michigan, 1935; LL.B, Yale University, 1941; honorary degrees from several universities including Michigan State University, Albion College, Aquinas College, Spring Arbor College; Lieutenant Commander, United States Navy Reserve; Attorney, 1941–49; member, Buchen and Ford, 1949–74; member 81st–93rd Congresses from 5th Michigan District, 1949–74, elected minority leader, 1965; vice president of the United States, 1973–74; president of the United States, 1974–77; delegate, Interparliamentary Union, Warsaw, Poland, 1959, Belgium, 1961; delegate, Bilderberg Group Conference, 1962; director, Santa Fe International, GK Technologies, Shearson Loeb Rhoades, Pebble Beach Corporation, Tiger International; member, American Bar Association, Michigan Bar Association; Grand Rapids Junior Chamber of Commerce Distinguished Service Award, 1948; United States Junior Chamber of Commerce Distinguished Service Award, 1950; Silver Anniversary All-American *Sports Illustrated*, 1959; Distinguished Congressional Service Award American Political Science Association, 1961. (See also *Current Biography* 1975)

FROHNMAYER, JOHN EDWARD (1942–). Born, Medford, Oregon; B.A., Stanford University; M.A., University of Chicago, 1969; J.D., University of Oregon, 1972; Served with United States Navy, 1966–69; associate attorney, Johnson, Harrang, and Mercer, 1972–75; partner; Tonkon, Torp, Galen, Marmaduke, and Booth, 1975–89; chairman, National Endowment for the Arts, 1989– ; editor-in-chief Oregon Law Review, 1971–72; board of directors, International Sculpture Symposium, 1974; member, Oregon State Bar Association, chairman, bar committee on domestic law 1975–76, procedure and practice committee, 1984–85; member, Oregon Arts Commission, 1978–85, chairman, 1980–84; member, National Endowment for the Arts Opera-Music Theatre; member American Bar Association; board of directors, Chamber Music Northwest, Western States Arts Foundation; board of directors, City Club Portland; founding member chamber choir, Novum Cantorum; fellow, American Leadership Forum; Order of the Coif, 1972; singer, has appeared in numerous recitals and various other musical productions. (See also *Current Biography*, 1990.)

HAIMAN, FRANKLYN SAUL (1921–). Born, Cleveland, Ohio; B.A., Case Western Reserve University, 1942; M.A., Northwestern University, 1945; Ph.D., Northwestern University, 1948; served with United States Army Air Force, 1942–45; Member, faculty Northwestern University,

1948–   ; chairman, department of communication studies, Northwestern University, 1964–75; professor of communication studies, Northwestern University, 1970–88; John Evans professor of communication studies, Northwestern University, 1988–   ; President, American Civil Liberties Union of Illinois, 1964–75; national board of directors, 1965, national secretary, 1976–82, national vice-president, 1987; Author: *Group Leadership and Democratic Action*, 1951; *Freedom of Speech: Issues and Cases*, 1965; *Freedom of Speech*, 1976; *Speech and Law in a Free Society*, 1981; co-author: *The Dynamics of Discussion*, 1960, 2d edition, 1980; editor: book series *To Protect These Rights*, 1976–77; contributes articles to professional journals.

KAGAN, DONALD (1932–   ). Born, Kurshan, Lithuania; naturalized, 1940; A.B., Brooklyn College, 1954; M.A., Brown University, 1955; Ph.D., Ohio State University, 1985; instructor, Pennsylvania State University, 1959–60; assistant professor, Cornell University, 1960–64, associate professor, 1964–67, professor, 1967; professor, Yale University, 1969–   ; master Timothy Dwight College, 1976–78, acting director of athletics, 1987–88; dean Yale College, 1989–   ; member: American Historical Association; American Association of Ancient Historians, American Philological Association; author; *The Great Dialogue*, 1965; *The Outbreak of the Peloponnesian War*, 1969; *The Archidamian War*, 1974; *The Sicilian Expedition*, 1981; *The Peace of Nicias and the Fall of the Arthenian Empire*, 1987; co-author, *The Western Heritage*, 1979.

LAY, DONALD POMEROY (1926–   ). Born, Princeton, Illinois; Student, United States Naval Academy, 1945–46; B.A., University of Iowa, 1948; J.D., University of Iowa, 1951; LL.D, Mitchell College of Law, 1985; Served with United States Naval Reserve, 1944–46; Associate attorney with Kennedy, Holland, DeLacy, and Svoboda, 1951–53; Quarles, Spence and Quarles, 1953–54; Eisenstatt, Lay, Higgins and Miller, 1954–66; judge, United States 8th Circuit Court of Appeals, 1966–   , chief judge, 1980–   ; board of governors, American Association of Trial Lawyers, 1963–65; faculty member on evidence, National College of Trial Judges, 1964–65; member, U.S. Judicial Conference, 1980–   ; Order of Coif, Delta Sigma Rho; member, American Bar Association, Nebraska Bar Association, Iowa Bar Association, Wisconsin Bar Association, American Judicature Society; University of Iowa Hancher-Finkbine medal, 1980; Significant Sig award, 1986; Herbert Harley Award, 1988; Member, editorial board: *Iowa Law Review*, 1950–51; contributes numerous articles to legal journals.

LEWIS, BERNARD (1916–   ). Born, London, England; naturalized citizen, 1982; B.A., University of London, 1936, Ph.D., 1939; Diplome des Etudes Semitiques, University of Paris, 1937; postgraduate work, University of London and University of Paris; honorary Ph.D. degrees from Hebrew University of Jerusalem, 1974, Tel Aviv University, 1979, State University of New York, University of Pennsylvania, Hebrew Union College, 1987; served with Royal Armoured Corps and Intelligence Corps,

British Army, 1940-41; Foreign Office department, 1941-45; assistant lecturer, School of Oriental Studies, University of London, 1938; professor, School of Oriental Studies, University of London, 1949-74; Cleveland E. Dodge professor of near eastern studies, Princeton University, 1974-86; professor Emeritus, Princeton University, 1986-   ; A.D. White professor-at-large, Cornell University, 1984-   ; visiting professor: University of California, Los Angeles, 1955-56; Columbia University, 1960; Indiana University, 1963; University of California at Berkeley, 1965; College de France, 1980; Ecoles des Hautes Etudes, Paris, 1983-86; University of Chicago, 1985; member: American Academy of Arts and Sciences; American Historical Society; American Philosophical Society; Council on Foreign Relations; Royal Historical Society; Royal Asiatic Society; associate member, Institut d'Egypte, 1969-   ; honorary member: Turkish Historical Society, 1972-   ; Atatuerk Academy of History, Language and Culture, 1984-   ; Societe Asiatique, 1984-   ; director, Annenberg Research Institute, 1986-   ; Athenaeum Club; Princeton Club; fellow, British Academy, 1963; citation of honor from the Turkish Ministry of Culture, 1973; Gottesman lecturer Yeshiva University, 1974; fellow of University College, London, 1976; Harvey Prize, 1978; honorary fellow School of Oriental Studies, University of London, 1986; professor emeritus, Princeton, 1986-   ; author of over thirty books dealing with Islam and the history of the Near East including, *The Origins of Islamism*, 1940, *Turkey Today*, 1940, *A Handbook of Diplomatic and Political Arabic*, 1947, *The Arabs in History*, 1950, *Istanbul and the Civilization of the Ottoman Empire*, 1963, *The Assassins*, 1967, *Islam in History, 1973, The Jews of Islam, 1984, The Political Language of Islam*, 1988; editor: *Land of Enchanters*, 1948; *The World of Islam*, 1976; *Encyclopedia of Islam*, 1956-87; *The Cambridge History of Islam*, 1971; author of numerous articles in scholarly journals.

LYMAN, PRINCETON NATHAN (1935-   ). Born, San Francisco, California; B.A., University of California Berkeley, 1957; M.A., Harvard University, 1959, Ph.D., 1961; international relations officer, Agency for International Development, 1961-64; program officer, United States Aid Mission, Seoul, Korea, 1964-67; research associate, Harvard University, 1967-68; chief, civic participation division, Agency for International Development 1968-71; director, Africa Development Resources 1971-76; director, United States Aid Mission, Addis Ababa, Ethiopia1976-78; director, planning office for Institute for Scientific and Technological Cooperation, 1978-80; lecturer, Johns Hopkins University, 1980-86; Deputy Assistant Secretary of State for Africa, 1981-86; Ambassador to Nigeria, 1986-89; director, Bureau of Refugee Programs, Department of State, 1989-   ; member: American Foreign Service Association, vice president, 1969-70; African Studies Association; American Political Science Association; Agency for International Development Meritorious Honor award, 1966, 1971, Superior Honor Award, 1970, 1986; Department of State Meritorious Honor award 1986; President's Superior Performance Award, 1983; President's Meritorious Service Award, 1989; author: *Korea: The Interplay of Politics and Economics*, 1971; chapter in the anthology *The Crisis and Challenge of African Development*, 1988; contributor to *Orbis*, *Pacific Affairs*; *Journal of Comparative Administration*; *Asian Survey*.

MANN, JONATHAN MAX (1947–   ). Born, Boston, Massachusetts; B.A., Harvard College, 1969, M.D. Washington University, 1974, M.P.H., Harvard University School of Public Health, 1980; state epidemiologist and assistant director of New Mexico health department, 1977–1984, director, Project SIDA in Zaire, 1984–1986; director, World Health Organization's Global Program on AIDS, 1986–1990; professor of Epidemiology and International Health, Harvard School of Public Health, and Director, International AIDS Center of the Harvard AIDS Institute, 1990–Present. Member, Santa Fe County Medical Society (treas. 1981–82, pres. 1983–84), U.S.–Mexico Border Health Assn., American Public Health Assn.

MATHEWS, JESSICA TUCHMAN (1946–   ). Born, New York, New York; B.A., *magna cum laude*, Radcliffe College, 1967, Ph.D., California Institute of Technology, 1973; Congressional Science Fellow of the American Association for the Advancement of Science, 1973; issues director for Morris Udall's presidential campaign, 1975–76; director, Office of Global Issues, National Security Council, 1977–79; member editorial board of the *Washington Post*, 1980–82; research director of the World Resources Institute, 1982–88, and vice-president, 1982–   ; member of the Board of the Federation of American Scientists, the Joyce Foundation in Chicago, the Population Reference Bureau in Washington, D.C., and the council of the Overseas Development Council. She is a distinguished fellow of the Aspen Institute, and a member of the Council on Foreign Relations and the Inter-American Dialogue.

MINOW, NEWTON NORMAN (1926–   ). Born, Milwaukee, Wisconsin; B.A., Northwestern University, 1949, J.D., 1950; LL.D., Brandeis University, 1963, University of Wisconsin, 1963, Northwestern University, 1965, Columbia College, 1972; Served with United States Army, 1944–46; Lawyer with Mayer, Brown and Platt, 1950–51, 53–55; law clerk, Chief Justice Fred M. Vinson, 1951–52; administrative assistant to Illinois Governor Stevenson, 1952–53; special campaign assistant to President Adlai Stevenson, 1952, 56; partner firm Adlai Stevenson, 1955–57; partner firm Stevenson, Rifkind, and Wirtz, 1957–61; chairman, Federal Communications Commission, 1961–63; executive vice president, Encyclopedia Britannica, 1963–65; partner, Sidley and Austin, 1965–   ; professor, Northwestern University, 1987–   ; director, Annenberg Washington Program, 1987–   ; former chairman, Chicago Educational Television; trustee, Mayo Foundation, 1973–80, Northwestern University, 1975–   , William Benton Foundation, 1981–83, Chicago Orchestral Association 1975–   ; chairman of the board, Jewish Theological Seminary, 1974–77; board of governors, Public Broadcasting Services, 1973–80; co-chairman presidential debates League of Women Voters, 1976, 1980; Trustee of Notre Dame University 1983–   ; one of Ten Outstanding Young Men in Chicago, 1960; one of Ten America's Outstanding Young Men, 1961;

George Foster Peabody Broadcasting Award, 1961; Northwestern Alumni medal, 1978; Ralph Lowell Award, 1982; Author: *Equal Time: The Private Broadcasters and the Public Interest,* 1965; co-author: *Presidential Television,* 1973, *Electronics and the Future,* 1977, *Four Great Debates,* 1987; contributor: *As We Knew Adlai.* (See also *Current Biography* 1961)

PEROT, H. ROSS (1930–   ). United States Naval Academy; Served with United States Navy, 1953–57; salesman, International Business Machine Corporation, 1957–62; founder, Electronic Data Systems Corporation, 1962; chairman, director, Electronic Data Systems Corporation, 1962–1986; now with The Perot Group, Dallas; founder, Perot Systems Corporation, 1988–   ; Recipient, Internationally Distinguished Entrepreneur Award, University of Manchester, 1988. (See also *Current Biography* 1971)

REDFORD, ROBERT (1937–   ). Born, Santa Monica, California; student: University of Colorado; Pratt Institute of Design; American Academy of Dramatic Arts; L.H.D., University of Colorado, 1987; Ph.D. University of Massachusetts, 1990; Broadway theatrical actor: *Barefoot in the Park*; *Tall Story*; *Sunday in New York*; film actor: *Barefoot in the Park,* 1967; *Butch Cassidy and the Sundance Kid,* 1969; *Downhill Racer,* 1969; *Big Fauss and Little Halsey, Tell Them Willie Boy is Here,* 1970; *Jeremiah Johnson,* 1972; *The Hot Rock, The Candidate,* 1972; *The Way We Were, The Sting,* 1973; *The Great Gatsby,* 1974; *The Great Waldo Pepper, Three Days of the Condor, A Bridge Too Far,* 1975; *All The President's Men,* 1976; *The Electric Horseman,* 1979; *Brubaker,* 1980; *The Natural,* 1984; *Out of Africa,* 1985; *Legal Eagles,* 1986; film director: *Ordinary People,* 1980; *The Milagro Beanfield War,* 1988; recipient, Golden Globe Award, 1981; Academy Award as Best Director, 1981; Audubon medal, 1989; Dartmouth Film Society Award, 1990. (See also *Current Biography,* 1982.)

REEDY, GEORGE EDWARD (1917–   ). Born, East Chicago, Indiana; B.A., University of Chicago, 1938; D.J.C. Nashota Seminary, 1981; served with United States Army Air Force, 1942–45; reporter, *Philadelphia Inquirer,* 1937; correspondent United Press International, 1938–41, 46–51; staff consultant armed services preparedness subcommittee U.S. Senate, 1951–52, staff director minority policy committee, 1953–54, staff director majority policy committee, 1955–60; special assistant to Vice President Johnson Lyndon Johnson, 1961–63; press secretary to President Johnson 1964–65; president Struthers Research and Development Corporation, 1966–68; special consultant to President Johnson, 1968–69; writer, lecturer, consultant 1969–   ; dean, College of Journalism, Marquette University, 1972–77, Nieman professor, 1977–   ; fellow, Woodrow Wilson International Center for Scholars, Smithsonian Institution; fellow in communication, Duke, 1973–74; Author: *Who Will Do Our Fighting for Us?* 1969; *The Twilight of the Presidency,* 1970; *The Presidency in Flux,* 1973; *Lyndon B. Johnson: A Memoir,* 1982; *The Twilight of the Presidency, Johnson to Reagan,* 1987; numerous articles on government and politics.

WATTLETON, (ALYCE) FAYE (1943–   ). Born, St. Louis, Missouri; B.S., Ohio
State University, 1964, M.S., Columbia University, 1967; instructor, Miami Valley Hospital School of Nursing, 1964–66; assistant director of
nursing, Dayton Public Health Nursing Association, 1967–69'; executive
director, Planned Parenthood Association of Miami Valley, Dayton,
1970–78; president Planned Parenthood Federation of America, Incor-
porated, 1978–   ; board member, National Urban League, 1979; board
member, Ohio State Alumni Association, 1980; member, American Public Health Association; American College of Nurse-Midwives; recipient of
numerous humanitarian awards including Citation for Outstanding
Achievement from State of Ohio House of Representatives; Citation for
Outstanding Achievement Ohio State University; citation from *MS.* magazine. (See also *Current Biography*, 1990.)

WIESEL, ELIE(ZER) (1928–   ). Born, Sighet, Transylvania; came to U.S.,
1956, naturalized; attended Sorbonne, University of Paris, 1947–50; honorary degrees, twenty-nine institutions; foreign correspondent at various
times for *Yedioth Ahronoth*, Tel Aviv, Israel, *L'Arche*, Paris, France, and
Jewish Daily Forward, New York City, 1949–   ; Distinguished Professor,
City College of the City University of New York, New York City,
1972–76; Andrew Mellon Professor in the Humanities, Boston University, Boston, Massachusetts, 1976–   ; Henry Luce Visiting Scholar, Yale
University, New Haven, Connecticut; chairman, U.S. President's Commission on the Holocaust, U.S. Holocaust Memorial Council; board of directors, National Committee on American Foreign Policy, Hebrew Arts
School, HUMANITAS, International Rescue Committee; board of governors, Oxford Center for Postgraduate Hebrew Studies, Ben-Gurion
University of the Negev, Haifa University, Tel-Aviv University; col-
league, Cathedral of St. John the Divine; member, Amnesty International; Writers and Artists for Peace in the Middle East; Phi Beta Kappa;
honorary chairman, National Jewish Resource Center; recipient, Prix Ri-
varol, 1964 , Jewish Heritage Award, Haifa University, 1965, Remembrance Award, 1965, Prix Medicis, 1968, Prix Bordin French Academy,
1972, Eleanor Roosevelt Memorial Award, New York United Jewish Appeal, 1972, Martin Luther King Jr. Medallion, City College of the City
University of New York, 1973, Faculty Distinguished Scholar Award,
Hofstra University, 1973–74, Jewish Heritage Award, B'Nai B'rith, Avo-
da Award, Jewish Teachers Association, Humanitarian Award, B'rith
Sholom, Jabotinsky Medal, State of Israel, International Literature Prize
for Peace, Royal Academy, Belguim, 1983, Congressional Gold Medal,
1984, Remembrance Award, Israel Bonds, 1985, Anne Frank Award,
1985; Jacob Javits Humanitarian Award, Freedom Cup Womens League
Israel, Nobel Peace Prize, Medal of Liberty Award Statue of Liberty Presentation, 1986, Profiles of Courage Award, B'Nai B'rith, Golda Meir
Humanitarian Award, 1987, Presidential Medal Hofstra University, Human Rights Law award International Human Rights Law Group, 1988;
fellow, Jewish Academy of Arts and Sciences, Timothy Dwight College,
Yale University; author of twenty-three books including *Night*, 1960,
Dawn, 1961, *The Accident*, 1962, *A Beggar in Jerusalem*, 1970, *Souls on Fire*,

1972, *The Fifth Son*, 1985, *Against Silence*, 1985, *A Song for Hope*, 1987, *The Nobel Speech*, 1987, *Tempete Twilight*, 1988, *The Six Days of Destruction*, 1988, *From the Kingdom of Memory*, 1990; editorial boards of *Midstream, Religion and Literature, Sh'ma: Journal of Responsibility*; (See also *Current Biography*, 1986.)

INDEX TO VOLUME 63 (1991)
BY SUBJECT

AFFIRMATIVE ACTION
About

Programs

AGED

Care and Hygiene

Family relationships

Medical Care

AIDS

Great Britain

'All heaven in a rage'. M. Daly. *History Today* My. '87. **63:4**

ANIMALS

Religious Aspects

Animal lib. T. Stafford. *Christianity Today* Je. 18, '90. **63:4**

Human vs. animal rights. J.M. Loeb, et al . *The Journal of the American Medical Association* N. 17, '89. **63:4**

Out of the cage: the movement in transition. M. Clifton. *The Animal Agenda* Ja./F. '90. **63:4**

Treatment

Why worry about the animals? J.B. Elshtain. *The Progressive* Mr. '90. **63:4**

ANTIFUR MOVEMENT

The fur flies. J. Kasindorf. *New York* Ja. 15, '90. **63:4**

Fuzzy-wuzzy thinking about animal rights. R. Conniff. *Outdoor Life* F. '91. **63:4**

BLACKS

Voting with his feet. *Time* My. 7, '90. **63:3**

Civil Rights

The Supreme Court and civil rights: has the tide turned? T. Marshall. *USA Today* (Periodical) Mr. '90. **63:3**

Education

Exclusive opportunities. J.H. Bunzel. *American Enterprise* Mr./Ap. '90. **63:3**

In ivory towers. R.W. Wilkins. *Mother Jones* Jl./Ag. '90. **63:3**

Is affirmative action still the answer? R.K. Landers. *Editorial Research Reports* Ap. 14, '89. **63:3**

Major supreme court decisions, January–June 1989. S. Rabinove. Je. 30, '89 **63:3**

You ain't the right color, pal. F.R. Lynch and W.R. Beer *Policy Review* '90. **63:3**

Employment

In ivory towers. R.W. Wilkins. *Mother Jones* Jl./Ag. '90. **63:3**

Strategies for a diverse and competitive America. D.M. Blandin. *Vital Speeches of the Day* Ja. 1 '91. **63:5**

Will diversity=opportunity+advancement for blacks? S.H. Tucker and K.D. Thompson. *Black Enterprise* N. '90. **63:3**

CHALLENGER (SPACE SHUTTLE) EXPLOSION, 1986

About

Shuttle pit stop. G. Freiherr. *Air & Space Smithsonian* O./N. '90. **63:2**

Suits and Claims

Whistle-blower. T. Chiu. *Life* Mr. '88. **63:2**

CUMULATIVE SPEAKER INDEX

1990-1991

A cumulative author index to the volumes of *Representative American Speeches* for the years 1937-1938 through 1959-1960 appears in the 1959-1960 volume, for the years 1960-1961 through 1969-1970 in the 1969-1970 volume, for the years 1970-1971 through 1979-80 in the 1979-1980 volume, and for the years 1980-1981 through 1989-1990 in the 1989-1990 volume.